Reviews and Reviewing: A Guide

Reviews and Reviewing: A Guide

Edited by A.J. WALFORD

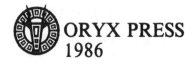

ORYX PRESS
1986

The rare Arabian Oryx is believed to have inspired the myth of the unicorn. This desert antelope became virtually extinct in the early 1960s. At that time several groups of international conservationists arranged to have 9 animals sent to the Phoenix Zoo to be the nucleus of a captive breeding herd. Today the Oryx population is over 400, and herds have been returned to reserves in Israel, Jordan, and Oman.

© Mansell Publishing Limited and the Contributors, 1986
Published in the United States, 1986
by The Oryx Press
2214 North Central Avenue
Phoenix, AZ 85004-1483

Published simultaneously in Canada

First Published in the United Kingdom by
Mansell Publishing Limited, 6 All Saints Street, London N1 9RL England

Library of Congress Cataloging-in-Publication Data

Reviews and reviewing.

   Bibliography: p.
   Includes index.
   1. Book reviewing. I. Walford, Albert John.
PN98.B7R5   1986   028.1   86-16371
ISBN 0-89774-390-3

Contents

Contributors

Margaret Girvan is Senior Assistant, Fine Arts Library, Westminster Public Libraries, London.

D.J. Grogan is Head, Department of Bibliographical and Community Studies, College of Librarianship, Wales, Aberystwyth.

Grace Hallworth was formerly Divisional Co-ordinator, Hertfordshire Library Service.

Helen P. Harrison is Media Librarian, Open University Library, Milton Keynes.

Anthony P. Harvey is Librarian, British Museum (Natural History), London.

Joan M. Harvey was formerly Senior Lecturer, School of Librarianship, Loughborough Technical College.

J.D. Hendry is Chief Librarian, Renfrew District Library Service, Paisley.

A.J. Walford is editor of *Walford's Guide to reference material*.

Michael J. Walsh is Librarian, Heythrop College, University of London.

Introduction

This collection of essays aims to provide guide-lines for the reviewing of books and audiovisual materials in a variety of disciplines. In addition, there are lists of reviewing journals, which are extensively annotated and which in themselves provide a guide to serials that carry reviews. Seen as a whole, the volume therefore provides a useful reference tool for reviewers, publishers and librarians amongst others — for example, by offering criteria for reviewing, by surveying potential sources for reviews of books and audio-visual materials, and by providing an aid for book and periodical selection.

Part One of the book provides an overview and contains two general chapters. The first looks at the art of reviewing and considers such topics as its history, definitions, techniques, the value of a review, and a reviewer's role and qualifications. The second chapter discusses the administrative role of the book-review editor.

Part Two deals with specialized reviewing and has 12 chapters. As a rule, each individual subject or subject area is divided into three sections. First, there is an introductory section which helps to set the scene, indicates the qualifications expected of a reviewer, offers reviewing guidelines, notes typical features of reviews such as level, slant, scope and style, cites review examples and so on. There follows a section for indexes to reviews, listing the main sources and noting significant features. The final section contains a list of reviewing journals with lengthy annotations. Journal titles are usually arranged by the number/quality of reviews carried. For a subject area such as Technology (see Chapter 8), the range is so extensive that the choice of journals for scrutiny is restricted to 20 representative titles, arranged in A–Z order. Chapter 9, 'Fine arts' is similarly arranged and deals chiefly with general art journals. Chapter 13, 'Children's books' has the reviewing journals subdivided into two broad-age divisions and a list of annual publications, while Chapter 14, 'Audiovisual materials' considers particular forms and audiences. Periodicals which feature in specific chapters in Part Two are mostly in English, although French and German titles do appear. Review articles are given much less attention than are book reviews proper. Comments concentrate on what reviewers look for and their reactions to individual books. The review editor's viewpoint is also expressed, in Chapter 2.

There are two appendices. The first provides a select list of indexes to reviews, which is arranged for convenience under three headings and contains over fifty items. The other appendix is a select and annotated bibliography, which has more than fifty entries. The book is completed by an index of authors, titles and subjects.

My warmest thanks go to the other contributors and I would like to add a special note of thanks to Anthony P. Harvey, who played such an important role at the start of this project and who gave such useful advice.

A.J. WALFORD

Part 1

Overview

Part I.

Overview

1. The art of reviewing

A.J. Walford

Definitions

Review

A published evaluation of a book, performance, and so on. According to King,[1] a book review serves two major functions — descriptive and evaluative: 'It can first of all indicate to the reading public some general idea of the contents and it can offer a critique, an evaluation of merit. These two functions are rather distinct and yet they belong together'. For him the majority of medical books can be reviewed adequately in between 250 and 500 words. Manten[2] allows 1,000 words if the item is of more than average importance (e.g. a new multi-volume encyclopaedia) and up to 1,500 words for books of exceptional merit.

Peer-reviewing is the procedure whereby a paper/article submitted to a journal editor is then passed to a person of equal status in the relevant field, for his judgement.

Review article

An essay of between 1,000 and 1,500 words, reviewing either a cluster of several books on a related topic or else a literature survey, with a lengthy list of references, such as that regularly featured in *British book news* and *Choice*. Virgo[3] distinguishes (1) the annual review (see below); (2) the critical review that 'selectively evaluates contributions to the solution of a common research problem'; and (3) data compilations.

Annual review of .../Advances in .../Progress in ...

A state-of-the-art summary of progress in a specific field, especially in science, technology and medicine (e.g. the Chemical Society's *Specialist periodical reports: reviews of the chemical literature*). Such surveys are often annual. The term 'state-of-the-art survey' may also apply to individual contributions in an annual review (e.g. 'The scholarly communication process', by P.J. Hills, in *Annual review of information science and technology*, (vol. 18, 1983). Woodward has discussed the role of scientific review literature in information transfer.[4]

Annotation

A mini-review or short description of the contents of a book, and so on, usually without evaluation. Its brevity (between 10 and 100 words) and absence of a critical note normally distinguish the annotation (as in *Aslib book list*) from the book review proper.

Abstract

Also a summary of contents, but customarily applied to the periodical article, and non-critical, as provided in an abstracting service. Abstracts may be either *informative* (i.e. sufficiently covering all the relevant points/arguments, data and conclusions in the original as to help the reader to decide whether to consult the original itself); or *indicative*, providing a bare statement of contents.

Digest

According to Harrod,[5] 'a methodically arranged compendium or summary of literary, historical, legal, scientific or other written matter'. *Book review digest* has descriptive and critical excerpts from reviews in 84 journals.

Literary criticism

The *Oxford English dictionary* defines criticism in its second sense as 'the art of estimating the qualities and character of literary or artistic work'. Literary criticism usually concerns belles lettres — poetry, drama, the novel and the literary essay. Literary reviews are now rarely able to afford the luxury of the lengthy essay 'as a catalyst to distill the reflections of well-stocked minds', such as Macaulay's. Leonard Woolf[6] has argued that reviewing is quite distinct from literary criticism: the reviewer 'has nothing to say to the author; he is talking to the reader'.

The review: its value

Macphail's article on 'Book reviews and the scholarly publisher'[7] summarizes the role of the review: 'A thoughtful, timely, well-written book review serves the shared interests of scholarly publishers and the scholarly community'. For publishers, the review is at least a method of promotion, by bringing books to the attention of likely readers, and a means of providing an evaluation of their product: 'Readers look to book reviews for news and appraisal of the latest work being done in their field of specialty. Very often, reviews suggest directions in which further study might proceed; this, in turn, stimulates research and future publication and the continued growth and advance of scholarship'. American librarians, we are told,[8] rely heavily on *Library journal* and *Choice* when choosing books for purchase, and scholarly publishers have noted a direct relationship between a good *Library journal* or *Choice* review and sales by library suppliers.

The editor of *The Russian review*[9] considers that book reviews are, or should be, compact sources of information in their own right: 'Book reviews are a good way of finding out what is in books that we will never read. There are also books, all too few, that I actually will read. Reviews are guides to selecting these'. It should be added that the specialist gains by noting reviews of books on subjects bordering on his own area of research.

The reviewer: role and qualifications

The reviewer can be seen as one of a quartet in which author, publisher and editor are the other members, each with responsibilities. On the reviewer's functions, Virginia Woolf[10] distinguishes between the 'Gutter' (the scissors-and-paste official) and the 'Taster' (who affixes his/her mark of approval or disapproval). It is assumed that the reviewer is a competent writer, with well-expressed ideas:

> He must know the subject under discussion and must be able to speak with 'authority' derived from efficiency in the field. He must be able to appreciate the validity of the points made, perceive the degree of adequacy in coverage, discriminate what is new and original from the derivative, evaluate the significance of the new. And he must be able to recognise errors. Ideally, he should not be too limited, in his narrow field, but have certain broader insights.[11]

Editors or book-review editors normally select their reviewers. Occasionally a 'books received' list in a journal carries a note inviting reviewers who are willing to review any of the titles listed to contact the editor. *College and research libraries* states that 'Reviewers willing to review books for the journal are invited to write to the editor indicating their special areas of interest and qualifications'.

Objectivity and anonymity

Conarroe,[12] writing on the reviewing process, warns of the 'unconscious biassing effects of reviewers knowing the age, sex, range or place of employment of authors, or of editorial boards knowing the same thing about reviewers'. Other motivations include an urge to curry favour with the author; also, using the cloak of anonymity, to stab at a rival. Harsh comments are more the arena of literary and art criticism, where tastes and preferences are in question. In the field of science, technology and medicine, on the other hand, reviewing has been labelled 'snug', 'for the good reason that STM books are so technical in content and language'.[13] If the reviewer is himself an author, he may be non-committal, for fear of retaliation.

In earlier times anonymous reviewing was the rule. Could Schiller have published his criticism of Goethe's *Egmont* if he had had to sign it? Distinguished writers have little wish to add acrimony to censure by endorsing reviews with their names. Signed reviews are now more usual, there being a suspicion that anonymity may conceal incompetence, cowardice or hack-work. (*Punch* discontinued anonymous reviewing in 1942; the *TLS*, in 1974; and *Choice*, as late as 1984.) Identified by name, circumspect reviewers have resorted to expressing adverse criticism indirectly or by implication.

Book selection and reviewing

The most current, non-evaluative sources of information on English-language books, for selection purposes, are checklists (e.g. *British national bibliography, The bookseller*, plus *Books of the month and books to come* and *Publisher's weekly*), advertisements in the media, and publishers' catalogues. But for critical, evaluative comment one must look to book reviews in journals. Budd[14] observes that, as the result of the spate of scholarly books in the 1980s, 'scholarly book reviews are more than time-savers; they can be indispensable'.

Writing on technical-book reviewing in 1948, during a period of shortage of paper and binding materials, Collison[15] lamented that the system of book reviewing had become a broken reed so far as the librarian was concerned: 'Reviews of technical books were never very plentiful, and those on which any reliance would be placed were rare indeed. Today they are almost non-existent'. The situation has since improved, but many worthwhile books are still not reviewed or are reviewed too tardily. With ever-tightening budgets, librarians look for critical reviews as a guide to what is really worthwhile purchasing. *The local historian*'s review-editor[16] sees a distinct advantage in providing reviews as sources of book selection in his field: 'To librarians it has proved an invaluable bibliographical tool, particularly useful for the attention it brings to bear on the work of local historical societies, very small publications and individuals who publish their own writings'.

The librarian may, on the other hand, refer to reviews to confirm, or otherwise, his or her selection, already made and partly prompted by publicity and anticipated public demand. Again, it may be argued that a fair proportion of popular books 'choose themselves'. Finally, the book-weeding process also involves evaluation/re-evaluation and decision-making, a problem elaborated by Whittaker.[17]

Time-lag

Can the librarian/book-selector afford to wait three to six months for an adequate review of the expensive item, a so-called revised edition, or a multi-volume work, in face of demand stimulated by media publicity? *A world history of art*, by H. Honour and J. Fleming, published in September 1982, was reviewed in *The Observer* on 25 November 1982; in *The listener* on 23 December 1982; in *British book news* in February 1983 and in *Apollo* in February 1984. Again, *Natural history manuscript resources in the British Isles*, published on 15 October 1980 and reviewed in *British book news* in February 1981, was not noticed in *Nature* until 30 April 1981. Yet Brightman,[18] discussing scientific and technical-book reviewing in general, argued that he would rather wait for an authoritative review before deciding to purchase a new book. (Time-lag and quantitative review-coverage are explored in detail by Chen[19] in his *Scientific and technical book reviewing*, based on a study of some 500 biomedical, scientific and technical reviewing-journals.)

Advance page proofs and pre-publication copies of forthcoming books facilitate early-warning reviewing. Hence the mini-review section, 'Forecasts', in the *Publisher's weekly* and the semi-monthly, loose-leaf *Kirkus reviews*,[20] which provides in-house reviews of books — mainly aimed at schools and public libraries — several months ahead of publication.[21] The monthly *Good book guide: new books list*[22] offers 10- to 25-word annotations for books due to appear during the month. In-house reviewing has the advantage, for the journal editor, of conforming more closely to editorial policy,[23] as well as producing early notices. CIP (cataloguing in advance of publication) involves the early provision of bibliographical details of new books by publishers.

Looking ahead, Martinelli[24] discusses the use of electronic media for making review-article material available to users, and Walby[25] outlines the possible advantages of transmitting text electronically to and from reviewers. 'The technology exists to connect author, editor and reviewer electronically in an interactive and online mode', he adds.

Techniques

Sarton's method[26] of reviewing science books was to read the book-to-be-read in the evening, making notes or simply jotting page numbers on a pad as he proceeded: 'My review takes shape during the night and I am ready to study my notes and write the material the following morning'. He summarized salient points thus:

1. What is the subject of the book?
2. What are the author's qualifications and the aim of the book?
3. How well is the book organized (e.g. contents; documentation; appendices; index)?
4. Evaluation: how far is the book's aim fulfilled? Does it contribute a new approach, based on primary sources, or is it a rehash of secondary sources only? How does the book compare with its competitors? Does it fill a gap or prove to be complementary to existing books on the subject?

For Stueart[27] a sound review should provide:

1. Bibliographical details, including previous editions (if any).
2. Author's qualifications.
3. Subject; aims; level of treatment.
4. Balanced assessment.

5. Comparison with similar books.
6. Readership recommended.
7. Signature and affiliation of reviewer.

In dealing with a composite or encyclopaedic work by various hands, the reviewer must appreciate the dangers inherent in sampling (Sarton's term is 'segment analysis'), which could be unrepresentative. It is wisest for the specialist reviewer to concentrate on the area with which he is truly familiar. Other hazards include the temptation to parade his or her knowledge of the subject rather than concentrate on the book in hand; a lazy reliance on the publisher's blurb; and indulgence in petty fault-finding.

Wolper[28] has admirably summarized ten golden rules:

1. The judgement should be an integral part of the analysis.
2. The reviewer should point out what the author has overlooked or conveniently forgotten.
3. A reviewer must back up his criticism.
4. The author's exact words must not be muffled.
5. If what an author has said is worth mentioning, the reader should be told what it is.
6. Cryptic titles must be explained.
7. Whatever the book, the reviewer must not forget that the reader may not have taken the same journey (e.g. provide a wider context to the subject of the review, if required).
8. Begin the review with a striking remark or quotation, if possible.
9. Avoid jargon, clichés, redundancy and ineptness.
10. Be accurate, even though verification is a mundane chore.

Aggrieved authors of books reviewed are not infrequently given the opportunity to protest in the journal's correspondence column against treatment considered unfair. The reviewer occasionally retorts, preferably in the same issue of the journal. At times the exchange of views has led to altered decisions and, more often, to broadened understanding. Sometimes, however, the damage done is irreparable.

Reviewing channels: the press

A survey made in October/December 1973[29] of the amount of space devoted to book reviews in the leading British daily and Sunday newspapers showed that biography and fiction were quite clearly the

most reviewed categories, followed by history, children's books and
politics. *The Sunday Times* was found to carry the most reviews and
give most space to them. The mid-1983 report made by Quentin
Oates in *The bookseller*,[30] attempting a qualitative approach, considered *The Sunday Times* review pages patchy: 'some good things, but
some awfully boring stuff'. For Oates, *The Observer* remained, 'so
far as the quality of the reviewing is concerned, still at the top of the
league'. Of the weeklies proper, *The listener* had by far the best
reviewing record, 'though I wish it would not at times suffer from the
TLS disease and be tardy with its reviews'. The literary editor of *The
Times*[31] states the media's angle rather than that of the bookseller:
'Book pages have to justify their existence as lively journalism in a
world in which journalism becomes livelier every day. Your hardened
journalist begrudges the precious space given to book reviewing'.
The introduction of book pages in the daily press, with stress on
readability, is indeed a comparatively recent innovation.

Reviewing of journals

The American *Serials review* (Ann Arbor, Mich., Pierian Press, 1975 –.
4 p.a.) performs a service for both established and new periodicals,
much as *RSR/Reference services review* (also from Pierian Press)
does for reference books. It surveys and provides reviews of periodicals in particular fields or on specific topics (e.g. 'Current justice journals: a review and annotated bibliography of selected scholarly journals', covering 30 titles, in vol. 11 [1], Spring 1985 issue), with an
index of journals reviewed elsewhere over a period. Its editor scans
about 200 journals for such reviews. Two other US sources give
reviews of new journals: *New magazine review* (North Las Vegas,
Nev., John Creighton, 1978 –. 12 p.a.) and *Periodically speaking*
(North Cohorton, NY, Moore-Cottrell Subscription Agencies, 1977 –.
4 p.a.). On a much smaller scale, *Choice* carries a regular section,
'Periodicals for college libraries'. The reviews (about seven per issue)
are signed, with affiliations, and average 250 words apiece. The
Choice periodicals-editor invites reviewers to contact him with
review copies or with offers to review new periodicals. Similarly, *Library journal*'s 'Magazines' feature gives prominence to some six
recent periodicals, some of which may have a subject in common
(e.g. music, opera and film journals; office-management journals).

In Britain, surprisingly little attention has been paid to reviews or annotated announcements of new or established journals in their current issues. A notable exception is *Nature*'s annual review (1–7 October 1981 –) of new science periodicals. That issue covered 124 journals whose first number was published or retitled between June 1978 and May 1980. Criteria for inclusion[32] involved frequency (at least three p.a.), language (major language: English) and availability of four issues for review (the first, the most recent and two others), for adequate assessment. The service was aimed at potential subscribers (especially librarians), authors and publishers. The preponderance of biological journals, among those submitted for review, continues. The reviews are signed, averaging 500 words each. *British book news* has featured 'Periodicals and serials' (the title varies) in most monthly issues since August 1981. The reviews – about six per issue and signed – average between 120 and 250 words in length. Scientific, medical and technical journals preponderate; serials, such as state-of-the-art annuals, are included. An appended 'Advance notice of other items to be reviewed' occasionally appears. *CABLIS* (Library Association Library, 1975 –) monthly notes 'New periodicals. A comprehensive annotated list of titles added to the LAL stock'. Subject coverage is librarianship and information science, nine new titles being dealt with in the March 1985 issue.

The *TLS* runs a series of critical reviews of current issues of some leading British, American and other journals, mostly literary. The series began on 12 August 1983; recently, no. 27 featured *Ariel* (Israel), on 3 May 1985. A review-article, 'Learning and learned journals', in the 16 December *TLS*,[33] consists of signed surveys of periodicals in the fields of physics, literature, music, social sciences, history, biology, art history and philosophy. A further *TLS* series, 'Journals received',[34] comments on recent issues of a selection of scholarly journals. The quarterly *Incorporated linguist* devotes between four and six pages to analysing recent issues of language journals, with brief commentary. *The music review* carries a 'Review of periodicals', in alternate quarterly issues, under country headings, and *The honest Ulsterman*, a small-format literary magazine praised in the *TLS*[35] for its 'bracing standards of critical acumen and seriousness', includes reviews of recent anthologies and issues of poetry magazines.

History

Printed criticism in England dates from the seventeenth century. According to McCutcheon,[36] most of the technical elements in reviewing are to be found, 'often in embryo, to be sure, but unmistakable', in the quarto newsbooks of the period 1641 to 1665. It was a period of pamphleteering, of political and theological controversy. In the latter part of the seventeenth century the earliest scholarly journals, usually shortlived, consisted primarily of book notices, 'to acquaint the learned with each other's work'.[37] The influential French *Journal des savants*, which has continued, with breaks, from 1665, 'marked the beginning of a long line of serials devoted to the abstracting of books for busy readers'.[38] Of the longer-lived early English journals, the *History of the works of the learned* (1691–1712) is noteworthy as being largely devoted to describing foreign books, and *The present state of the Republic of Letters* (1728–36) covered English books. A tradition, then, of periodical reviewing was in process of creation by the beginning of the eighteenth century. Addison's critical essays on Milton in *The spectator* of 1712, which were unexpectedly popular, suggest that a new kind of critical audience was growing up.[39]

The gentleman's magazine (1731–1907) was founded by the publisher Edward Cave as a periodical of miscellaneous literature, setting the pattern of the review of literature, antiquities and science. At first its chief feature was the analysis, by Cave himself, of 'the two hundred half sheets which the London press then threw up monthly'.[40]

Of the main reviews of the pre-*Edinburgh review* period (1788–1802), Roper[41] gives prominence to the Whig and Nonconformist *Monthly review* (1749–1845) and its rival Tory and Established Church *Critical review* (1750–1817), which was supported by Johnson, Smollett and Robertson. The *Monthly review,* dealing throughout its long career with science and literature, as well as with literary criticism, began to assume more of the style of the modern review. Dr Johnson[42] drew a distinction between the two types of journal thus: 'The Critical reviewers, I believe, often review without reading the books through, but lay hold of a topic,   and write chiefly from their own minds. The Monthly Reviewers are duller men, and are glad to read the books through'.

It was *The Edinburgh review* (1802–1929), established by Jeffery, Scott, Horner, Brougham and Sidney Smith, that opened a new era in literary criticism. *The Edinburgh*'s contributors included Macaulay and Carlyle, both remarkable for their lengthy, subjective reviews, and the Lake Poets were a particular butt. *The quarterly review* (1809–1967), its Tory rival, mustered among its contributors, over the years, Canning, Scott (who reviewed himself), Southey, Sir John Barrow and Isaac Disraeli, and was notorious for Croker's attack on Keats's *Endymion*. (Roper[43] notes that these famous quarterlies were not always quick to spot new talent.) *Blackwood's [Edinburgh] Magazine* (1817–1973), a monthly rival of *The Edinburgh* and less weighty than *The quarterly*, directed its literary attacks against the 'Cockney School' of Hazlitt, Lamb and especially Leigh Hunt.

As to style, the mid-nineteenth century vogue of the leisurely 'polite' essay reached its zenith, given ample room for critical comment, in the authoritative, solemn and rotund voice of Macaulay: 'A generation later Arnold and Bagehot gave the form its final refinement; with Pater it was already in decline, expressive and subtle, but overwrought and literary'.[44]

Of the literary weeklies *The examiner* (1808–81) was one of the earliest. Its reputation owed much to a succession of such writers as Leigh Hunt, Albany Fonblanque, John Forster and Henry Morley.[45] The long-lived *Spectator* (1828–) gained respect for its sound judgement and authoritative criticism in both politics and literature — a status enhanced under J. St Leo Strachey's editorship. A third weekly, *The Saturday review* (1855–1931), devoted many of its pages to articles of pure criticism. Its reviewers were known as 'the Saturday revilers'.

Between 1870 and 1880 English newspapers, originating in the eighteenth-century 'pamphlet of news', began to pay increased attention to literary and artistic criticism, and gradually the daily press became a formidable competitor in this field to the weekly review, if not the monthlies and quarterlies. Hugh Chisholm continues:[46]

> Books are 'reviewed' in the Press for literary reasons partly as a *quid pro quo* for publishers' advertisements; and the desire for 'something to quote', irrespectively of the responsible nature of the criticism, became in the early 'nineties a mania with publishers... Unfortunately the enormous output of books made it impossible for editors to have them all reviewed, and equally impossible for them to be certain of discriminating properly between those which were really worth reviewing or not. The result has been that the work of book-reviewing in the newspapers is often hastily and poorly or very spasmodically done.

There were some notable exceptions. *The New York Times book review* (1896–) and *The Times literary supplement* (1901–) were 'the most serious attempt by any newspaper to deal seriously with letters'.[46]

Writing in the 1920s, F.R. Leavis[47] (editor of the influential quarterly review, *Scrutiny*, 1932–53) lamented that there was no longer a body of critical opinion. The fact that *The Edinburgh review* and its rivals 'pronounced a vigorous aesthetic creed and were, therefore, of the greatest benefit to a lively interest in poetry, is forgotten, because they were sometimes ungentlemanly, and their place has been taken, but not filled, by the torrential journalistic criticism that is poured out daily, weekly and monthly'. In general, reviews are considerably shorter than they were in the nineteenth century — more lively, but less critical.

An American analysis of book-reviewing in 1972–74 and 1978–80[48] found that the majority of reviews in six key US journals used extensively for book selection by librarians were favourable. Main factors in prevailing conditions are the flood of book production (51, 355 items in the UK alone in 1984), increasing subject specialization and the relatively small amount of space available for reviews, because of high costs. The present situation is one in which scholarly and professional journals continue to serve their particular clientèles, whereas the press, radio and television have gained ground at the expense of the literary and general weeklies, monthlies and quarterlies.

As to the future, Almargo[49] identifies three areas in which the value of book reviews could be enhanced:

1. A co-operative effort between editors and reviewers to shorten the present time lag between the publication of the book and the appearance of its review;
2. Co-ordination between publishers to avoid excessive duplication of reviews;
3. An increase in the number of books reviewed.

References

1. King, Lester S. 'The book review', *JAMA*, vol. 205, 1968, p. 343.
2. Manten, A.A. 'Book reviews in primary journals', *Journal of technical writing and communication*, vol. 5 (3), 1975, p. 232.
3. Virgo, Julie A. 'The review article: its characteristics and problems', *The library quarterly*, vol. 41 (4), October 1971, pp. 275–91.
4. Woodward, Anthony M. 'The roles of reviews in information transfer', *Journal of the American Society for Information Science*, vol. 25 (11), May 1977, pp. 178–80. Also; his 'Review literature: characteristics, sources and output in 1972', *Aslib proceedings*, vol. 26 (9), September 1974, pp. 367–76.

5. Harrod, L.M. *Harrod's librarians' glossary.* Aldershot, Hants., Gower, 1984, p. 238.
6. Woolf, Leonard, 'Note', in Virginia Woolf, *Reviewing.* London, Hogarth Press, 1939, p. 29.
7. Macphail, Bruce D. 'Book reviewers and the scholarly publisher', *Scholarly publishing,* vol. 12 (1), October 1980, p. 55.
8. Macleod, Beth. '*Library journal* and *Choice*: a review of reviews', *The journal of academic librarianship,* vol. 7 (1), March 1981, p. 23 (citing Friedland, Abbot. 'Reviews: who needs them?', ALA Conference, Chicago, July 1976).
9. Field, Daniel. 'Reviewing books', *The Russian review,* vol. 42 (4), October 1983, pp. v–viii.
10. Woolf, Virginia. *Reviewing.* London, Hogarth Press, 1939, p. 15.
11. King, Lester S. *op. cit.,* p. 343.
12. Conarroe, Joel, in *Earth and life science editing,* no. 20, September 1983, p. 10.
13. Lincoln, Tim. 'The book review business', *Nature,* vol. 302, 28 April 1983, p. 757.
14. Budd, John. 'Book reviewing practice of journals in the humanities', *Scholarly publishing,* vol. 13 (4), July 1982, pp. 363–71.
15. Collison, R.L. 'The art and technique of book reviewing. 3: Book reviews and the librarian', *Aslib proceedings,* vol. 1 (2), August 1949, pp. 128-32.
16. *The local historian,* vol. 16 (3), August 1984, p. 131.
17. Whittaker, Kenneth. *Systematic evaluation,* London, Bingley, 1982, pp. 132–8.
18. Brightman, R. 'The art and technique of book reviewing. 2: The reviewing of scientific and technical books', *Aslib proceedings,* vol. 1 (2), August 1949, pp. 125–7.
19. Chen, Ching-chih. *Biomedical, scientific and technical book reviewing.* Metuchen, NJ, Scarecrow Press, 1974. Also: Schutze, Gertrude. 'Time interval between book publication and review', *Special libraries,* November 1947, pp. 297–9.
20. *Kirkus reviews.* New York, Kirkus Reviews, 1933–. 6 p.a.
21. Katz, Bill, and Katz, Linda Sternberg. *Magazines for libraries,* 4th edn. New York, Bowker, 1982, p. 181.
22. *Good book guide: new book list.* London, Braithwaite and Taylor, 1985–. 12 p.a.
23. Culver, Marguerite R. 'Too much time lag in technical book reviews', *Library journal,* vol. 74 (10), May 1949, pp. 805–6.
24. Martinelli, L.W. 'Book reviews in scholarly journals', *Journal of research communication studies,* vol. 3, 1981–82, pp. 387–91.
25. Walby, Basil J., in *Earth and life science editing,* no. 20, September 1983, p. 10.
26. Sarton, George. 'Notes on the reviewing of learned books', *Isis,* vol. 41, July 1950, pp. 149–58.

27. Stueart, Robert D. 'Reviews and reviewing', in *Encyclopedia of library and information science*, vol. 25, 1978, p. 316.
28. Wolper, Roy S. 'On academic reviewing: ten common errors', *Scholarly publishing*, vol. 16 (3), April 1985, pp. 269–75.
29. Noble D.H., and Noble, C.M. 'A survey of book reviews', *Library Association record*, vol. 76 (9), May 1984, p. 96.
30. Oates, Quentin. 'Critics crowner', *The bookseller*, 4 August 1984, pp. 625–6.
31. Howard, Philip. 'Crowner in the dock', *The bookseller*, 9 March 1985, pp. 1036–7. Also: Gissen, Max. 'Commercial criticism and punch-drunk reviewing', *Antioch review*, vol. 2 (2), Summer 1942, pp. 252–63.
32. *Nature*, vol. 306, 6 October 1983, p. 478. Also: Glen, John W. '*Nature* reviews new journals', *Earth and life science editing*, no. 15, January 1982, pp. 15–16.
33. *TLS*, no. 4211, 16 December 1983, pp. 1397–402.
34. *TLS*, no. 4280, 23 November 1984, p. 1355.
35. *TLS*, no. 4245, 10 August 1984, p. 834.
36. McCutcheon, R.P. 'The beginning of book reviewing in English periodicals', *Proceedings of the MLA*, vol. 37, December 1922, pp. 691–706.
37. Young, Arthur P. 'Scholarly book reviewing in America', *Libri*, vol. 25 (3), 1975, pp. 174–82.
38. Graham, Walter. *The beginnings of English literary periodicals*, New York, Oxford University Press, 1926, p.2.
39. Watson, George. *The literary critics*, 2nd edn. London, Woburn Press, 1973, p. 56.
40. *Encyclopaedia Britannica*, 11th edn. Cambridge University Press, 1910–11, vol. 5, p. 573; vol. 21, p. 152.
41. Roper, Derek. *Reviewing before the 'Edinburgh', 1788–1802*. London, Methuen, 1978, p. 242.
42. Boswell, James. *Boswell's life of Johnson*. London, Oxford University Press, 1946, vol. 2, p. 23.
43. Roper, Derek. op. cit., p.244.
44. Read, Herbert. *Collected essays in literary criticism*, 2nd edn. London, Faber, 1951, p. 11.
45. *Encyclopaedia Britannica*, op. cit., vol. 19, p. 562.
46. *Encyclopaedia Britannica*, op. cit., vol. 19, p. 548.
47. Leavis, F.R. *Towards standards of criticism*. London, Wishart, 1933, p. 25.
48. Serebnick, Judith. 'An analysis of publishers of books reviewed in six library journals', *Library and information science research*, vol. 6 (3), July/September 1984, pp. 289–303.
49. Almargo, Bertha R. 'Book reviewing in medical journals', *The serials librarian*, vol. 9 (2), Winter 1984, pp. 121–31.

2. The administrative role of the book-review editor

J.D. Hendry

In my view, there are two kinds of book-review editors: the first can make a comparatively light task of his editorship, merely acting almost as a 'post-box', requesting books in an undiscriminating way and, equally, channelling copies of books submitted for review to a wide range of possible reviewers and assessors in a manner which is designed primarily for his own convenience; the second, however, is an editor of high standards whose editorship can attract both a high calibre of reviewer who feels honoured or academically recognized by an invitation to review, and this editor, too, has earned the esteem of authors and of publishers. The administrative problems, the skills and the wide range and depth of knowledge required of a book-review editor of stature, are considerable. The administrative role of such an editor is now considered.

The most fundamental, guiding principle of a review editor in preparing and publishing a review, must be to provide a valid academic assessment of integrity and standing. In my experience, if one consistently accepts less, then one not only has sub-standard quality in individual reviews, but the integrity and academic standards of the review journal and its editor, are equally diminished. Beyond this, one's guiding principles must be to take particular account of the range and level of the readership of one's journal, and in considering this factor, to bear in mind that a great many readers of such a journal peruse it as a current-awareness service and guide to its specialized literature, as may wish to dwell on its academic papers (which will likely appear at the front of the journal). For the purposes of this chapter, it is assumed that in the main, journals of an academic character containing both reputable articles and a substantial review section, are being discussed. There are, of course, a few journals which are devoted exclusively to reviews, but it is hoped that the comments made here will also be substantially relevant to such journals.

Any review editor can face a number of dilemmas in considering titles for review. His first problem may be in receiving a great many unsolicited books for review. There is no obligation to return such books — and, indeed, it may prove expensive to do so — if they are not to be reviewed. Nevertheless, it is a matter both of courtesy and a sound investment for the future if such works are returned to their publisher with a succinct note indicating the reasons why such a title is not appropriate for consideration for review purposes. This can thereafter have the advantage of saving both the editor's time, and that of the publisher, and will signal clearly to the publisher the policies and standards of the review journal. A publisher who persists in forwarding titles not relevant to such a journal can thereafter be ignored with a relatively clear conscience.

It is extremely important that an editor of integrity should show clearly what his policies and standards are. If, however, a title submitted in such a way is considered to be reasonably within the scope of a journal's areas of interest, it can be helpful to both readers and publishers if this work is listed in a general 'List of publications received'. Readers therefore know of its existence. Any further conclusions or assessments can then be made by the individual reader concerned in following up an individual investigation of this entry. The normally accepted bibliographical details should be included, and recommendations relating to such details are contained in this paper. The unsolicited title, however, can be the most clear-cut aspect of a review editor's work. Inevitably, an editor has a whole range of informal contacts with publishers, academics, practitioners and others involved in the production of books on almost any subject. Editors can be approached informally by authors, agents or publishers, to give consideration to reviews: equally, editors can learn informally of the planned or forthcoming publication of a title and may be interested in assessing such a work for review. In such situations, there is no hard-and-fast rule; only integrity, and mutual trust and respect. Where an editor requests a book for review, either formally or informally, he has a duty to have this work reviewed. Otherwise he should indicate to the publisher the reason why he is unable to do so. Equally, a request to have a review journal placed on a publisher's mailing list brings an obligation either to review or return.

In selecting reviewers for books which the editor considers that he wishes to see reviewed and published in his journal, there can be a number of varying practices. One school of thought holds to the view that many of the best, well-thought-out and critical reviews are undertaken by bright young academics and professionals on their way up, so to speak. It is an intrinsic part of an editor's work to be aware of such young talent. In many cases such potential reviewers may be as knowledgeable in their fields, because they are likely to be as directly and closely involved in their specialist field of work as their more eminently regarded counterparts of an older generation. This is not always the case, however, and it would be a great pity if a substantive work were done less than justice because a bright young man did not live up to his apparent promise. Another problem is in having reviews returned on time from busy academics and practitioners. Many in this category are extremely busy, but do not like to refuse a reasonable request to review. Frequently, too, they may be amongst the best in their field. Here again there is no simple solution. A series of polite but consistent reminders, starting at an early date, and a degree of personal intervention, are often the most effective devices. Editors have to realize, however, that there are times to cut their losses and reconcile themselves to an inability to obtain a review of a work on time. This is always a great pity, and an experience from which an editor learns as he develops his knowledge both of publishers and, especially, potential reviewers.

There are certain basic bibliographical facts which should always be presented clearly in any review. Regrettably, although these seem known to most librarians, they are not always recognized by academics and, in some cases, by academic review-editors:

(1.)   The names and initials of authors and/or editors.
(2.)   Their designations, if relevant.
(3.)   The title, and if there is such, the subtitle of the work.
(4.)   The series (if applicable).
(5.)   Edition, or related detail (e.g. *2nd edition, revised*).
(6.)   Year of publication or, failing which, year of copyright.
(7.)   Publisher.
(8.)   Place of publication and international standard book number (ISBN).
(9.)   Number of tables, plates, diagrams, and so on.
(10.)   Price; here price in country of origin should be stressed; prices can vary widely from one country to another.

The substance of a review is the most important element in any review which hopes to be considered objective *and* critical. Unfortunately, but understandably, many editors are under pressure of space to include as many short, pithy reviews as possible, in any given issue of their journal. There are arguments in favour of imposing on a potential reviewer the discipline of writing a review within the parameters of, say, 500 words for a short review, 1,000 words for a longer and more critical review, and perhaps 1,500 for a wide-ranging or in-depth assessment. The critical factor, however, for any editor, should be in most cases, to know his reviewer, and with this, to ascertain the significance of an author and his work, in a general sense. Again there are no hard-and-fast rules. A combination of long-developing judgement and instinct should in most situations equip an editor with the knowledge to judge the length and depth of treatment which a review should take. In some instances, however, I would go beyond this. Many academics at the peak of their careers and their intellectual and administrative powers may be frustrated and stultified by an over-restrictive number of words given in guidelines for review. In so many cases a wide-ranging and in-depth review and academic discussion have emerged, as a result of a knowledgeable editor allowing a reviewer of standing to have the space he requires to do justice to a new and potentially notable work. Such reviews, when they do emerge, can often be landmarks in the development of a subject or theme, referred to by many researchers in years to come. I would caution, therefore, against the too-rigid imposition of a set number of words in reviews, although I appreciate the need for such discipline in many circumstances.

It should go without saying, that the substance of any review should actually tell the reader what the book is about, by giving a fair and succinct summary of its contents, and whether the author's aims, and the contents, reasonably match each other. Together with this, one expects an assessment of the level at which the book is aimed, and to what extent the author has succeeded in reaching this audience or readership. Regrettably, such factors do not always manifest themselves, and while an editor has a responsibility in soliciting, and then publishing reviews which might then turn out to be less than satisfactory, it must sometimes be recognized that a poor review may say a great deal more about the reviewer than about the author of the original work (or even the book-review editor). Weak and slackly written reviews have to be suffered from time to time. More difficult, however, is the garrulous and self-opinionated reviewer, who is more interested in his own point of view and self-esteem than in disciplining himself to a proper and critical assessment of the value of a work. To a degree, but not consistently, such reviews may have to be borne, more as a reflection of the reviewer than anything else. Nevertheless, any firm review-editor will not tolerate acidic remarks, personal diatribes or the personalization of academic or professional issues. It is not the role of a reputable review journal to act as a vehicle for such shoddy behaviour. A pointed, or perhaps a brief but diplomatic note, to such a reviewer, may not always win friends, but it will maintain the integrity and standards of the review journal.

Further, in considering the substance of a review, it is quite appropriate to remark on layout, quality of paper, illustrations, diagrams and tables, pricing, indexing and type-face. Each of these factors can be important in evaluating the use of a book, or even in the degree of value and ease of use, which may be considered in deciding whether to purchase a book or to request one's institution to seek to obtain it.

The physical layout of reviews is something which all too often spoils the overall impression of a book-review section. There are two aspects to be considered: firstly, the positioning of individual reviews, and groups of reviews, in relation to each other; and secondly, the physical layout of spacing, headings, type-face and general page-design and art-work.

Many editors tend to list reviews by length (in the first instance). Thus the 'long' reviews come first, followed by those of middle length and finally the short reviews. I have known a number of review editors who have used this format as a vehicle to edit badly written reviews, or those of poor substance, in order to bury these at the end of the short-reviews section. While having some sympathy for this, it is not a practice I would recommend. If reviews have to be edited, because of the types of problem I have mentioned above, they should nevertheless be grouped with their subject. My own inclination, and one I have found attractive to many who follow reviews consistently, is to begin a review section with one long, discursive and critical review, contributed by a reviewer of some stature, usually in consideration of a work which is, in itself, potentially of significance. Here I would provide a title or apt quotation for the review, followed by the name of the reviewer. There would then follow the author, title and other bibliographical details of the work being considered, with the author and short or initial title in bold-type. The body of the review would follow in normal-type. This review would be separated clearly from other reviews by the use of white space, line or other devices such as asterisks – or simply to lay out the review, if possible, to finish at the end of a page. My preference beyond this initial review would be to group like-subject reviews together, arranging these alphabetically by author. The reviewer's name and a brief description of his position or standing, should be placed at the end of each review. A 'List of publications received' might be placed at the end of these reviews.

It cannot be stressed too often, that the impact and effect of a book-review journal or section can be spoiled, and the substance of the reviews badly received, by a poor physical layout. Clearly, a review editor must conform to the overall style and layout of the parent journal. Nevertheless, a close working relationship with the printers and graphic artists involved in the layout and printing of a journal can be a fruitful and aesthetically satisfying investment. Too many academic and professional journals are physically staid in appearance. There is surely no need to appear dull in order to be academically reputable.

There can also be a feeling or impression, amongst the editors of academic and professional journals, that the book-review section is rather a poor relation, an appendage tacked on to a journal to fill in space. Nothing should be further from the truth, as many practitioners in specialist fields use such journals primarily as a source to assist them to remain abreast of current literature and, in the case of many librarians and other book selectors, in gaining guidance as to availability and value for money. A good book-review section is of considerable importance to a journal and should be treated accordingly, and the review editor must be the first to recognize this.

In summary, a book-review editor must always maintain a sense of objectivity and integrity. It is too easy to seek reviews from one's friends, to solicit reviews from those whom one knows will provide a 'comfortable' review in the knowledge that the cynicism which afflicts many closely-knit academic and professional groupings will ensure that a similarly sympathetic review will be reciprocated in times to come. Nor should a review editor ever forget the bitterness and anguish which an author may experience when he feels that his book has been unfairly or cavalierly treated.

There are times when authors are wounded because, or perhaps despite the fact, that their works are reviewed fairly and vigorously. However, a review editor's ultimate task, for every work that appears in his journal, is to ensure that he maintains the highest standards of intellectual honesty and academic integrity. It is a considerable responsibility.

Bibliography

Budd, John. 'Book reviewing practices of journals in the humanities', *Scholarly publishing*, vol. 12 (4), July 1982, pp. 363–71.

Freeman, Susan Tax. 'On responsibility in reviewing', *American anthropologist*, vol. 79 (2), June 1977, pp.441–2.

Simon, Rita James, and Mahan, Linda. 'A note on the role of book review editor as decision maker', *Library quarterly*, vol. 39 (4), October 1969, pp.353–6.

Part 2

Specialized reviewing

3.   Reference books

A.J. Walford

The field covered by the term 'reference book' is indeed wide: it comprises bibliographies and indexes, handbooks and manuals, encyclopaedias, directories, biographical sources, histories, gazetteers, atlases, yearbooks.[1] For the purpose of this brief survey, reviews of general bibliographies and encyclopaedias have been singled out for comment. Language dictionaries are considered in Chapter 11 and specialized encyclopaedias, dictionaries and bibliographies figure under the subjects concerned.

The reviewing apparatus for reference works is a flourishing one in the United States. Certain periodicals and annuals are wholly devoted to such reviewing: *American reference books annual* (*ARBA*) (1970–), *Reference sources* (1977–), *Reference and subscription books reviews*, 1968/70 (1970–) and *RSR/Reference services review* (4 p.a.). Other US journals run regular reference-book review sections — *Choice*,[2] *Library journal*,[3] *Wilson library bulletin*, *RQ* and *College and research libraries*.[4] *The journal of academic librarianship* (Ann Arbor, Mich., Mountainside Publishing, Inc., 1975–6 p.a.) has a regular 'Reference material' mini-reviews section. Librarians and academics dominate the US reviewing scene.

The British reference-book reviewing apparatus is, by comparison, fragmentary. *Refer* is the one periodical wholly concerned with reference items and resources. *Library review* (1927– 4 p.a.) allots a diminishing number of its pages to reference material. *British book news: a monthly review of new books*, excellent of its kind, does not sectionalize reference books, although it carries a regular review-essay on a particular topic or area. The *TLS*, similarly, provides general coverage, with one issue annually highlighting reference items,

British and foreign (e.g. no. 4282, 26 April 1985). *Good book guide* (1977–.3 p.a., with 2 supplements) has a regular, if small, reference-book section, with periodic comparative round-ups of English-language encyclopaedias, dictionaries and atlases. The annual *Good book guide to children's books* has a 'Reference' section.

Qualifications of a reference-book critic are enumerated by Kister[5] as follows:

1. The ability to write clearly, succinctly and sometimes quickly.
2. A thorough and comparative knowledge of reference materials and their make-up, characteristics and uses.
3. An objective stance towards the material under review.
4. An honest and independent spirit.

Bibliographies

Bibliographies provide easy targets for comment in terms of coverage, arrangement, detail (including annotation) and supporting indexes. Colaianne[6] distinguishes between annotated bibliography and descriptive and analytical bibliography. Both of the latter are based primarily on the study of format. Points for evaluating a bibliography have been outlined by the Committee of the Reference Services Division, American Library Association,[7] under nine heads: (1) subject matter; (2) scope within subject matter; (3) methodology; (4) organization; (5) annotations, abstracts; (6) bibliographic form; (7) timeliness; (8) accuracy; and (9) evaluation of format.

The valuable review-article by Cave,[8] 'Besterman and bibliography: an assessment', discusses at length Theodore Besterman's concept of bibliography, as expressed in his monumental *A world bibliography of bibliographies* (Lausanne, Societas Bibliographica, 1963–66, 5 vols.) which ran to four editions in 30 years. Cave describes this compilation as a masterpiece of enumerative work, but flawed by some of Besterman's theories. Coverage excluded bibliographies not separately published on the theory that lists of value were only *occasionally* in serials and other works. Besterman also rejected annotated entries; instead he painstakingly recorded the number of items in each volume of a bibliography as 'an alternative to critical annotation'. A third major criticism by Cave is of Besterman's adopting A–Z subject and country arrangement for entries, on the theory that classification schemes become obsolete, being modified to meet individual needs. But subject (and country) headings, too, can suffer modification, and the inadequacy of cross-references in *A World bibliography* underlines this deficiency.

The 120-word mini-review of Gavin Higgens's *Printed reference material* (2nd edn. London, Library Association, 1984) in *Current awareness bulletin*[9] hardly allows for more than concise descriptive notes and a concluding appraisal: 'An essential volume for any library'. But the reviewer errs in declaring the handbook to be 'an exhaustive guide for reference librarians'. What bibliographic guide can claim to be 'exhaustive' or, for that matter, 'the ultimate'?[10] ('Comprehensive' would have been a better term.) The 800-word review in *Refer*[11] gives the writer ample room and verge enough to dissect, comment on and then detail shortcomings that the compiler could bear in mind when planning a third edition of *Printed reference material*. Thus the *Refer* review notes the absence of 'old favourites' and certain other 'indispensable' tools, naming them. A composite work such as the Higgens volume, with its 19 contributors, is bound to show some unevenness and inconsistencies, as well as gaps in coverage. The *Refer* review states that 'the greatest disappointment with Higgens must be the neglect of audiovisual material and microforms'. Higgens 2 already admits chapters on 'Online information retrieval systems' and 'Videotext information and communication systems'. What, pray, do we mean by *printed* reference material?

Encyclopaedias

The role of the multi-volume English-language general encyclopaedia tends to have a diminishing scholarly appeal in an age of subject encyclopaedias. Of those general encyclopaedias, the majority are published, using continuous revision, in the USA. The Reference and Subscription Books Review Committee of the ALA has listed eleven points to be considered in evaluating general encyclopaedias:[12] (1) authority; (2) subject coverage and emphasis; (3) structure, with particular attention to access to particulars, and display of related data; (4) accuracy; (5) objectivity; (6) currency; (7) style, with attention to vocabulary levels; (8) bibliography; (10) physical format; and (11) special features.

Dahlaus[13] opens his review of *The new Grove dictionary of music and musicians* with the confession: 'Dictionaries and encyclopaedias are, strictly speaking, scarcely reviewable. The merits that distinguish them and the deficiencies that mar them reveal themselves only during the course of years — or even decades — of use'.

The Daily Telegraph review of the sixth edition of *Everyman's encyclopaedia* (London, Dent, 1978, 12 vols.[14] is headed 'All you need to know', and it praises the set as 'everything that a compact work of reference for the home should be... an ever-present help in the hour of homework'. The reviewer does point out that the *Everyman's* policy of avoiding long articles continues, that illustrations are now *in situ* instead of being bunched, and affirms that the encyclopaedia has the 'virtue of ease of reference'. He admits, however, that many articles have been left substantially as they were in the fifth edition (1967). While *Everyman's encylopaedia* (6th edn) certainly contains numerous sound, concise articles by British academics on a variety of subjects, one important drawback has been overlooked in *The Daily Telegraph's* 200-word review: the absence of an index. Such an omission is possibly acceptable in a one-volume general encyclopaedia of the calibre of *The new Columbia encyclopaedia* (4th edn. New York, Columbia University Press, 1975) — similar in wordage, price and number of articles, with 66,000 cross-references — but it is inexcusable in a 12-volume general encyclopaedia with a defective apparatus for cross-referencing and awkward division of volumes. The heavily-contoured atlas appended to volume 12 of *Everyman's* appears to be an afterthought; it has no link with the main text as a locator of places.

The 1974 edition of the *New encyclopaedia Britannica* ('Britannica 3') was a basic reorganization into three parts: *Propaedia* (1 vol.), *Micropaedia* (10 vols.) and *Macropaedia* (19 vols.). It elicited a remarkable number of critical reviews. The well-balanced 4,000-word appraisal by Cole in *Wilson library bulletin*[15] has sections on structure, approach and coverage, format, difficulties in use, and sampling searches. The conclusion reached is that Britannica 3 contains much excellent material, but ease of use is not one of its merits. The division of contents between *Micropaedia* and *Macropaedia* makes it necessary to consult another volume in most cases. Indeed, 'it is our experience that even simple searches might involve eight or nine volumes...The form of subject headings can create difficulties for users...By far the greatest source of difficulty in the use of Britannica 3 is the indexing, and in this encyclopaedia the use of the index is absolutely essential'. Cole concludes that Britannica 3 should be purchased for its detailed coverage of the contemporary world, but that it will not entirely replace any printing of the *Britannica* since 1970.

Indexes to reviews

Two annuals, *American reference books annual* (see below) and *Reference sources*, both act as indexes to reviews of reference books. *Reference sources*[16] (Ann Arbor, Mich., Pierian Press, 1977–) covers items reviewed in over 600 library and non-library journals. Entries are in one A–Z author sequence, with cross-references from titles. The 1977 volume has 20- to 60-word annotated entries for 3,500 books, citing a single reviewing source in each case. *Book review digest*[17] (New York, H.W. Wilson, 1906– 10 p.a., quarterly and annual cumulations), *Book review index* (Detroit, Mich., Gale, 1965–, 6 p.a., annual cumulation) and *Library literature* H.W. Wilson, 1931–. 6 p.a., annual cumulation) index the leading US reference reviewing journals.

Reviewing journals

American reference book annual (Littleton, Colo., Libraries Unlimited, 1970–. Annual) is devoted to reviews of reference books published or distributed in the United States. As the largest of the current reference-service reviews *ARBA* employs several editor-reviewers, all with library-science background. Vol. 15, 1984 (xxvii, 793 pp.), has 1,534 numbered and signed entries in 43 categories (1. General reference works...43. Military science), citing ten US reviewing library journals. A list of about 300 contributors states their affiliations. The reviews, 300 over 1,000 words long, are analytical, critical and comparative. *ARBA* excels in its longer reviews. *Academic American encyclopedia* (New York, Grolier, 1982 [revised annually], 21 vols.) provides bibliographies for only 40 per cent of its articles and is less strong on science and technology: 'Overall, AAE is a sound purchase for high schools and undergraduate libraries for use as a ready-reference tool. It cannot be thought of as a replacement for World Book, Americana or Collier's (the main competitors), but rather as a supplement to these works. It is a good buy for the money but it does need to be used with caution'. Bibliographical data in *ARBA* entries lack only full pagination. Its index covers authors, titles, forms and subjects; cumulations are for 1970–74 and 1975–79. About one-third of *ARBA* reviews are reprinted, suitably geared, in *Reference sources for small and medium-sized libraries* (4th edn. ALA, 1984).

Choice (Chicago, Ill., Association of College and Research Libraries, ALA, 1964–. 11 p.a. Circulation: 5,090) is 'a monthly book and non-print selection journal', with about 300-word reviews of some 8,000 items p.a. and aimed primarily at American undergraduate libraries. Vol. 22 (6), March 1985 (pp. 755–896), has about 750 reviews in 30 main sections, of which the 'Reference' section (pp. 791–801) comprises 51 entries. The book reviews, signed, with affiliations, are analytical, critical and frequently comparative, indicating readership. Thus *An atlas of African affairs*, by Ieuan Ll. Griffiths (London, Methuen, 1984) is described as 'a handy reference that will best serve to accompany other research reading, giving graphic, continent-wide information on a broad range of topics' and for possible classroom use. For libraries, it supplements Colin McEvedy's *Penguin atlas of African history* (London, Lane, 1980) and J.D. Fage's *Atlas of African history* (2nd edn. London, E. Arnold, 1978). It does not replace R. Van Chi-Bonnardel's *Atlas of Africa* (New York, Free Press, 1973), although there is some ovelap with *Africa today: an atlas of reproducible pages* (Wellesley, Mass., World Eagle, 1983). While Griffiths supplies more narrative data on events, *Africa today* has larger maps and charts.

Choice's bibliographical details invariably quote CIP data. Other features of *Choice* include 'Periodicals for college libraries', a bibliographical essay or review article and 'Letters' (including authors' or others' comments on reviews). Each issue carries author, title and advertisers indexes, cumulated per annual volume and for vols. 1–10, March 1964 to February 1974.

Reference and subscription books reviews (Chicago, Ill., ALA, 1958/60–. annual. Circulation: 37,000) cumulates reviews in the twice-monthly (monthly in July and August) *RSBR* — within the same covers as the ALA's *Booklist*. The 1982/83 volume (vii, 108 pp.) has 289 'Reviews and notes' ranging from mere references to 1,600-word book-reviews, plus three 'Omnibus articles' (e.g. 'Six multi-volume adult encyclopedias', each surveyed under 11 heads). Reviews are closely analytical, critical, indicating readership, and comparative, with appended descriptors. The belated review of the 20-volume *The illustrated encyclopedia of mankind* (London, Marshall Cavendish, 1978) gives editorial details before describing coverage: 'a synthesis of information usually accessible only in the collections of academic libraries'. 'Criticism should be tempered by the fact that it provides, as it was intended to do, an excellent synoptic overview of extant peoples and cultures in fewer than 2,700 pages', although the editors do not state their criteria for selecting cultural and linguistic groups represented in the 500 entries: 'It will...give reference departments of all types of libraries something heretofore not available — a simple compendium of ethnographic information for a representative sample of world cultures'. Bibliographical data in *RSBR* omit full pagination and ISBNs. A title index precedes the text. The 1983/84 annual has a changed title: *Reference books bulletin*. It lists titles of items reviewed under 23 subject and form headings, with an appended A–Z subject and form index.

RSR/Reference services review (Ann Arbor, Mich., Pierian Press, 1972–. 4 p.a. Circulation: 2,000) aims 'to provide reference librarians and subject bibliographers with information essential to discerning and judicious book selection, as well as guidance in the use of existing reference sources'. Vol. 12 (2), Summer 1984 (112 pp.), groups reviews under state-of-the-art surveys (e.g. 'Birds of a feather: a covey of field guides') and the regular 'Reference serials'. The 1,000-word review of *The ALA glossary of library and information science*, edited by Heartsill Young (Chicago, Ill., ALA, 1983) is a thorough revision of the 1943 *ALA glossary* and has at least twice as many terms. It is praised for its 'excellent syndetic features, its list of published sources consulted and its affordable price [$20]'. *Harrod's librarians' glossary*, by L.M. Harrod (5th edn. Aldershot, Hants., Gower, 1984) is more encyclopaedic, with extended definitions and entries for names of organizations. *RSR* bibliographical data omit only full pagination. Each issue carries a very selective index.

Library journal (New York, Bowker, 1876–. 22 p.a. Circulation: 26,634) regularly features book reviews, with a short section, 'Reference books'. vol. 110 (2), 1 February 1985 (120 pp.), has reviews on pp. 86–115, including 10 reference-book reviews. Comments average between 150 and 250 words, are signed, with affiliations, and are evaluative, indicating readership. A handbook on the birds of Australia is graded 'for the novice' and faulted for its inappropriate large format, detracting from its use as a field guide. *The Macmillan book of business and economic quotations*, edited by Michael Jackman (London, Macmillan, 1985) is criticized for omitting dates and citations of sources. *A dictionary of economic quotations*, edited by Simon James (London, Croom Helm, 1981) is preferred. Bibliographical details in *LJ* omit place of publication and full pagination. Each issue has an index of 'Book reviews and professional reading'. The 15 April issue each year features 'Reference books of 19--', compiled by the ALA's Outstanding Reference Books Committee, Reference and Adult Services Division.

Wilson library bulletin (New York, H.W. Wilson, 1914–. 10 p.a. Circulation: 23,000) is for small and medium-sized general libraries. Vol. 59 (7), March 1985 (pp. 435–512), has a 'Current reference books' section of 24 items on pp. 499–504, by a university librarian. The 150- to 200-word reviews are briefly analytical and comparative, indicating readership. *The encyclopedia of American political history*, edited by James P. Greene (New York, Scribner) has 90 lengthy articles, the scholarly contributors being encouraged 'to take a strong personal line of interpretation'. As such, the books, with its extensive index and bibliography, complements the narrower articles in the Scribner *Dictionary of American history* (1976–77, 7 vols. and index). Bibliographical data in *WLB* reviews lack ISBNs and full pagination. The annual index has a heading 'Reference books, reviews of', with author and title entries.

RQ (Chicago, Ill., Reference and Adult Services Division, ALA, 1960–. 4 p.a. Circulation: 6,000) is particularly helpful to reference librarians. Vol. 24 (2), Winter 1984 (pp. 131–248), has a 'Reference books' section, with an editor, pp. 224–36. The 21 reviews, between 350 and 600 words apiece, signed, with affiliations, are analytical and critical, indicating readership. *The bibliography of Mexican-American history*, edited by Malt S. Meier (Westport, Conn., Greenwood Press, 1985) is strongly recommended, although material published in the 1980s is not well represented. Bibliographical details in *RQ* omit full pagination and ISBNs. The annual volume-index includes author–title entries for books reviewed.

College and research libraries (Chicago, Ill., Association of College and Research Libraries, ALA, 1939–. 6 p.a. Circulation: 11,000) features a half-yearly (January, July) section of reviews: 'Selected reference books of...', edited by Eugene P. Sheehy. Vol. 46 (1), January 1985 (100 pp.), covers the second part for 1983–84 (pp. 55–67), with 25 initialled entries, each between 250 and 350 words in length, and arranged under 14 headings (Bibliography...Psychology). Comments are descriptive and evaluative, the selection being intended for 'reference workers in university libraries'. *The encyclopedia of historic places*, by Courtland Canby (New York, Facts on File, 1985) is compared unfavourably with the Webster and Columbia–Lippincott gazetteers and with *The new Columbia encyclopedia*. Bibliographical details omit full pagination. The annual index has entries for authors and reviewers.

British book news: a monthly review of new books (London, British Council, 1944–. 12 p.a. Circulation: 5,000) is a major selection tool for British books. The March 1985 issue (pp. 129–92) has 205 reviews, of which perhaps 10 per cent concern reference items. Reviews are between 200 and 500 words long, signed, but without affiliations, and briefly analytical, indicating readership. *Longman dictionary of the English language* (Harlow, Essex, Longman, 1984) 'may be safely recommended to anyone whose needs are no longer satisfied by a concise dictionary, but who find the *Shorter Oxford English dictionary* [3rd edn. Oxford, Clarendon Press, 1973, 2 vols.] insufficiently up to date'. However, no comparison with competitive dictionaries by Chambers and Collins is offered. Bibliographical details omit full pagination. Authors and titles of books reviewed are indexed monthly and annually.

Refer: journal of the RSIS (Reference, Special and Information Section) (London, Library Association, 1980–. 2 p.a. Circulation: 6,250) 'a forum for news, views and comment on all aspects of reference and information work', specifically concerns itself with British reference material and resources. Apart from the lengthy review of Higgens's *Printed reference material* (see above), it carries a valuable regular feature, 'Reference books you may have missed' (pp. 9–13), covering 25 items; for example, *British government publications: an index to chairmen and authors*, vol. 4 (1979–82), edited by Stephen Richard (London, Library Association, 1984), and the international version of the *Aslib directory: libraries, information centres and databases in science and technology: a world guide* (Munich, etc., K.G, Saur, 1984), the latter being arranged by countries, but the subject indexing is far too broad and most entries 'have no indication of subject'. *Refer* gives ISBNs for items, but not full pagination. Volumes 1 and 2 have a combined index.

References

1. Covey, Alma A. *Reviewing of reference works*. Metuchen, NJ, Scarecrow Press, 1972, pp. 20–36.
2. Schmitt, John D. 'An assessment of *Choice* as a tool for selection', *College and research libraries*, vol. 44 (5), September 1983, pp. 374–80.
3. Macleod, Beth. '*Library journal* and *Choice*: a review of reviews', *The journal of academic librarianship*, vol. 7 (1), March 1981, pp. 23–8.
4. Rettig, James. 'Reviewing the reference reviews', *RSR*, vol. 9 (4), October/December 1981, pp. 85–102. Also: Ream, Daniel. 'An evaluation of four book review journals', *RQ*, vol. 11 (2), Winter 1979, pp. 149–53.
5. Kister, Ken. 'Wanted: more professionalism in reference book reviewing',*RQ*, vol. 19 (2), Winter 1979, pp. 144–8.
6. Colaianne, A.J. 'The aims and methods of annotated bibliography', *Scholarly publishing*, vol. 11 (4), July 1980, pp. 321–31.
7. 'Criteria for evaluating a bibliography', *RQ*, vol. 11, Summer 1972, pp. 359–60.
8. Cave, Roderick. 'Besterman and bibliography: as assessment', *Journal of librarianship*, vol. 10 (3), July 1978, pp. 149–61,
9. *Current awareness bulletin*, vol. 2 (2), February 1985, p.18.
10. *American libraries*, vol. 8 (3), March 1977, p.129.
11. Dixon, Diana. 'Printed reference material: Higgens 2 reviewed', *Refer*, vol. 3 (3), Spring 1985, pp.7–8.
12. *Reference and subscription books reviews, 1982–1983*. Chicago, Ill., American Library Association, 1983, p.94.
13. Dahlaus, Carl. 'The new Grove', *Music and letters*, July/October 1981, p. 249.

14. *The Daily Telegraph*, 14 December 1978, p. 12.
15. Cole, Dorothy Ethlyn. 'Britannica 3 as a reference tool: a review', *Wilson library bulletin*, vol. 48 (10), pp. 821–5.
16. *Reference sources for small and medium-sized libraries*, 4th edn. Chicago, Ill., ALA, entry 166.
17. Palmer, Joseph W. 'Review citations for best-selling books', *RQ*, vol. 19 (2), Winter 1979, pp. 154–8.

4. Religion and philosophy

Michael J. Walsh

First I ought to declare an interest. Too many years ago to recall now with comfort, one of my tutors assured me that if my history degree did nothing else, it would equip me to review books. Soon afterwards I began. The first volume upon which my animadversions appeared in print was, I think, a study on the theology of work. It had been passed on to me by another of my mentors, whose eyesight would no longer permit him to pick his way among small type. From that time onwards I have always had upon desk or mantleshelf a collection of books awaiting my perusal — and a deadline.

But I have another perspective on the art of reviewing. For a short period I was acting as a publisher. I had to organize publicity and media coverage, and choose suitable journals to which to send the handful of books for which I was responsible. Only one journal, the *Theologische Revue* as I recall, ever returned a book as unsuitable for their publication. Otherwise one sat back and waited for a notice of the book to appear. Sometimes they did; sometimes they did not — but that, too, I have come to understand during the dozen and more years I have served as the review editor to the *Heythrop journal*.

This last experience has taught me a great deal, especially, perhaps, about the haphazard nature of reviewing. Some books, most obvious among those classed as religion rather than philosophy, will scarcely ever be noticed in the type of journal discussed later in this chapter. I am thinking in particular of books intended for devotional reading, of which there are myriads and whose popularity is unquestioned despite their being ignored by the academic world. But for the other, more reviewable titles, so much depends upon chance: upon the knowledge of the review editor and his or her advisors; upon being the first to approach the obvious person with suitable terms (I am speaking of length and copy-date and not of finance); upon the chance encounter and the discovery of a new facet to an established reviewer's range of interests. And even when an apparently appropriate person has been cajoled into accepting, there is still no guarantee that satisfactory copy will be returned, though, to be truthful, that is possibly the least of the worries of a review editor in a learned journal.

And there is a fourth aspect to my interest in reviews of books. I have long been a librarian. In that office I have often had to depend upon notices of books in learned journals before deciding whether to spend meagre resources upon this one expensive, scholarly volume or upon those three relatively cheap undergraduate texts. I have friends in the publishing world who tell me that, in the academic sphere, reviews do not sell books. I have others who assure me they do, and it is with the latter group that, as a librarian, I side, with the proviso that, in the academic field, even books which receive bad notices can prove to be indispensable.

That at least seems to be true of the humanities. I have been struck by how little attention has been given to the art of reviewing, and of reading reviews, by those authors who have surveyed the topics of philosophy and religion and presume to give advice. My own introduction to *Religious bibliographies in serial literature: a guide*[1] does not recommend the use of reviews, though the description of the 177 journals listed is careful in each case to mention the importance of the review section.

Otto Lankhorst, in his *Les revues de sciences religieuses*, devotes some five pages to 'recensions' without suggesting that they may be of importance to the study of religion.[2] Indeed, he appears to be doubtful about the value of journals in general:

> Les études sur le contenu des revues en sciences exactes montrent comment les publications spécialisées servent à l'avancée de la science. Or en sciences religieuses, sans se citer les uns les autres au plan international et sans se copier d'ailleurs, les articles des revues se répètent. La prolifération des revues n'augmente pas l'information. Les instruments bibliographiques existent tant en sciences religieuses qu'en sciences exactes. Mais alors que dans ces dernières elles sont utilisées, ceux des sciences religieuses laissent le chercheur indifférent[3]

He may be right. Wilson and Slavens' *Research guide to religious studies*[4] scarcely mentions periodicals.

They order things differently in philosophy. In his *Philosophy: its nature, methods and basic sources*, Sebastian Matczak writes:

> Magazines are of great importance for scholars. They find in them the elaboration of specific problems which can hardly be published in book-form because of their limited scope ... In these magazines also the most recent literature on topics which might be of significant value for our own prospective writings or our own writings in progress are listed and examined[5]

He then devotes over thirty pages to 'Periodicals in general', 'General philosophical magazines' and 'Special philosophical magazines', this last section being divided up both geographically and by discipline within the general area of philosophical study. This view of the importance of journals is shared by Richard De George, and he puts it even more forcefully:

> Periodicals are the lifeblood of contemporary philosophy, and provide a ready outlet for the writings of philosophers ... Many philosophical journals list new books in philosophy as they appear, often giving brief summaries of them and carrying review articles of the more important and significant ones. By following the journals one can keep abreast of new books and can often decide from the summaries and reviews which to read, buy, or recommend to a university or public library[6]

Dr De George has a somewhat optimistic view of the 'up-to-dateness' of philosophical reviewing. Both the philosophical and theological journals noticed below clearly have backlogs of reviews awaiting publication – or their reviewers are singularly dilatory in sending in their copy. Both factors may apply, but from my experience it is the former rather than the latter reason which accounts for most of the delay. Journals simply cannot cope with the number of books which are sent. When I calculated, some ten years ago, the number of books received by the *Heythrop journal* over a period of years, the figure for 1974 was 368. In that year the number of works actually reviewed was 166. In 1984 the number of books reviewed had risen slightly, to just under 200, taking into account those covered by the *Journal*'s 'Notes and Comments' section, but the number of books logged as having been received that year was 637. Clearly, rather less than a third of these will be noticed in the pages of the *Journal*, other than by a listing under 'Books received'.

It would of course be possible to notice rather more books were the length of individual reviews to be reduced. As will be seen later, this is a solution followed by some of the journals discussed, both in philosophy and religion, and the short notice can respond to the need, expressed above by De George, for information upon which to base decisions about what to read or purchase. But this raises a question about the nature of reviewing in scholarly journals in general, and perhaps in particular about the type of review which ought to be published by academic journals in philosophy and theology. For in both of these disciplines the facts are rarely in dispute. What matters is the argumentation and the conclusions to be drawn from the facts. It is not enough to tell the reader in brief form what an author says: a reviewer has to evaluate the argument and enter into debate with the author. It is this which makes a journal a forum for discussion, just as much as the article section which, almost always, precedes the reviews. The *Review of metaphysics* (see below) at one time provided the brief abstract type of review: I have noted with interest that of late it has moved into the evaluative type.

Religion

Indexes to reviews

Religious index one: periodicals (Chicago, Ill., American Theological Library Association, 1977–. 2 p.a., cumulated 2-yearly), successor to the *Index to religious periodical literature*, 1949–76 (1953–77, 12 vols.), is considered the single most comprehensive index of its kind. Section 3, 'Book reviews', carries about 7,000 entries p.a. Its emphasis is on Western religions, particularly Protestant Christianity, but with Catholicism and Judaism well represented. *The Catholic periodical and literature index* (Haverford, Pa., Catholic Library Association, 1930–. 6 p.a., cumulated 2-yearly) and *The index to Jewish periodicals* (Cleveland, Ohio, College of Jewish Studies Press, 1963–. 2 p.a.) are also of value. The *Arts and humanities citation index* (1978–. 3 p.a.) and the *Internationale Bibliographie der Rezensionen* (1971–. 2 p.a.) are leading general review-indexing services that cover a wide range of religious periodicals.

Reviewing journals

In the description which follows of the individual journals, I have taken four things for granted. I presume that in each case the journals name the authors of the reviews which they publish; that the academic affiliation — or some other form of address — is provided for each reviewer; that there is a list of reviews published in each issue of the journal; and that there is an annual index of reviews and/or reviewers. Not all the journals display all these features. When they do not I shall say so.

I shall start with the *Heythrop journal* (Heythrop College [University of London], London, 1960–. 4p.a. Circulation: 800), not because it is the one which, obviously, I know best but because it is a type of journal, once more common than it is now, produced by Roman Catholic seminaries and reflecting their teaching. Roman Catholic clergymen at one time spent at least half as much time studying philosophy as they did studying theology: the magazines produced by the colleges in which they pursued their studies were therefore interested in both disciplines. The *Heythrop journal* publishes about 200 reviews annually (see above) of which about 50 are philosophical. The theological reviews cover the whole spectrum of religious studies, and the philosophical ones do likewise for their own discipline, but there is a slight emphasis, given the *Journal*'s Jesuit origins, upon continental philosophy, which is not common in other British publications. The review section constitutes approximately half of each issue, and is divided into 'Reviews' and 'Short notices', the latter section containing book notes of only half a page or so (about 250 words). These are signed by initials. There is a backlog of about 18 months to two years: it is longer for those works published in the autumn simply because so many appear at about that time. (Publishers believe that the autumn is the best time for selling books — or at least for launching them. It has occurred to me to wonder about the effect of this *embarras de richesses* upon a book's chances of finding a reviewer.) Reviews which appear in the main book pages average around 750 words, and their authors are encouraged to provide critical commentary upon the works they have undertaken to consider, rather than simply supply an outline of content. Works in foreign languages, particularly German and French, are noticed quite frequently. Full bibliographical details are supplied — apart from the ISBN, which in my experience is very rarely noted in any journal. It would be improper for me to make comparisons between this publication and the others to be discussed except to remark that the number of reviews published is rather higher than for most other comparable journals.

The *Heythrop journal* covers both philosophy and theology: it does not particularly specialize in the philosophy of religion. Two rather similar journals that do so are the *Journal of religion* (University of Chicago Press, 1882–. 4 p.a. Circulation: about 2,000) and *Religious studies* (Cambridge University Press, 1965–. 4 p.a. Circulation: 1,300). The former, which is produced by the Divinity School of the University of Chicago, welcomes contributions from scholars in theology (biblical, historical, ethical and constructive) and in other types of religious studies (literary, social, psychological and philosophical) according to its 'Statement of policy', and that appears to apply to its review section as much as to the articles it publishes. There are some limitations, however. Books on scripture, especially those of a technical, exegetical sort, do not figure prominently, whereas religio-literary works are regularly noticed, as are books on the philosophy of religion. Not that many books of any kind are reviewed. The total seems to be about 75 a year, though there has occasionally appeared an 'Editor's bookshelf' — a survey of a large number of books in a few words. In the January 1985 issue a new feature appeared entitled 'Books notes', a selection of short reviews. Bibliographical detail is properly supplied, but the delay on the appearance of reviews seems to be at least two years. In addition to the reviews themselves, there are regular 'Review articles', of up to some 3,000 words or so. The normal reviews are considerably shorter, though very occasionally they run to a similar length.

Religious studies likewise publishes lengthy reviews — notices of up to 1,000 words are not uncommon, and all in a particularly elegant format. There is no list of books received and no special index of books reviewed, though I calculate approximately 100 are noticed annually. As with the *Journal of religion*, books from the United States and the United Kingdom predominate, but in *Religious studies* there is, perhaps, rather more chance of a review appearing of a work from a less common source such as India. The journal has, from its foundation, been edited by a philosopher of religion, and works within that particular branch of philosophy are well represented in the review pages. But the editorial board has upon it a number of members who were specialists in comparative religion, as it used to be called until 'religious studies' became the more fashionable and, perhaps, more accurate term. One can therefore expect to find rather more notice taken of books on non-Christian religions in *Religious studies* than even in the *Journal of religion*. There is also a quite surprising number of books on ecclesiastical history covered. Adequate bibliographical details are given, albeit a little haphazardly. The currency of the books noticed is rather better than for the *Journal of religion*, and both provide notices of a similarly high academic level.

Though not as old as the *Journal of religion*, probably the most prestigious of English-language periodicals in the field is the *Journal of theological studies* (Oxford University Press, 1899–. 2 p.a. Circulation: 1,500). 'Theology' is taken very broadly, and books noticed can cover the whole range of Christian studies, including philosophy in so far as this discipline is linked to theology. Both 'reviews' and 'short notices' are published, the former being listed in the contents, the latter not. 'Short notices' are a standard 250 words or thereabouts, but the review section can contain notices which vary from about 750 words, and occasionally less, to about 2,000. Bibliographical details are full, and a wide variety of languages is covered. There is a delay of some two years in noticing a book, but all works received are listed promptly. About 150 reviews appear in the two parts which make up the plump annual volume.

In none of the journals so far considered, I think, can any denominational bias be observed, either in coverage or in choice of reviewer. That would not be quite so true of the *Nouvelle revue théologique* (Tournai, Casterman, 1868–. 6 p.a. Circulation: 4,600), which is produced by the Jesuits' Centre de Documentation et de Recherches Religieuses at Namur. As a guide to publications in French, and indeed in almost any of the European languages, it is invaluable. It notices approximately 400 titles a year either in its 'Bibliographie' or in its 'Notes bibliographiques'. Under the former rubric, reviews extend to 500 words or more and are signed, under the latter they are some 200 words long and only have initials appended. In neither case is any academic affiliation indicated, but this seems to be because reviewing is undertaken rather as a team effort: the same names turn up time and again, which makes the speed of the appearance of reviews — usually a year or less from the publication of the book being noticed — all the more surprising and commendable. The quality of review does not noticeably decline, although in perhaps only half of the reviews does its author enter into debate with the thesis of the book. Bibliographical information is excellent and generally includes the book's size, though not the ISBN. There is a list of books sent, which reveals that few English ones find their way to the reviewers' shelves. That is unfortunate. On the continent of Europe I know that the *Nouvelle revue théologique* is counted by theological librarians as a prime source of information upon which to base purchases.

The journals so far noticed concern themselves with a wide range of topics within the general area of religious studies, but the number of more specialized publications is considerable. The *Journal of ecumenical studies* (Temple University, Pa., 1964–. 4 p.a. Circulation: 3,000) is perhaps the most academically orientated periodical with its particular specialization in English. And 'ecumenism' is understood in the wide sense to embrace relations between Christianity in general and non-Christian religions, as well as the more common understanding of the term. Its reviewers tend to be drawn from a wide denominational base, though not from a wide geographical one: the majority of those who review the around 200 books a year are teaching in North American institutions. The journal stays close to its theme in the review section and in the regular review articles, and the approach is academic. There is a slight tendency observable to follow fashionable interests, aided by the commendable speed with which reviews appear: the delay is little more than a year. Satisfactory bibliographical details are given, and foreign-language, especially perhaps German, works are covered to some extent. One disadvantage is the small type in which the reviews are printed

Though something like the *Revue biblique* may be more prestigious, little compares to the *Journal of biblical literature* (Chico, Calif., Scholars Press, 1882–. 4p.a. Circulation: 6,000) for its coverage of material in the scriptural field. The reviews, rather more than 100 a year, are arranged chronologically according to the subject matter of the book under consideration. The periodical sticks very closely to its specialism and rarely strays outside the second century CE. Foreign-language publications, especially German ones, feature prominently, and top-class reviewers engage in serious discussions with the texts they are noticing. As a result, reviews can be quite lengthy: 1,500 words is not uncommon. A feature of the *Journal* is the occasional 'Collected essays' section, in which a single reviewer considers briefly volumes of collected essays and lists their contents. The time-lag on publications is some two years or more.

The *Journal of ecclesiastical history* (Cambridge, Cambridge University Press 1950–. 4 p.a. Circulation: 1,200), in its 'Reviews' and 'Short notices' sections covers some 175 publications a year. They are arranged in chronological order of subject matter and can be on the longish side — 1,000 words or more is not uncommon in the 'Reviews' part of the periodical. Foreign-language material is frequently noticed — indeed, there are occasional reviews in a foreign language — but the books are for the most part English or American. Reviews are listed in the contents, and adequate bibliographical detail is given. Reviewers in the *Journal of ecclesiastical history,* for the most part English academics, seem to have developed a particularly gentlemanly style of their own.

There is a quite different style to the *Revue d'histoire ecclésiastique* (Louvain, Université Catholique de Louvain, 1900–. 4 p.a. Circulation: 1,800), which reviews perhaps two dozen titles per issue at any length, but then notices considerably more, country by country, under the rubric 'Chronique'. Adequate bibliographical detail is provided in either section of the journal. The reviews are always in French, as is the 'Chronique', and the whole has a distinctly Roman Catholic feel to it — though it would be going too far to describe it as a bias. No serious theological library is going to be without the annual bibliography which is received as part of the *Revue,* so its pages are excellent ones for reviews to appear in. And the chances of that happening are good: perhaps as many as 750 books and other publications are noticed annually, if sometimes very briefly.

A very different kind of periodical from the *Revue* is the *Journal for the scientific study of religion* (Storrs, Society for the Scientific Study of Religion, University of Connecticut, 1961-. 4 p.a. Circulation: 3,500), which is highly technical and replete with graphs and tables of percentages and variables. Luckily its review section is more intelligible to the general reader while remaining fairly technical: it does not in general review books unless they are within the fields of the sociology or the psychology of religion. Reviews range from around 500 words to 1,500 or more, and adequate bibliographical detail is given for the 50-or-so titles noticed each year. It is highly recommended for its specialized field, its chief drawback being the distressingly small type in which the reviews are presented on double-columned pages.

In religious studies as in other disciplines there are a number of journals devoted wholly to the reviewing of books. The *Theologische Literaturzeitung* (Berlin [DDR], Evangelische Verlagsanstalt, 1876–. 12 p.a. Circulation unknown) and the *Theologische Revue* (Aschendorff, Münster, 1902–. 6 p.a. Circulation unknown) represent, respectively, the Lutheran and the Roman Catholic Churches. Both are very similar in presentation, with a long opening review article or articles, followed by highly technical reviews often of 1,000 words or more. Both notice approximately the same number of books per issue — about 50 — which obviously gives the *Literaturzeitung* a considerable advantage in that it appears twice as often as the *Revue.* The denominational bias of each is evident, though not too obvious. Much more obvious is the distinctly German-language selection of books covered. Since Germans are pre-eminent in the fields of systematic theology and, to a degree, of scriptural exegesis, this is not necessarily a disadvantage. It is my impression, however, though it can be no more than an impression, than non-German works do not fair particularly well in the pages of either journal. Both cover all aspects of religious studies, but the emphasis is upon theological and historical works. Currency for both is good: books are frequently noticed within a year of their appearing, and editors can hardly be blamed for reviewers who hand in their material late.

Currency is not so good for *Religious studies review* (Waterloo, Ontario, Council for the Study of Religion, Wilfrid Laurier University, 1975–. 4 p.a. Circulation: 2,400), which now appears to have an 18 month to two-year backlog. This is surprising in that each issue covers about 250 books in its 'Notes on recent publications' section, and a variable number, but perhaps as many as fifty more, in the series of review articles which precede the 'Notes'. But it is the 'Notes' section which is of importance, and it has a style of its own. Though reviewers may occasionally stray beyond the limits set, the average notice appears to be in the region of 200 to 250 words in length, excluding, that is, the full bibliographical details which are conscientiously provided. Again it can only be an impression, but it seems that this limitation, which does not allow the author of a review to develop his or her ideas about the work under consideration, not infrequently leads to rather brusque dismissals of books. Coverage is of all branches of religious studies, arranged under a variety of headings, and a good deal of space is given to non-Christian religions, particularly Judaism. Though foreign-language books are frequently noticed, there is an obvious American bias in the choice of works considered and, especially, in the choice of reviewers. There is also a special section on the Americas, and coverage of indigenous (North) American religions. One helpful feature is the tendency of reviewers to indicate the level, as well as the value, of the book they are considering. All in all, a most useful bibliographical resource, which might be greatly improved by the addition of a list of books reviewed in each issue, as well as the invaluable annual index.

Philosophy

Indexes to reviews

The philosopher's index: an international index to philosophical periodicals and books (Bowling Green, Ohio, Philosophy Documentation Center, Bowling Green State University, 1967–. 4 p.a., cumulated annually) is the main review-indexing service, covering about 350 philosophical and related journals in English, French, German,

Italian and other languages. The book-review section follows subject and author (including abstracts) sections, and the whole service is available online. The *Arts and humanities citation index* cites reviews in 83 philosophy journals, and the *Internationale Bibliographie der Rezensionen* adds its quota.

Reviewing journals

Nothing quite like the *Religious studies review* appears to exist within the discipline of philosophy, though there are, of course, a number of journals devoted solely to reviewing. There is, for instance, *Philosophical books* (Oxford, Blackwell, 1960–. 3 p.a. Circulation: 900), an off-shoot of the journal *Analysis*, also published by Blackwell. Its purpose is to provide prompt, scholarly reviews of new professional books and journals in philosophy and the history of the philosophy, and it offers more extensive review coverage than other journals in this field. It includes a regular discussion feature in which the authors of selected titles have the opportunity to reply to reviews. That at least is its claim, yet for a journal devoted entirely to reviews, apart from the discussion article which usually opens each issue, it covers surprisingly few books, perhaps a couple of dozen in every number. They are, however, relatively prompt in appearing — quite often reviews are printed within the year of a book's publication. The style of reviewing tends to the descriptive, and though they are not uncritical, the notices are almost always polite, falling well within the English philosophical tradition of attractive writing. The choice of books is very main-line philosophy, again almost always Anglo-American, and are presented in two sections, 'History of philosophy' and 'Contemporary philosophy'. The former is not aptly named, since it rarely seems to deal with specifically historical studies. A better division might be into people, mainly dead, and topics, usually current. Reviews are 750 words or more, and are headed with full bibliographical details minus, as almost always, the ISBNs.

A somewhat similar publication is *Canadian philosophical reviews* (South Edmonton, Alberta, Academic Printing and Publishing, 1981–. 6 p.a. Circulation unknown) which notices some 120 books a year, reviews being published either in English or in French. The choice of title noticed is somewhat eclectic: it may be that the journal has not yet existed long enough to establish a clear policy. So far its policy is stated rather oddly (though it must be said it reads rather better in the French version): 'The editors will consider for publication submitted reviews of publications that are strictly educational textbooks'. The reviewers are mainly North American, though there are a few from elsewhere, and the style seems to favour the competent rather than the technical. Arrangements of content is alphabetical by order of the author of the book reviewed, which makes for some odd juxtapositions. It is a fairly useful tool for the choice of books, but it is not especially quick in taking note of new publications.

Currency is rather worse for the *Review of metaphysics* (Washington DC, Catholic University of America, 1947–. 4 p.a. Circulation: 2,700), which is a pity, because on other counts this is an excellent source of information for librarians and professional philosophers. Indeed, it remains such despite the two-to-three year (or more) delay in noticing books and despite its religious origins. These last are not particularly obvious in the review section — entitled 'Summaries and contents' — apart from a refreshing interest in continental philosophy and in philosophy of religion. The *Review* denies association 'with any school or group', but 'is interested in persistent, resolute enquiries into root questions'. That may be true of the body of the journal, but the review section, which is unlike any other noticed in this survey, is more wide-ranging. The introduction to the review section says that 'Books received are acknowledged in this section by a brief resume [sic], report, or criticism. Such acknowledgement does not preclude a more detailed examination in a subsequent Critical Study'. In practice such critical studies have become infrequent almost to the point, now, of non-existence, and, as was noted earlier, the style has changed. Before December 1982 the summaries were signed by initials only, and it was claimed they were provided by the (named) managing editor 'and staff'. That claim is still made, though since that date reviewers have been named, and have been chosen from all over the United States. Nonetheless, though it is inclining more to the critical comment, the review section continues to present reasonably careful accounts of a book's content rather than the traditional form of review. Bibligraphical details for the 50-to-60 works noticed in each issue are provided in a standard format, and the expertly done reviews seem to be getting longer, but, at the time of writing appear to be about 600 to 700 words in length. One drawback of this otherwise very useful survey is the absence of any list of books covered, either in the quarterly contents or the annual index.

It is my general impression that philosophical journals on the whole do not dedicate quite as much space as do theological ones to the review section. The distinguished periodical *Mind* (Oxford, Blackwell, 1876–. 4 p.a. Circulation: 3,800) notices less than 50 books a year, although, because the journal is very much open to philosophical debate, a number of other titles are noticed, as it were, in passing. A very large number of books are listed as received, perhaps as many as eight times those reviewed, and the chances of a book being considered for review are clearly higher if it is in English, and particularly if it is English. Reviews are prompt, often within a year of the book's publication, and thorough. They can indeed be very technical and sometimes quite sharp in their tone. Length varies from the long (about 1,000 words) to the very long, and good bibliographical detail is provided.

From the same publisher comes *The philosophical quarterly* (Oxford, Blackwell, 1950–. 4 p.a. Circulation: 1,500), which also provides highly technical reviews, though in rather smaller numbers — perhaps 40 a volume. As with *Mind,* the contributors tend to be British, and the reviews tend to be a little shorter than with the senior publication: between 750 and 1,000 words being more common, although there were at one time a number of 'critical studies' published which constituted very lengthy (up to 5,000 words or so) discussions of major books. Seven of these were published in 1983, only two the following year and, halfway through 1985, none have so far appeared. *The quarterly* itself is a forum for philosophical debate of a high order and attracts distinguished contributors: it is an excellent place to be noticed, and a prompt one. The delay can be a year or less.

At a very similar level there is *The philosophical review* (Ithaca, Cornell University, 1892–. 4 p.a. Circulation: 3,600) which notices about 75 books a year. A fault is that reviews are slow in appearing, possibly up to three years, but on the plus side they are long, perhaps 2,500 words, and in many cases are thorough debates of issues raised. Footnotes are common, which is unusual in the review section of any journal. Also unusual, but much to be welcomed, is the provision of the bibliographical detail of the periodical at the head of each review, and as well as being listed in the quarterly contents, the notices appear in the annual index. One failure, which is comparatively easy to correct, is a lack of standardization in the detail provided of each book. Prices are rarely given. The contributors are for the most part teaching in the United States.

From the other side of the world comes the *Australasian journal of philosophy* (Victoria, La Trobe University, 1923–. 4 p.a. Circulation: 1,200), a substantial periodical which commits itself to publishing 'original articles of high quality in any area of philosophy, which is of sufficient interest to the readers...Reviews and critical notices of important recent books in philosophy which are likely to be of interest to Australasian philosophers will also be published'. That amounts to around 50 titles a year, mainly from American or European (British in particular) publishers, though the reviewers are usually from Australasia. It is an impressive journal which gives space to major, often highly technical, discussion of new writing in any branch of philosophy, and sometimes at some length — 1,000 words or more.

It was remarked earlier that the *Review of metaphysics* was unusual in its interest in continental philosophy. But that was of English-language works on French, German, Italian and other philosophers. The other journals hitherto mentioned display little concern for philosophy outside the Anglo-Saxon tradition. The *Archives de philosophie* (Paris, Beauchesne, 1923–. 4 p.a. Circulation: 800) shows considerable interest in books published in English, especially those from publishers on the continent of Europe, though not only these. Its particular strength, naturally, is in the European philosophers, and it regularly prints critical surveys of recent works on, for example, Spinoza, Hegel or Descartes. It is difficult to be precise about the *Archives*. Reviews proper vary very considerably in length, and are often long delayed. Though reviews are listed in the quarterly contents, there is no annual index and no mention of the works surveyed in the bulletins on individual philosophers, which makes it next to impossible to turn to the *Archives* as a work of reference. More often than not the academic affiliation of the reviewer is not given, which indicates that he is a staff member of the Jesuit Centre Sèvres in Paris, though no religious bias is observable in the journal itself.

Also concerned with continental philosophy is the somewhat maverick *The independent journal of philosophy* (Paris, George Elliot Tucker, 1977–. Irregular. Circulation unknown) which belongs to its editor and has moved around with him. Originally it announced itself as a quarterly, and declared an interest 'in dialogue with especially the idealist, phenomenological and existentialist traditions', which are otherwise not well represented in English-language philosophical journals of standing. Unlike most of the journals noticed, it appears to solicit book reviews, though it warns authors to contact the editor before submitting them. In so far as any picture emerges after only four issues, the 'Book reviews' section has three parts: 'Review articles', 'Critical notices' and 'Short notices'. But the shortest notice I noticed ran to about 500 words, and as there is little difference between any of the sections, they might best be described as extremely long, very long, and long reviews. Unusually, bibliographical details frequently include ISBNs. Contributors have been predominantly North American, though there have been a good number from the continent of Europe, the occasional Australian and a solitary Irishman. I detected none based in the United Kingdom.

Finally, two specialized reviews. The *British journal for the philosophy of science* (Aberdeen, Aberdeen University Press, 1950-. 4 p.a. Circulation: 1,600) covers perhaps a score of books each year, although there is also the occasional review article. Books seem to be carefully selected from the many received — the book list itself is lengthy — and do not stray outside the *Journal's* professed specialization. The reviews are usually of moderate length, 750 words and upwards, and are quite frequently footnoted. Titles are covered within a year or two of publication and are listed in the annual index. There is the occasional failure to standardize bibliographical detail.

The *Journal of the history of philosophy* (St Louis, Washington University, 1963-. 4 p.a. Circulation: 1,550) notices approximately 50 titles a year, and from a variety of sources — French and German titles occur regularly. The currency is hard to determine: works occasionally are noticed quite quickly, but there is often a three-year, or perhaps even four-year wait. When they eventually appear, however, they are of very high quality and sometime of considerable length —up to 2,000 words or so. The contents are arranged and, somewhat oddly, indexed, in chronological order of the topic they discuss — usually, though not always, a philosopher: 'history', it seems to me, does not mean quite the same to a philosopher as it does to a political historian.

This survey does not lend itself to any real conclusion except that a book falling within the field of religion has rather more chance of being reviewed than one within the discipline of philosophy. Perhaps one should not be surprised by that. *Ulrich's international periodicals directory* lists more than five times as many journals under the rubric 'Religions and theology' than it does under 'Philosophy'.

References

1. Walsh, Michael J., with others. *Religious bibliographies in serial literature: a guide.* London, Mansell, 1981.
2. Lankhorst, Otto. *Les revues de sciences religieuses.* Strasbourg, Cerdic, 1979, pp. 208–13.
3. *Ibid.*
4. Wilson, John F., and Slavens, Thomas P. *Research guide to religious studies.* Chicago, Ill., American Library Association 1982.
5. Matczak, Sebastian. *Philosophy: its nature, methods and basic sources.*

New York, Learned Publications, Inc., 1978, p. 187.
6. De George, Richard. *The philosopher's guide to sources: research tools, professional life and related fields*. Lawrence, Kans., Regents Press, 1980, p.118.

5. Social Sciences

Joan M. Harvey

'The book-review is an important form of professional communication, if for no reason other than the scholar's difficulty in coping with the knowledge explosion', state Riley and Spreitzer.[1] Indeed, all need assistance in selecting from the flood of new books in the social sciences those few that will really serve our particular purposes but, as Snizek and Fuhrman say,[2] 'Despite its important functions, the book-review suffers from a markedly low status among scientific publications'. This is particularly so in the social sciences; largely as a result of what Riley and Spreitzer[3] believe to be the emphasis on 'primary' publications, rather than 'derivative' literature, book reviews are generally 'grouped with such prosaic forms as abstracts, indexes and bibliographies'. On the other hand, Peter Berger[4] states that because of the political and economic structure of academic life, scholars tend to be judged by their productivity, the number of books and articles publishers are willing to accept, and that 'as a result the sensible person reads the sociological journals mainly for the book-reviews'. Champion and Morris[5] consider that 'While Berger's position may be considered by some to be extreme, there is little doubt that book-reviews...do exert some significant degree of influence upon the discipline. For instance, textbook adoptions for classroom use are probably influenced significantly by the reviews the books receive. In addition, professional sociological libraries are probably guided in part by reviews' — and no doubt the same could be said of other fields of social science.

Reviewers of books in the social sciences are predominantly academics and, to a lesser extent, practitioners working in the same

fields as the authors of the books, possibly as colleagues or com-
petitiors. This makes for knowledgeable reviews, but there is,
perhaps, a danger of *noblesse oblige*. Research done in the 1970s on
book-reviewing in the main American sociological journals by
Snizek and Fuhrman[2] found that the age and professional experience
of both author and reviewer, as well as the prestige of their past and
present institutional affiliations, may affect the likelihood of a book
being reviewed more or less favourably, and also that no one journal
publishes a disproportionate number of more favourable or
unfavourable reviews, and there is no evidence to substantiate the
hypothesis that earlier reviews influence later reviewers of the same
book. Snizek, Fuhrman and Wood[6] found some evidence that members of the same theory-group are the most critical of an author's
work. However, Merton's[7] 'Matthew effect', that high-status
authors tend to have their books reviewed more critically than low-
status authors, has been refuted by Hirsch and Potter-Efron,[8] who
reported that 'There is virtually no relationship between the status of
authors and the favourableness of the reviews' and 'The higher-
status reviewers on the average wrote more favourable reviews than
did the lower-status reviewers', and this was regardless of the status
of the authors whose books were reviewed.

Certainly, the reliability of reviews is very important. Woodbury[9]
writes: 'If a single word were to summarize the role of the reviewer,
it would be "responsibility". Reviewers accept heavy responsibility
to their colleagues to represent a book fully and fairly, balancing the
author's aims against the results', going on to say that 'Reviewers
also have a responsibility to authors, to make no unfair, irrelevant,
personal, or unsupportable criticisms'. Sarton[10] wrote that 'Every
honest book deserves some respect in spite of its imperfections'. Even
so, reviewers can approach their task in many different ways, from
many different viewpoints.

The review of John W. Work's *Race, economics, and corporate
America* (Wilmington, Del., Scholarly Resources, 1984) in *Choice*[11]
is predominantly descriptive:

> In a pioneering study of racial discrimination against blacks within the
> internal labor markets of corporate America, Work argues that discrimi-
> nation against blacks is less in entry-level jobs and in jobs with relatively
> low education and skill requirements. Discrimination is greater with
> respect to upward mobility and is particularly strong for blacks with rela-
> tively high educational, skill, and seniority qualifications...These conclu-
> sions are supported by a unique empirical analysis of data on 2,721 man-
> agerial employees of an unidentified major US corporation. The analysis

generally supports the conclusions, but, as is usually the case with empirical studies of this sort, the results are suggestive rather than conclusive.

In a letter published a few months later, another academic criticized the above review as 'excessively generous':

Regretably [sic], the only scholarly thing about this book is the name of the publisher. It is regrettable that the few discernibly useful notions presented here about the importance of institutional racism to the corporate careers of blacks have intuitive plausibility but receive neither carefully reasoned theoretical support not well-executed empirical research support. The book contains just enough citations to respectable writing by economists and other social scientists along with more than enough statistics to give it an aura of credibility and persuasiveness for the novice. In truth, the book is replete with unsupported assertions, weakly documented criticism of extent theories of racial discrimination, incorrect usage of generally understood terminology (e.g. supply and demand), chic phraseology, pedantic writing and important caveats buried in footnotes. Perhaps most distressing for the professional reader is the woefully inadequate analysis of the data from an anonymous corporation...No self-respecting neoclassicist, institutionalist, or radical economist would embrace the superficial (and sometimes incorrect) criticisms presented in this volume.[12].

Bibliographical descriptions preceding the individual reviews usually include sufficient information to permit easy identification of the books reviewed, but seldom is there any mention of other useful information. ISBNs, for instance, are included in fewer than ten of the review sections of the journals mentioned below, so that for reasons of space their inclusion, rather than their exclusion, has been noted. Inclusion of indexes and bibliographies are indicated even less frequently, but some reviewers do at least make a point of mentioning the inclusion or omission; for example, a review of two books in International affairs[13] ends: 'The reviewer found it very frustrating that neither volume carried an index, a forgivable omission in the cheaper publication, but not so in a book selling at £30'.

Format and typography are seldom mentioned by the reviewer, but typographical errors, the fault of poor proof-reading, are often mentioned and are increasing at a rate that would seem to be unacceptable in scholarly publications. A review in the Canadian journal of political science[14] ends: 'The format and the typography of the book are excellent. Quite commendable is that footnotes are placed at the foot of each page — a practice that is now regrettably almost obsolete. Yet there are more typographical errors than one would expect from a quality press'; and again, in *International affairs*:[15] 'The writing of the book must have required great toil. It is therefore regrettable that the proofreading of Middle Eastern personal and place names was inadequate. More than 60 such errors were counted'.

Style of writing, which may enhance or damn the reading of a book, is also important, although it is considered to be unimportant to social scientists if the following extract of a review in *Political theory* is true: 'I want to conclude with a few words about the book's grammatical and stylistic failings. To be fair to the author, social science in general has cared so little about elegance in prose that his own prose does not in the slightest way compromise the field'.[16]

Hargrave,[17] comparing reviews of books in the social sciences in general and in scholarly periodicals, studies accuracy/inaccuracy, objectivity/bias, insight/lack of insight, organization, clarity/confusion, comparison and style; also omissions, documentation, methodology, 'sensationalism' and inclusion of quotations from the book, — all of which are merely exemplary aspects indicating a well-written or poorly written book-review. The following[18] is offered as an example of a good critical review, clear and informative, of *Information sources in politics and political science: a survey worldwide*; edited by Dermot Englefield and Gavin Drewry (London, Butterworths, 1984):

> This substantial volume comprises twenty-four densely packed contributed chapters grouped into four parts covering general resources, approaches to the study of politics and government, topic-by-topic treatment of the United Kingdom, and separate descriptions of other individual countries and regions. The style is discursive, the authors presenting the sources they describe within their respective subject or jurisdictional contexts. Depending on the reader's purposes this can either be a help or a hindrance...Many pages (e.g. pp. 313–40) consist of almost unrelieved lists of books, punctuated occasionally by such comments as 'The following are useful' (p. 313). A wide sampling of the titles listed shows them to be generally up to date and well selected; publisher, edition and date are given for most...Quick reference is certainly not well catered for by the modest seven-page index...Equally inexcusable is the dearth of information on electronic media, particularly in view of the series editors' observation that 'Computerized data bases...are now well established and quite widely available for anyone to use' (p. vi)...Despite its expository shortcomings (and its price, [£38]), however, this book will have its place on library shelves since it brings together so much information in one place.

This survey of book-reviewing in the social sciences is restricted to about 20 journals each in the fields of sociology, politics and economics, 13 in education and 8 in law. Even with such subject limitations, coverage is by no means comprehensive, the aim being to select for inclusion the more important journals in each field, from the book-reviewing point of view. The five sections are not totally exclusive either; there is considerable overlap between them, particularly between sociology, politics and economics. Just as the articles in a journal do not stay rigidly within one particular subject field, so the selection of books to be reviewed is wider than the title of the journal indicates. *Soviet studies*, for instance, is concerned with politics and, to a lesser degree, sociology as well as economics; *International affairs*, while relating mainly to international affairs in particular and to politics more generally, also includes some economics.

Periodicals selected are the more scholarly ones; the more journalistic publications, such as *New society, New statesman* and *The economist*, have been omitted, although *The Times educational supplement* and *The Times higher education supplement*, perhaps somewhat illogically, are included. In the field of sociology, *Contemporary sociology* stands out as the major reviewing journal, with its fairly brief but up-to-date reviews. *Sociology, Sociological review* and the *British journal of sociology* are also important because they deal with more British publications, whilst *Contemporary sociology, American journal of sociology* and *Social forces* are the main American journals in the field. Also included are the more specialized journals on social policy, the family, ethnic and racial studies, social work and social history.

The combined book-review sections of the British *International affairs* and the American *Foreign affairs* and *American political science review* cover the most important works published in English, followed by the *Annals of the American Academy of Political and Social Science*. Other important American titles are *Perspective* and *Political science quarterly*, important British titles being *Political quarterly* and *Political studies*. More specialized journals concentrating on a particular geographical area are *The journal of Commonwealth and comparative politics* and *West European politics*. Finally, there are two journals dealing with government.

The journal of economic literature is quite the most important reviewing journal in the economic field, *Economic journal* being the most prestigious British journal in economics, but others included below are excellent journals. Surprisingly, there are five journals devoted to economic history, all included here, as are two other specialized journals dealing with industrial relations. Not included, because the contents are annotations and not reviews, but which should be more widely known, is the quarterly *Economics books: current selections*, published by the Department of Economics and University Libraries at the University of Pittsburgh (1974–), which endeavours 'to annotate all books that appear in the English language in the area of economics'.

Two journals in the field of education that are not included in the following pages (because not really appropriate) are *Resources in education* and *Review of educational research*. *Resources in education* (1966–. 12 p.a. Circulation: 5,000), compiled by the ERIC (Educational Resources Information Center, Washington, DC) is an abstracting journal announcing recent report literature in the field of education and covering about 25,000 documents a year. *Review of educational research* (American Educational Research Association, Washington, DC, 1931–. 4 p.a. Circulation 16,000) does not include book-reviews as such but is a journal of 'integrative reviews and interpretations and educational research literature on both substantive and methodological issues'. Two examples of its review-articles are 'Teacher evaluation in the organizational context: a review of the literature' (vol. 53 [3], Fall 1983, pp. 285–328), with about 160 references, and 'Reviewing the reviewers on literacy and reasoning: some selected theses and references' (vol. 54 [4], Winter 1984, pp. 682–8), which was an attempt to highlight briefly some themes which appeared to run through the previous review-article in that issue.

Law journals are usually aimed at either the academic readership, such as *The Cambridge law journal* and *Harvard law review,* or at practising lawyers, such as *Law quarterly review* and *ABA journal,* but this does not mean that there is a firm dividing line. Reviewers may be practitioners or academics. International law is very important these days, and the final three journals included in this chapter are devoted to international and Commonwealth law.

Indexes to reviews

Of the ten indexing services mentioned here, no less than five are published by H.W. Wilson, New York. *Social sciences index* (1974–. 4 p.a., cumulated annually), *Business periodicals index* (1958–. Monthly, except August, and cumulated annually), *Education index* (1929–. 12 p.a., cumulated annually), *Index to legal periodicals* (1958–. 11 p.a., cumulated annually) and *Book review digest* (1965–. 10 p.a., cumulated annually). The last-mentioned has excerpts/digests or reviews in more than 80 US, British and Canadian periodicals, provided that non-fiction reviews are recorded in at least two sources. In the case of H.W. Wilson indexes proper, the 'Book-reviews' section follows the main sequence.

Entries in *Social science citation index*, 1970– (Philadelphia, Pa., Institute for Scientific information, 1973–. 3 p.a.) use the symbol '+' to indicate reviews. *Book review index* (Detroit, Mich., Gale, 1905–. 10 p.a., cumulated quarterly and annually) has the advantage of both author and subject indexes to reviews in over 600 journals, as well as a master cumulation for 1969–79 (1980–81, 7 vols.). *Reference sources* (Ann Arbor, Mich., Pierian Press, 1977–) also claims to cover 600 journals, but its annual appearance detracts from its currency, and the same applies to *American reference books annual* (Littleton, Colo., Libraries Unlimited, 1970–).

Internationale Bibliographie der Rezensionen wissenschaftlichen Literatur (Osnabrück, Dietrich, 1971–. 2 p.a.) is the major general review-indexing source for scholarly journals, covering about 3,000 titles in various languages. *British humanities index* (London, Library Association, 1963–. 4 p.a., cumulated annually) does include a number of social-science periodicals in the 313 titles covered, but book-review indexing is restricted to review-articles.

Sociology

Indexes to reviews

Social science citation index (*SSCI*), which indexes the vast majority of social-science journals, includes review-articles and also book-reviews. Of the more conventional indexes, *Social sciences index* covers most sociology journals, *Internationale Bibliographie der Rezensionen* and *Book review index* record a reasonable number, and *Book review digest* and *British humanities index* , a few, but not *Humanities index*. The majority of the journals listed in the following section also issue annual or volume indexes, including indexes of book-reviews.

Reviewing journals

Contemporary sociology (Washington, American Sociological Association, 1972–. 6 p.a. Circulation: 10,000), subtitled 'a journal of reviews', is devoted to the reviewing of sociological literature, a service previously included in *American sociological review.* Vol. 14 (1), January 1985 (pp. 1–144), includes 17 review essays on pp. 9–14, and 100 book-reviews, signed, with affiliations, on pp. 40–139. Reviews, which are arranged in subject groups, are usually brief

(400–1,500 words in length), with occasionally more extended treatment. They are evaluative and critical, if somewhat breezy. One reviewer comments: 'This is the most important book on sociology of science published in the still-going 1980s, which is not to say that most readers will agree with its message'. The reviews have generally been requested by the editors and reviewed by academic sociologists; selection has a definite US bias. Bibliographical details are given in full. *Current sociology* includes only English-language books, but it is planned to include, in future, review essays on books in foreign languages not yet translated into English.

Sociology (London, The British Sociological Association, 1967–. 4 p.a. Circulation: 2,200) is the official journal of the major British association in the discipline. Vol. 18 (4), November 1984 (pp. 475–628), has seven reviews, signed, with affiliations, on pp. 588–99, and 22 shorter notices on pp. 600–25. Length of reviews range from the 500- to 1,750-word bracket to shorter reviews between 500 and 1,000 words. Reviews are critical; for example, 'The questions underlying the title theme of the book are vital and interesting but the author, unfortunately, does not pursue them'; 'Despite these defects, however, the book does raise important issues'; and 'The book leads the reader into confusion and does not point to the exit'. Full bibliographical details are given. One or two review-articles are included each year. In future it is intended to carry some reviews of older books that 'may be worth revisiting' (vol. 19 [3], February 1985). There is a review editor, and the volume index includes a list of books reviewed and of books included in shorter notices.

American journal of sociology (Chicago, Ill., University of Chicago Press, 1895–. 12 p.a. Circulation: 8,000), often referred to as 'the *AJS*', is a prestigious journal, formerly the organ of the American Sociological Society. Vol. 91 (1), July 1984 (pp. 1-246), has a five-page review essay with 12 references, and 21 reviews, signed, with affiliations, on pp. 197–246. Of medium length (750–1,500 words), the reviews are written by American academics and, following full bibliographical details, concentrate on the subject content of the books, being both critical and evaluative. The review of a book on the Dutch experience of minority groups includes the comment, 'Although I applaud the author's efforts to make comparative references, comparing the Maoris in New Zealand with the Moluccans in the Netherlands seems inappropriate'. Another review commences: 'In a rather lengthy introduction which should have been edited more carefully, he makes dubious statements'. The volume index includes separate listings of review essays and symposia, and books reviewed.

There is also a list of reviewers. Cumulative indexes are published at regular intervals; that is, vols. 1–70 (1895–1965) and vols. 71-5 (1965–70).

The sociological review (Henley-on-Thames, Routledge and Kegan Paul, 1908–. New series, 1953–. 4 p.a. Circulation: 2,000), edited at the University of Keele, publishes learned articles on a wide range of sociological topics, short notes on sociological research and critical comments on articles previously published in the *Review.* Vol. 32 (2), May 1984 (pp. 185-447), includes a 23-page review-article on books by Norbert Elias, and 22 reviews, signed, with affiliations, on pp. 390–442 by academics from various UK universities. Length of reviews range from 500 to 1,500 words, with an exceptionally long one at about 2,000 words in length. Reviews are critical and analytical (e.g. 'Despite some very considerable flaws, is a valuable contribution to a fairly wide debate...specific fault...: over-reliance on written accounts...lack of personal research and observation'). Currency is rather poor, some books published in 1981 and 1982 being reviewed in 1984. Full bibliographical details are given. The annual index has a separate listing of books reviewed.

The British journal of sociology (Routledge and Kegan Paul, for the London School of Economics and Political Science, 1950–. 4 p.a.) is the leading British journal in the field of sociology and related areas, and international in scope. Vol. 35 (3), September 1984 (pp. 315-472), includes a 10-page review-article with 17 references and 14 reviews, signed, with affiliations, on pp. 462–72. Length of reviews ranges from 300 to 500 words, the majority being about 500 words. Reviewers are mainly British academics reviewing mainly British books, although a few are American, and the brief content is mostly descriptive, with some criticism or praise. Bibliographical details lack place of publication. The volume index (cumulated 10-yearly) has separate listing of reviews.

L'Année sociologique (Paris, Presses Universitaires de France, 1952–. Annual) devotes more than half its space to a selective survey of the significant literature of sociology, the signed reviews varying in length from brief analyses to extensive essays surveying significant contributions in a given subject area; it is international in scope, with an emphasis on French sociology. Volume 34, 1984 (476 pp.), has a third part, 'Analyses bibliographiques et notes critiques' (pp. 241–476) divided into nine subject-sections, each having an individual editor. Some items included are literature reviews on a specific subject (e.g. Durkheim) and some are signed book-reviews. All contributions are in French and the majority of books reviewed are also in

French, with a few in other European languages. Bibliographical details omit prices.

Sociology and social research (Los Angeles, Calif., University of Southern California, 1916–. 4 p.a. Circulation: 2,600) is subtitled 'an international interdisciplinary journal' and is America's second-oldest sociological journal. Each issue normally includes a specially commissioned lead review-article, four or five research-articles, and book-reviews. Vol. 69 (1), October 1984 (pp. 1-169), has a 21-page lead article reviewing Robert Park's theory, with 61 references dating from 1921 to 1984, and 36 reviews, signed, with affiliations, on pp. 127–66, averaging 500 words each. Books reviewed are often the results of research and surveys. Comments are critical and may indicate readership; for example, 'This book is rich in meaning and treatment and should prove invaluable to students of contemporary social theory' and 'This is a book that should receive wide attention among students of organisation and public administration. It is conceptually ambitious, empirically rigorous, and quite well-written for its genre'. There is a book-review editor. Bibliographical details lack prices. The volume index includes lists of review-articles and reviewed books.

Social science quarterly (Austin, Texas, University of Texas Press, 1920–. 4 p.a. Circulation: 2,500), formerly *Southwestern social science quarterly*, is the journal of the Southwestern Social Science Association, dealing with all aspects of the social sciences but mainly with sociology. Vol. 66 (1), March 1985 (pp. 1-240), includes 25 reviews, signed, with affiliations, of about 150 words in length on pp. 227–40. The reviews are concise and well-written, descriptive rather than critical and include recommendations on type of readership. There are full bibliographical details. The annual index includes a section 'Book reviews and reviewers'.

Social forces (Chapel Hill, NC, University of North Carolina Press, 1922–. 4 p.a. Circulation: 5,000) is subtitled 'an international journal of social research associated with the Southern Sociological Society'. Vol. 63 (2), December 1984 (pp. 307–621) has 30 reviews, signed, with affiliations, on pp. 576–617. Both reviewers and books reviewed are usually American. Length of reviews ranges from 300 to 1,000 words, and there is wide subject coverage. Reviews are usually favourable, clearly descriptive and mildly critical; for example, 'This book does not make easy reading. It irritates and grates on one's sense of logic...Yet it is not without merit'. Full bibliographical details are given. The volume index (cumulated for 1922–72) includes a listing of books reviewed.

Canadian review of sociology and anthropology/La Revue canadienne de sociologie et d'anthropologie (Montreal, Canadian Sociology and Anthropology Association, 1964–. 4 p.a. Circulation: 1,800), the official journal of the Association, publishes scholarly material pertaining to Canadian society as well as articles on international sociological significance. At least one issue of every volume is devoted to a specific area of sociology. Vol. 21 (3), August 1984 (pp. 247–370), has 15 book-reviews, signed, with affiliations, on pp. 344–70, reviewed mainly by Canadian academics. Book selection emphasizes works dealing with Canada. Books in French are reviewed in French; English books, in English. Bibilographical details are sometimes incomplete, omitting prices or year of publication. Length of reviews ranges between 500 and 1,000 words. The annual index includes a list of books reviewed.

The Jewish journal of sociology (London, Heinemann, 1959–. 2 p.a.), published on behalf of the Maurice Freedman Research Trust, aims to provide an international vehicle for serious writing on Jewish social affairs, not only for sociologists but for social scientists in general. Vol. 26 (2), December 1984 (pp. 93–176), has nine reviews, signed, without affiliations, on pp. 145–66. The reviews range in length from 500 to 1,000 words and, as do the articles, relate to Jewish social affairs. Full bibliographical details are given. The annual index has a list of books reviewed and a list of reviewers.

Society (New Brunswick, NJ, Rutgers State University, 1963–. 6 p.a. Circulation: 15,000), subtitled 'social science and modern society', formerly titled *Trans-action*, is produced primarily for the general adult audience in the field of sociology. Vol. 21 (4) (whole number 150), May/June 1984 (pp. 1–104), includes five lengthy, 1,500- to 2,000-word signed book-reviews, with affiliations and some CVs on pp. 92–104. Reviews are scholarly and critical; for example, 'The author begins from an odd premise' and 'The format is one I have never encountered previously. This is a book without an author, joint authors or editor — that is, no one is "in charge"...there is no consistent voice'. Full bibliographical details are included, and there is a book-review editor. The annual index includes a listing of books reviewed, and there is a cumulative index to vols. 1 to 5.

Journal of social policy (Cambridge University Press, 1972–. 4 p.a. Circulation: 1,300), the journal of the Social Administration Association, is international in scope, with scholarly papers analysing all aspects of social policy and administration. Aimed primarily at those who do research or teach in the field of public administration, Vol. 13 (3), 1984 (pp. 255–382), includes 16 book-reviews, signed, with affiliations, the books being on political, social and/or economic matters. Reviews of between 500 and 1,250 words in length are descriptive and analytical, with some criticism; for example, 'It is disappointing...that a writer clearly so familiar with the literatures...does not give greater attention to some of the excellent evidence available' and one article in a yearbook needing 'strong editing before becoming a respectable academic piece...the author treats us to a display of Kung-fu which is entertaining but full of bad temper, crudities and irrelevant taunts'. No indexes but the annual contents-list records reviewed books. Reviews are indexed in *Social sciences index* and *Social science citation index*.

Social policy and administration (Oxford, Blackwell, in association with the University of Exeter, 1979–. 3 p.a. Circulation: 600) continues *Social and economic administration* (1967–78). Vol. 18 (2) Summer 1984 (pp. 127–210), has thirteen book-reviews, signed with affiliations, on pp. 189–208. The reviews, ranging from 500 to 1,000 words in length, are mainly by British academics and are scholarly, with added references, and critical; for example, 'it is difficult to do justice to the subtlety and complexity of the arguments and the range of the scholarship deployed to provide evidence in such a short summary, but for all that the case seems to me to be incomplete and deeply flawed', and 'Because it upsets traditional distinctions and patterns of thought, the book is probably of the greatest value to people who are most familiar with the literature of social policy. It has its vices, but its virtues outweigh these, and at its best, it is original, provocative and unsettling'. There is a book-review editor, and full bibliographical details are given. The volume index includes a separate listing of books reviewed.

Journal of marriage and the family (Mineapolis, Md., National Council on Family Relations, 1939–. 4 p.a. Circulation: 11,000), formerly *Marriage and family living*, is a scholarly journal — the main American research journal in its field, intended primarily for scholars, instructors and students. Vol. 46 (1), February 1984 (pp. 1–269), includes seven reviews, signed, with affiliations. There is a book-review editor and selection of books for review has a strong US bias. Reviews range from 500 to 1,250 words in length, and bibliographical details are full. The annual index includes cumulated tables of contents (by quarters), including book-reviews. Reviews are indexed in *Social sciences index*, *Book review index*, *Book review digest* and *Social science citation index*.

Ethnic and racial studies (Henley-on-Thames, Routledge and Kegan Paul, 1978–. 4 p.a. Circulation: 1,000) is devoted to the relationship between ethnic and racial groups in Western, communist and Third World societies, emphasis being on theoretical debate and fundamental research by social scientists and historians. Vol. 7 (3), July 1984 (pp. 321–446), has a review-article of about 2,000 words and four short book-reviews, signed, with affiliations, on pp. 440–6, ranging from 300 to 1,200 words in length. Reviews are critical; for example, 'This is a particularly disappointing and frustrating book on a fascinating topic by a well-read race relations specialist', and 'How all these heady ideas help to establish what the book is really about is not clear'. Some of the reviews have added references; bibliographical details are full. The annual index includes a list of books reviewed.

Social history (Andover, Hants., Methuen, 1976–. 3 p.a.) relates mainly to British social history, aiming to publish studies that encourage an interdisciplinary approach to historical questions. vol. 10 (1), January 1985 (pp. 1–146), includes 13 book-reviews, signed, with affiliations, on pp. 105–38, ranging between 900 and 1,600 words in length, and six shorter notices, also signed, on pp. 139–44. Review-articles are included in some issues (two in 1984). Books selected for review usually relate to British social history, but reviewers are British and American academics. Reviews are mainly descriptive but include some criticism; for example, 'the author's argument is certainly plausible, but he lacks convincing evidence'. Full bibliographical details are given, and many reviews also have footnotes referring to other publications, and so on. The annual index includes a listing of books reviewed.

Journal of social history (Pittsburgh, Pa., Carnegie-Mellon University Press, 1967–. 4 p.a. Circulation: 1,900) is scholarly and interdisciplinary. Vol. 18 (3), Spring 1985 (pp. 343–512), has 17 book-reviews, signed, with affiliations, on pp. 483–512). Length ranges from 600 to 1,500 words. Reviews, written by British and American reviewers, are descriptive, with mainly favourable criticism. Occasionally, they also include comments on production, style, and so on; for example, 'Except for the introduction this is a well-written book, and it is attractively produced. The index in inadequate...but the presentation of statistical data in maps instead of tables is a refreshing change'. Bibliographical details are full. The volume index (really contents pages) does not index reviews, for which see *Social sciences index, Social science citation index* and *Internationale Bibliographie der Rezensionen.*

British journal of social work (London, New York, etc., Academic Press, 1971–. 6 p.a. Circulation: 3,000), the official journal of the

British Association of Social Workers, offers a broad view of developments in social work, with particular emphasis on research findings and descriptive accounts of practice. Each issue includes about five articles, a section of abstracts on a particular subject taken from recent periodical literature, and book-reviews. Vol. 14 (2), 1984 (pp. 101–210), has 10 reviews, signed, with affiliations, of books on social-work subjects, including delinquency, family, welfare, hospices, and so on, on pp. 189–205. Reviews are descriptive, with some criticism; about 50 per cent have references appended; type of readership is also indicated. Bibliographical details are full. *BSJW* lacks an index and the contents lists do not record book reviews, although there is a book-review editor. Reviews are indexed in *Social science citation index*.

Social work (New York, National Association of Social Workers, 1956–. 6 p.a. Circulation: 90,000), the official journal of the Association, with the largest circulation in its field, is a professional journal committed to improving practice and expending knowledge in social work and social welfare. It is useful to students, faculty, administration and practitioners. Vol. 29 (5), September/October 1984 (pp. 419–96), has 10 reviews, signed, with affiliations, of 13 books on pp. 490–4. These reviews, ranging from 300 to 1,000 words in length, are mainly descriptive. Full bibliographical details are given. Volume author-index includes books reviewed.

Political Science

Indexes to reviews

Here again, the vast majority of political-science journals are indexed in *Social science citation index*, including review-articles and book-reviews. Over 50 per cent of the titles listed in the following section are also covered in *Social sciences index* and *Internationale Bibliographie der Rezensionen. Book review index, British humanities index* and *Book review digest* include a few. Surprisingly, three of the journals that follow are not dealt with in any of these indexing services.

Reviewing journals

International affairs (Guildford, Surrey, Butterworths, for the Royal Institute of International Affairs (Chatham House), 1922–. 4 p.a.) is a prestigious British journal with wide coverage of all aspects of international affairs, emphasis being on political and economic aspects.

The book-review section, containing review-articles, book-reviews and lists of books received, is an important source for the more notable contributions to political and economic literature. Vol. 61 (1), Winter 1984/85 (pp.. 1–196), includes a three-page review-article on one book, with footnotes listing earlier items, and 83 book-reviews, signed, with affiliations, on pp. 133–90. Reviews are arranged in subject groups, preceded by a section on Chatham House books and followed by a 'Bibliography and reference' section and a list of books received. Length of reviews ranges from 500 to 1,000 words, with shorter reviews (100–500 words) in the 'Bibliography and reference' section. Reviews are scholarly and clearly written; they can be critical (e.g. 'It would be very difficult to recommend this book to any but the most avid enthusiast'), or complimentary (e.g. 'At the level at which it has been approached this is a very successful biography indeed') or in a lighter vein: (e.g. 'the editors are to be congratulated on having produced a fascinating hotch-potch'). Bibliographical details are full, including the existence of indexes, bibliographies, and so on. The annual index does not list reviews, which are, however, covered in *Social sciences index, Social science citation index* and *Internationale Bibliographie der Rezensionen.*

Foreign affairs (New York, Council on Foreign Relations, Inc., 1922–. 5 p.a. Circulation: 85,000) aims to inform American public opinion by a broad hospitality to divergent ideas, and includes a section 'Recent books on international relations'. Vol. 61 (2), Winter 1984/85 (pp. 219–440), has 87 book-reviews on pp. 411–32, arranged by subject or geographical area. Each section has a named reviewer, but without affiliation, and reviews are short (50–300 words) and mainly descriptive. Comments also tend to be short; for example, 'This book deserves high praise'. More an alerting than a reviewing service, with the advantage that the books included are more up-to-date in their reviews than those included in journals with longer, more learned reviews. There is a review editor, but no volume index; contents lists in each issue record books reviewed. Reviews are indexed in *Social sciences index* and *Social science citation index.*

American political science review (Washington, American Political Science Association, 1906–. 4 p.a. Circulation: 20,000) is the official journal of the Association, covering international relations, political theory, public administration, American politics, comparative politics and political methodology. Vol. 78 (1), March 1984 (pp. 1–296), has 108 book-reviews, signed, with affiliations on pp. 207–95, arranged in five subject groups. Reviews are short, about 500–1,000 words in length, with clear descriptions and reasonable criticisms and praise; for example, 'This thoughtful and timely book' and 'well-conceived and executed book. I highly recommend it'. A section headed 'Annotations', with brief notes of 50–100 words describing books, and review essays are included in some issues. There is a book-review editor and editorial board. The annual index includes in one sequence authors of articles, books reviewed or annotated, and book reviewers.

Annals of the American Academy of Political and Social Science (London, Beverley Hills, etc., Sage Publications, for the Academy, 1899–. 6 p.a. Circulation: 15,500) has articles on a single prominent political or social problem, usually germane to US politics and written at the invitation of the editor, in each issue. The 'Book department', however, is not restricted to America or politics. Vol. 478, March 1985 (pp. 1-223), includes 35 book-reviews, signed, with affiliations, arranged in subject groups on pp. 183–214. Reviews are short (about 400–500 words), and concise, with useful criticisms and recommendations; for example, 'the author's purpose is apparently more historical and descriptive than evaluative. As such, the treatment is scholarly, fair and comprehensive. The result is an important and useful study that should serve as a point of departure for future research to come'. One of the longer reviews ends, 'The book is well-written, well edited, with excellent documentation, bibliography, tabular summaries, and...maps...It is recommended reading'; while another commences: 'This is not a book for beginners'. Bibliographical details are full. There is a five-yearly cumulative index. Reviews are covered in *Social science index*, *Book review index*, *Book review digest*, *Social science citation index* and *Internationale Bibliographie der Rezensionen*.

Political science quarterly (New York, Academy of Political Science, 1886–. 4 p.a. Circulation: 11,000), the journal of the Academy, claims to be non-partisan and devoted to the study of contemporary and historical aspects of government, politics and public affairs. American bias is pronounced. Vol. 99 (1), Spring 1984 (pp. 1–191), has 72 book-reviews, signed, with affiliations, on pp. 93–189, and a list of reference books and source materials received (pp. 190–1). The reviews, each about 500 words in length, are critical and evaluative; for example, 'This is a careful study. Nevertheless, the reader should be aware of two features of the book which may be disappointing' and 'The authors also show a lamentable tendency to overlook earlier, related work by others'. Books reviewed are mostly American, published a year or two earlier. The annual index includes a list of books reviewed.

Perspective (Washington, DC, Heldref Publications, 1972–. 8 p.a. Circulation: 1,200), subtitled 'monthly review of new books on government/politics/international affairs', reviews books on politics, international relations, political theory and methodology. Vol. 13 (7), October 1984 (pp. 145–60), has a two-page feature review of one book, and 26 reviews, signed, with affiliations, on pp. 148–59, followed by an author index to the books reviewed. Reviews are grouped by geographical area and by subject, mainly of American books, reviewed by American academics. Length of reviews ranges from 500 to 1,000 words. Reviews are good descriptions, often including some CV on the author and, although short, are critical; for example, 'This book fails to meet the purposes described by the editors. Its greatest strength lies in the very extensive citations among the notes following each chapter. Generally, chapters are neither well written nor clear, and often suffer from a bureaucratic type of double talk'; and of a biography, 'This is a good, highly readable book...written in journalistic style'. Full bibliographical details are given. The annual index, in the centre-fold of the following January issue, lists reviewed books under authors, A–Z.

Revue française de science politique (Paris, Fondation Nationale des Sciences Politiques and L'Association Française de Science Politique, with assistance from Centre National de la Recherche Scientifique, 1951–. 6 p.a. Circulation: 3,500). Vol. 34 (3), June 1984 (pp. 413–600), includes 11 book-reviews, signed, with affiliations, in a section headed 'Notes bibliographiques', on pp. 491–510, and 126 brief annotations headed 'Informations bibliographiques', on pp. 511–42. Arrangement of both sections is by eight subject-groups. Reviews are in French, as are most of the books reviewed and annotated (with a few in English and German). Scholarly, critical reviews are by academics. The annual index does not list book-reviews, these being covered in *Social science citation index* and *Internationale Bibliographie der Rezensionen*.

Millennium (London, Millennium Publishing Group, London School of Economics and Political Science, 1971–. 3 p.a. Circulation: 900) has research articles on international relations theory, foreign-policy analysis, strategic studies, comparative government studies, and so on. Vol. 13 (3), 1984 (pp. 245–347), includes a six page review-article and nine signed book-reviews on pp. 331–47. The reviews, which vary in length from 575 to 1,300 words, are written mainly by academic professors and lecturers, but also by some third-year and research students. Books selected for review are mostly British but some are American, recently published, and many are basic texts for the teaching of students. Reviews are critical; for example, 'This work will not stand up to such scrutiny...intellectually shoddy' and 'this book is more than disappointing, it is often misleading, whilst the gap in the bibliography, not to mention its tendentiousness will make it of dubious teaching value'. There would appear to be no annual indexes.

The political quarterly (London, The Political Science Quarterly Publishing Co., Ltd., 1940–. 4 p.a. Circulation: 3,500), founded with backing by George Bernard Shaw, aims to provide expert commentary on international social and political problems from a progressive point of view. Vol. 56 (1), January/March 1985 (pp. 1–109), includes a 'Book-reviews' section on pp. 91–108, with seven reviews, signed, but without affiliations and ranging from 200 to 2,500 words in length. There is a literary editor. Bibliographical details lack place of publication. The annual index lists books reviewed, and there is a cumulative index covering 1930–78.

Policy studies journal (Tallahassee, Fl., Florida State University, 1972–. 4 p.a. Circulation: 2,400), subtitled 'the journal of the Policy Studies Organization and the Policy Sciences Program, Florida State University', is an important journal in its field, aiming to show how political and social sciences can be relevant to government programmes. It includes a section of 'Literature reviews'. Vol. 13 (1), September 1984 (pp. 1–241), has 'Literature reviews' on pp. 205–31, commencing with the review editor's 'Comments', followed by two four-page review-essays relating to three books each, and 'Book notes' (pp. 219–29) of 46 books arranged A–Z by authors — brief unsigned abstracts (50-100 words). Finally, there are notes on 'Literature reviews' authors. Volume index includes reviewers and authors of reviewed books in the author index and titles of books reviewed in the subject index.

The journal of Commonwealth and comparative politics (London, Cass, 1961–. 3 p.a. Circulation: 716), titled *Journal of Commonwealth political studies* prior to 1974, is concerned with the study of Commonwealth politics and history, and also comparative politics and history of other areas. Vol. 22 (3), November 1984 (pp. 221–330), has six reviews, signed, with affiliations, on pp. 318–28 of books published in 1981, 1982 and two books in 1983. Length of reviews ranges from 600 to 1,650 words. Some issues include review-articles. Reviews can be critical; for example, 'This 150,000-word book would have been twice as good if it had been half as long', the reviewer complaining that the author did not stick to the subject of the title; and of a paperback, widely advertised as intended for the general reader, 'This book is not quite what its publishers have sought to make it appear'. Poor production, including poor proof-reading, is also criticized in some reviews. The volume index has a list of books reviewed, followed by a list of reviewers.

Canadian journal of political science/Revue canadienne de science politique (Waterloo, Ontario, Wilfred Laurier University Press, for the Canadian Political Science Association, 1968–. 4 p.a. Circulation: 3,200) supersedes the *Canadian journal of economics and political science*, published to 1967. Vol. 18 (1), March 1985 (pp. 1–228), includes 39 book-reviews, signed, with affiliations, on pp. 167–222 and five brief reviews on pp. 223–6. Length of reviews ranges from 500 to 1,500 words. A list of books reviewed precedes the review section. Written in the language of the books, French or English, by Canadian academics, the reviews are critical and clearly written, the main focus being on Canadian issues, but some international topics also figure. The annual index includes lists of reviewed books and of reviewers.

World politics (Princeton, NJ, Princeton University Centre of International Studies, 1948–. 4 p.a. Circulation: 4,000), subtitled 'a quarterly journal of international relations', is devoted to problems in international relations and comparative politics, each issue usually including two or three review articles. Vol. 36 (3), April 1984 (pp. i–iv, 309–460), includes three review-articles on pp. 407–60, the first dealing with a book published in 1981, the second, with 12 books published between 1978 and 1982, and the third, with four books published between 1977 and 1981. Reviewers are professors at American universities currently doing research, and the articles are scholarly and critical, although devoted as much if not more to the subject matter rather than to the books reviewed. Bibliographical details lack prices. Preliminaries contain a list of contributors (with affiliations), books published, and so on, and abstracts of the articles and review articles. The annual index records in one sequence authors of articles and review articles and books reviewed.

Journal of politics (Gainesville, Fl., Southern Political Science Association, University of Florida, 1939–. 4 p.a. Circulation: 4,100), is mainly concerned with American politics and government. Vol. 47 (1), February 1985 (pp. 1–145), includes in its 'Book section' (p. 292–338) a review-essay and 17 book-reviews, signed, with affiliations (pp. 305–80), preceded by a list, 'Book review contents' of the reviews. Not all issues include review-articles; some (one in 1984) carry 'Briefer notices', each between 30 and 40 words in length. There is a book-review editor. Reviews, 600 to 2,000 words in length,

are scholarly and critical; for example, 'Despite its conjectural quality, this very readable book...deserves careful consideration, for its
intriguing speculations promise to stimulate further research'. The
volume index includes a list of books reviewed and reviewers.

Political studies (Guildford, Surrey, Butterworths, 1953–. 4 p.a.
Circulation: 2,400), the journal of the Political Studies Association
of the UK, is devoted to comparative politics. Vol. 13 (1), March 1985
(pp. 1–180), includes two review-articles (pp. 122–35) and 88 book-
reviews, signed, with affiliations, on pp. 136–78, arranged in four
subject-groups. Each group is followed by a list of books received in
that subject field. Reviews (between 200 and 500 words in length)
are brief and to the point, up-to-date and with full bibliographical
detail, including ISBNs. The annual index (cumulated 10-yearly)
includes a list of books reviewed.

Political theory (London, Beverly Hills, etc., Sage Publications,
1973–. 4 p.a.), subtitled 'an international journal of political
philosophy', is intended to serve the entire political theory community having no particular affiliation or orientation. Vol. 12 (4),
November 1984 (pp. 467–638), has seven signed reviews in the
'Books in review' section, pp. 605–31. The reviews, between 1,000
and 2,000 words in length, are scholarly and can be very critical, covering much on the subject in general as well as on the books content.
The reviewer of one book, after somewhat devastating criticism of
the author's book and his views on the subject, ends, 'I want to conclude with a few words about the book's grammatical and stylistic
failings'; but a further reviewer writes of another book, 'In this book
the author presents a clearly written, meticulously argued, judicious
and sympathetic reading of and commentary on the entirety of Rous-
seau's *Social contract*'. There is a reviewed editor. Full bibliographical details are given. The volume index includes reviewers with
authors, and there is also a list of books reviewed.

West European politics (London, Cass, 1978–. 4 p.a.) is a leading
academic journal in its field, devoted to the discussion of political
and social issues relating to Western Europe. Vol. 8 (1), January 1985
(pp. 1–126), has nine reviews, signed, with affiliations, on pp. 119–
26. The reviews are shortish (250–500 words in length), up to date,
and in English, although some of the books reviewed are in other
European languages. Review-articles appear in some issues, and
there is a review editor. Reviews are descriptive and mildly, usually
favourably, critical. The first three reviews in this issue begin, 'This is
a welcome contribution to an area of comparative sociology', 'The
clear and informative tone of this book is set in the first chapter' and

'This is a very interesting book indeed'. The annual index does not list reviews.

Science and society (New York, S & S Quarterly, Inc., 1937–. 4 p.a. Circulation: 3,800), subtitled 'an independent journal of Marxism', publishes articles on politics and economics from the Marxist perspective by international contributors. Vol. 48 (3), Fall 1984 (pp. 257–381), includes an eight-page review-article, with many footnotes, and eight book-reviews, signed, with affiliations, on pp. 358–80. Length of reviews ranges from 750 to 1,750 words. The reviews are well written, interpreting the books from a Marxist angle, and books selected provide wide subject coverage. A 'Book note' on p. 381 is a brief review of an annotated bibliography on the nuclear power debate. Full bibliographical details are given. the volume index has sections listing review-articles and books reviewed.

Government and opposition (London, Government and Opposition, with the assistance of the London School of Economics and Political Science, 1965–. 4 p.a. Circulation: 1,500) is a scholarly journal subtitled 'a quarterly journal of comparative politics'. Vol. 20 (1), winter 1985 (pp. 1–143), has two review-articles, with footnotes, devoted to one or two books (pp. 104–17) and five signed reviews on pp. 118–41. Very often several books figure in one review. Reviewers' affiliations are given in the list of contributors. Reviews (ranging widely from 500 to 3,500 words) are scholarly, evaluative and very readable. Thus two books are compared on much the same subject; the reviewer finds one a better buy that the other: 'cheaper, longer, more vividly written and presenting more background to events and about personalities', whereas the other author's style is 'dry and sparse, able to gut a document for an apt quotation but making dramatic events seem dull'. Full bibliographical details are given. The volume index includes books reviewed and reviewers. Cumulative indexes cover vols. 1–5, 6–10.

Parliamentary affairs (Oxford University Press, for The Hansard Society for Parliamentary Government, 1947–. 4 p.a. Circulation: 2,000), subtitled 'a journal of comparative politics', is an established academic quarterly devoted to parliamentary democracy and covering all aspects of government and politics directly or indirectly connected with Parliament and parliamentary systems in Britain and throughout the world. Vol. 37 (3), Summer 1984 (pp. 243–352), has a book section on pp. 327–52, with six critical review-essays, each reviewing between one and seven books, brief descriptive unsigned reviews of between 100 and 300 words on seven reference books, and a list of recent books on British and Western European government and politics. Length of review essays ranges from 750 and 2,000 words. Bibliographical details lack date of publication and are given in footnotes. The annual index lists authors and titles of review essays and books reviewed.

Economics

Indexes to reviews

Almost all economic journals are included in *Social science citation index*, with probably about 50 per cent being indexed in *Internationale Bibliographie der Rezensionen* and fewer in *Book review index*, *British humanities index* and *Book review digest*. Only four of the journals noted below are indexed in *Business periodicals index* indicating, perhaps, that the businessman is more interested in production and marketing than in economics.

Reviewing journals

The journal of economic literature (Nashville, Tennessee, American Economic Association, 1963–. 4 p.a. Circulation: 26,000) is edited from the Department of Economics at Stanford University and is the major reviewing, indexing and abstracting journal in the field of economic literature. It continues the service previously included in *American economic review*, the most prestigious US economic journal. Vol. 22 (2), June 1984 (pp. 507–1006), includes 38 book-reviews, signed, with affiliations, on pp. 581–636, and also about 330 books and 14 new journals, with unsigned annotations of between 100 and 150 words in the section 'New books: an annotated listing', on pp. 638–719. The rest of the journal contains articles, communications, contents lists of periodicals and selected abstracts of articles in periodicals. Book-reviews range from 350 to 1,600 words in length and have classified arrangement. Reviewers are mostly American academics, and reviews are critical; 'Yet for all its brevity [xv, 138 pp.] the book is repetitious' and 'A conscientious reviewer cannot omit mention of the incredibly large number of typographical errors that eventually become distracting and on occasion seriously impede one's understanding'. There is also praise: 'This volume contains a wonderful collection of papers. With one exception...the articles included...deliver what the editor promises in his "Preface"; and, 'The book is forcefully written...Extensive notes and an index are provided'. Full bibliographical details, with ISBNs and *JEL* references, are given. The volume index has a general index listing books reviewed and an author index that includes book authors and reviewers.

The economic journal (Cambridge University press, 1891–. 4 p.a. Circulation: 7,000) is the prestige journal of the Royal Economic Society, covering all fields of economics, theoretical and applied, and representing all schools of thought. It carries original articles, notes and comments, and an extensive section of reviews and signed notes on new books. Vol. 93 (177), March 1985 (pp. 1–283), has 23 book-reviews, signed, with affiliations, on pp. 206–43, and 74 shorter 'Book notes' on pp. 245–72. 'Book notes' is arranged in subject groups, with descriptive comment (about 200–400 words apiece) and in smaller type than the rest of the journal. Average length of reviews is 1,000 words (one reaches about 1,800 words). Reviews are thoughtfully written, critical and evaluative, and very readable. One reviewer writes, 'This is an exceedingly honest book. The problems and assumptions are clearly stated...The authors, however, have been completely oblivious to developments in macroeconomics over the last 10 years'. The reviewers can also praise: 'Overall, this is an interesting and timely book that begins to fill a major gap...The exposition is good and the combination of theory and practice particularly attractive'. Bibliographical details are full. The annual index (cumulated for 1931–80. 1983) includes a listing of books reviewed and a list of reviewers.

Journal of political economy (Chicago, Ill., University of Chicago Press, 1892–. 6 p.a. Circulation 7,000) is an old-established journal with wide subject coverage, designed for the exchange of views among professional economists. Vol. 92 (4), August 1984 (pp. 565–790), has three lengthy book-reviews, signed, with affiliations, on pp. 781–90, each of about 2,000 words. Reviews are usually very critical. The reviewer of a book on Keynes' *General Theory* writes, 'Anyone looking at the title of this book would naturally expect to find a survey of the development of macroeconomics after the publication of *General theory* in 1936. At least so it was with me. But in fact it is not that kind of book at all. The author's intention is much better described by the subtitle'. The reviewer ends, however, by stating that it is a provocative and interesting piece of work. Reviews are in many cases supported by references and notes. Full bibliographical details are given. The volume index includes a list of books reviewed.

Economica (London, The London School of Economics and Political Science, 1921–. 4 p.a. Circulation: 4,000) is devoted to economics, economic history, statistics and closely related problems. Apart from original articles, it endeavours to provide for its readers reviews of the most important works published in its field. Vol. 52 (205), February 1985 (pp. 1–140), has ten book-reviews, signed, with affiliations, on pp. 123–35, of between 800 and 1,000 words in length. There is a review editor, and reviews are scholarly, descriptive and to some extent critical; thus, 'This is a scholarly and thoughtful collection...well-written, elegant and presents a stimulating combination of economic and historical analysis'; and 'To say that these essays deserve great attention, however, is not to say that their exposition is as full as one might wish';or, 'A small blemish of the work is presented by the standard of proof-reading'. Bibliographical details are full. The volume index includes a listing of books reviewed and a list of reviewers.

Southern economic journal (Chapel Hill, NC, Southern Economic Association and University of North Carolina, 1913–. 4 p.a. Circulation: 2,500) is a learned academic journal aimed mainly at southern universities in the United States. Vol. 51 (2), October 1982 (pp. 319–653), has 25 book-reviews, signed, with affiliations, on pp. 615–45, mostly of American publications, reviewed by academics from the southern universities, and often written with university-student readers in mind, or for academic teaching. Reviews are supported by reference to other works, although they are, in the main, descriptive, with some criticism. Review-length varies between 800 and 1,600 words. Full bibliographical details are given. The volume index includes a separate listing of books reviewed.

The Manchester School of Economics and Social Studies (The Manchester School, Economics Department, the University, Manchester, 1930–. 4 p.a. Circulation: 1,500) contains articles and book-reviews by academics worldwide. No. 2, June 1984 (pp. 123–237), has 20 book-reviews, signed, with affiliations, on pp. 211–36. There is a book-review editor, and a list of books reviewed precedes the reviews, which are arranged A–Z by authors. Reviews, though short, are critical and average about 500 words in length. Bibliographical details are full. An annual index is lacking and contents lists do not list reviews. Reviews are indexed in *Social sciences index, Social science citation index* and *Internationale Bibliographie der Rezensionen*.

Soviet studies (Harlow, Essex, Longman Group, Ltd., for the University of Glasgow, 1949–. 4 p.a. Circulation: 1,700), subtitled 'a quarterly journal of the USSR and Eastern Europe', is a scholarly journal devoted to the social sciences, particularly economics and political science, relating to the Soviet Union and other Eastern European countries. Vol. 37 (2), April 1985 (pp. 152–303), includes 16 book-reviews, signed with affiliations, on pp. 281–301, and nine book notices on pp. 301–2. Books reviewed are usually British or American publications, and the reviews, which are critical, are in English, ranging from 750 to 1,500 words in length. Book notices are unsigned and descriptive (50–100 words in length). Full bibliographical details are given. The annual contents list includes lists of books reviewed, but not book notices. Reviews appear in *Humanities index, Social science citation index* and *British humanities index.*

Journal of international economics (Amsterdam, North Holland Publishing Co., 1971–. 4 p.a.) is a highly specialized journal aimed at the widest professional readership in the area of international economics. Vol. 17 (1/2) August 1984 (pp. 1–200), has five book-reviews on pp. 185–200. Length varies considerably, from 700 to 2,750 words each. Books are usually British or American in origin, and reviewers are American and, to a lesser extent, British academics (but one review in this issue is by a Japanese). There is a review editor, and reviews are descriptive and generally mildly critical. Full bibliographical details are given. An annual index to the reviews is lacking, but reviews are indexed in *Social sciences index, Social science citation index* and *Internationale Bibliographie der Rezensionen.*

Canadian journal of economics/Revue canadienne d'économique (Toronto University Press, 1968–. 4 p.a. Circulation: 4,300), the journal of the Canadian Economics Association, publishes papers and reviews in both French and English. Vol. 17 (2), May 1984 (pp. 191–411), includes a review-article (pp. 386–98) based on one book, but with 24 references, and a 'Review of books' section of four book reviews, signed, with affiliations. Length of reviews ranges from 1,000 to 2,000 words. Books reviewed may be in English or French, and there is a strong Canadian bias in selection for review. There is a book-review editor, and reviews are critical and evaluative. Full bibliographical details are given. The annual index (cumulated for vols. 1–10), includes a 'Reviews of books' and a list of reviewers.

Weltwirtschaftliches Archiv/Review of world economics (Tübingen, Federal Republic of Germany, J.C.B. Mohr (Paul Siebeck), 1913–. 4 p.a.), the journal of the Kiel Institute of World Economics (Institut für Weltwirtschaft Kiel), is a leading German economic journal focusing on international economics. Vol. 121 (1), 1985 (pp. 1–202), includes a 'Literature' section, with three review-articles on pp. 142–75 (one in English, two in German), twelve signed book-reviews on pp. 176–97, a list of books received and a list of contributors, both authors and reviewers, with their addresses and affiliations. The reviews, in German or English, range from 500 to 1,500 words in length and are scholarly, with mainly favourable criticism, often indicating likely readership; thus, 'It is clear that this book raises more questions than it answers but this can only act as a catalyst to further investigation. It will be of interest to anyone interested in international financial theory and institutions', and 'its main value is to help students and researchers to keep up with a large and growing body of theoretical literature, a task that the book achieves admirably'. Bibliographical details lack prices. Annual index (cumulated at intervals) lists review-articles and reviewed books, and also lists authors and reviewers.

Economic development and cultural change (Chicago, Ill., University of Chicago Press, 1952–. 4 p.a. Circulation: 3,700) is international in coverage, being devoted to the problems of Third World countries and aiming to relate capital and technological structures to social and cultural systems. Vol. 33 (1), October 1984 (pp. 1–222), includes a review-article on pp. 173–7, relating to two books, and eight book-reviews, signed, with affiliations. Reviews are lengthy (1,200–2,500 words each, and occasionally more), critical and evaluative; in some cases 'Notes' list references or bibliographies. Bibliographical descriptions are full. The annual index (cumulated for vols. 1–15) has one sequence of authors, reviewers and authors of reviewed books.

Economic record (Boondura, Vic., The Economic Society of Australia, La Trobe University, 1924–. 4 p.a. Circulation: 4,400) is highly thought of in the field of international economics. Vol. 60 (169), June 1984 (pp. 111–202), has eight book-reviews, signed, with affiliations, on pp. 192–202, averaging 800–1,000 words in length. Reviews are critical and books either relate to Australia or are reviewed from an Australian point of view; thus, 'Australian economists...will find the lack of interest in these issues...remarkable'. Full bibliographical details are given. Most issues also include lists of books received, with useful short abstracts. The annual index includes a list of books reviewed.

Kyklos (Basle, Switzerland, Kyklos-Verlag, 1948–. 4 p.a. Circulation: 3,400) is subtitled 'internationale Zeitschrift für Sozialwissenschaften/Revue internationale des sciences sociales/International review for social sciences', which is somewhat misleading in that the publication relates to economics and its interaction with other disciplines. It is designed for the graduate scholar. Vol. 37 (3), 1984 (pp.

363–526), has a section containing 30 reviews on pp. 470–517, a list of books received, and a list of authors and of reviewers, with affiliations and addresses. Length of reviews ranges between 400 and 1,000 words. Books reviewed are predominantly in English, but several are in German and some in French, the language of the review not necessarily corresponding to that of the book. Reviews are descriptive, often with quotations from the books reviewed, and critical. Criticism can be complimentary; a reviewer comments on a book on Keynes thus: 'Only those dreary economists who regard economic theory and measurement as the sum and substance of their discipline will fail to derive great pleasure and instruction from this fascinating, wide-ranging and well-written volume'. The annual index lists reviews by author and reviewer of book reviewed.

Journal of comparative economics (New York, Academic Press, 1977–. 4 p.a.) is the journal of the Association for Comparative Economic Studies, publishing theoretical and empirical articles on the comparison of economic systems and subsystems, both contemporary and historical. Vol. 8 (3), September 1984 (pp. 237–352), includes seven book-reviews, signed, with affiliations, on pp. 335–52, ranging from 600 to 1,000 words in length. Reviews are by academics throughout the English-speaking world and are generally descriptive, with some favourable criticism; for example, 'This brief but solid and informative monograph' and 'This provocative and well-documented essay', and even 'In spite of the limitations of this study in terms of scope, dating, etc., it is a valuable contribution to the literature'. The annual index includes a list of books reviewed during the year; reviewers appear in the author index.

The journal of economic history (Wilmington, Del., The Economic History Association at the University of Iowa, 1941–. 4 p.a. Circulation: 3,714) is international in scope and concerned with economic history and related aspects of history and economics. One issue each year is devoted to papers given at the Association's annual meeting. Vol. 44 (4), December 1984, pp. 919–1165), has two review essays (one of 2½ pages on the *Cambridge economic history of India,* vol. 2; the other, of nearly six pages on three books on the Habsburg monarchy). The 38 signed book-reviews on pp. 1105–55 provide a substantial source of information on new books on economic history. Reviews are between 600 and 1,500 words in length, more descriptive than critical, and include many books in foreign languages. All reviews are in English. The annual index has a separate list of books reviewed.

History of political economy (Durham, NC, Duke University

Press, 1969–. 4 p.a. Circulation: 1,500) is a scholarly journal edited by the Department of Economics, Duke University. Vol. 16 (4), Winter 1984 (pp. 489–649), has six book-reviews, signed, with affiliations, on pp. 639–49. The reviews, mainly by American academics, range from 200 to 1,500 words in length. There is a book-review editor and reviews are critical. Thus a very short review of a book on Adam Smith states, 'The weakness of the book is that neither Smith nor the atmosphere of eighteenth-century Britain comes to life'; on another book,'This book (if that is what it is) begins curiously and as it continues gets curiouser and curiouser until it claims one's attention not for what it aspires to do and fails, or sought to have been and is not, but for the curio it is'. Full bibliographical details are given. Annual contents includes a list of books reviewed. There is a cumulative index for vols. 1–15 (1969–83).

The economic history review (London, The Economic History Society, 1927–. [2nd series, 1967–.] 4 p.a. Circulation: 5,000) is an important journal for both economist and historian, being devoted to the study of all aspects of economic and social history, history of economic thought and related disciplines. Surveys of the literature on specific topics are frequently included, and there is an annual 'List of publications on the economic and social history of Great Britain and Ireland'. Vol. 37 (3), August 1984 (pp. 319–471), includes 'Essays in bibliography and criticism, XCI: Recent work on the economic history of nineteenth-century France' (pp. 417–34), with a bibliography of 214 items. The 35 book-reviews, signed, with affiliations, on pp. 435–71, are presented in two sections, 'Great Britain' and 'General'. There is a book-review editor and length of reviews ranges from 300 to 1,000 words. Reviews are descriptive and evaluative; for example 'The volume's stress on intellectual history and on its interpretation in the civic humanist tradition lessens the attention given to two other aspects needed for a satisfactory interpretation'. Style and production are criticised; for example, 'spoiled at times by poor English and deficiencies in the quality and style of referencing and labelling'. Full bibliographical details are given. The annual index (cumulated for 1927–48, 1948–70) list books reviewed.

The journal of European economic history (Rome, Banco di Roma, 1972–. 3 p.a. Circulation: 3,500) is devoted to the study of the economic history of Europe and the various European countries. Vol. 13 (3), Winter 1984 (pp. 464-705), has 10 book-reviews, signed, with affiliations, on pp. 665–87. Arranged A–Z by authors, the books are mainly in English but include a few Italian titles; reviewers are usually British or American academics. The reviews, between 900 and 1,500 words in length, are pleasantly critical, with many comments and quotes. The annual index includes a list of books reviewed and of contributors and reviewers.

Business history review (Boston, Mass., Havard Business School, 1926–. 4 p.a. Circulation: 2,650) is a scholarly journal devoted to the historical evolution of business in the United States and abroad. Vol. 58 (2), Summer 1984 (pp. 153-316), has a five-page review-article, 'Urbanization of the American West', reviewing five histories of individual Western cities, and 38 book-reviews, signed, with affiliations, on pp. 302–16. Reviews, by American academics, are shortish (about 800 words in length), but critical and reasonably up-to-date and intended for an academic audience. The annual index (cumulated throughout the year and 5 yearly) has a list of books reviewed.

British journal of industrial relations (Oxford, Blackwell, 1961–. 3 p.a. Circulation: 2,000), edited at the London School of Economics and Political Science and subtitled 'a journal of research and analysis covering every aspect of industrial relations in Britain and overseas', is the leading British academic journal in its field. Vol. 23 (1), March 1985 (pp. 1–178), has 11 book-reviews, signed, with affiliations, on pp. 159–73. There is a book-review editor and British bias in book and reviewer selection. The reviews, between 450 and 1,000 words in length, are mainly descriptive, although they can be critical. Thus the review of a book written in the style of a company history ends, 'If the organisation wanted this sort of book, it would have been better left to a professional ghostwriter'. Full bibliographical details are given. The volume index (cumulated for vol. 1–19: 1963–81) has a list of books reviewed, A–Z by title.

Industrial and labor relations review (Ithaca, N Y, New York State School of Industrial and Labor Relations, Cornell University, 1947–. 4 p.a. Circulation: 4,200) is an interdisciplinary journal. Vol. 38 (1), October 1984 (pp. 1–153), includes a list of 'Recent publications' (pp. 106–18) and a section of 19 book-reviews, signed, with affiliations, on pp. 119–41, arranged in 12 subject-groups. Reviews are between 600 and 1,100 words in length and often include comments on the author's background as well as the subject, with critical comment; for example, 'This is that scholarly rarity, an interesting bad book', and 'sweeping conclusions based on a wholly inadequate data base'. Full bibliographical details are given. The volume index (cumulated for vols. 1–20: 1947–67) includes a list of books reviewed.

. **Education**

Indexes to reviews

Most journals in the field of education are indexed in *Education index*, which includes book-reviews. Reviews arè also covered in *Internationale Bibliographie der Rezensionen* and *Social science citation index;* a few appear in *Book review index* and *Book review digest. British education index,* unfortunately, does not index book-reviews.

Reviewing journals

British journal of educational studies (Oxford, Blackwell, under the auspices of the Standing Conference on Studies in Education, 1952–. 3 p.a. Circulation: 1,300) is aimed at the general reader rather than the specialist. Vol. 32 (3), October 1984 (pp. 199–290), has 14 book-reviews, signed, but without affiliations, in the 'Reviews' section on pp. 265–90. The reviews (450–1,500 words in length) are usually critical, with indications that the reviewers are familiar with the literature of the subject. Comments can be biting; for example 'The best parts of this book are the first and last chapters. Probably both could have been written without the dubious support of the research which is reported in between'. Full bibliographical details, occasionally including ISBNs, and very often supported by references, are given. The annual index lists books reviewed.

American journal of education (Chicago, Ill., University of Chicago Press, 1893–. 4 p.a. Circulation: 3,928), formerly *School review,* publishes thoughtful and scholarly theoretical articles on all aspects of education at every level. Vol. 92 (4), August 1984 (pp. 391–550), has 11 signed book-reviews on pp. 503–50, of between 1,500 and 2,500 words in length. Book selection has a strong American bias. Full bibliographical details are given, and there are copious footnote references and CVs of the reviewers. The annual index has a list of books reviewed and of reviewers.

Harvard educational review (Cambridge, Mass., Havard Educational Review, 1931–. 4 p.a. Circulation: 14,250) is a journal of opinion and research in the field of education. Vol. 54 (4), November 1984 (pp. 389–502), has two essay reviews of 7 and 4½ pages, each reviewing two books and including references, notes, and so on; six book-reviews, signed, with affiliations, on pp. 452–64; and 20 'Book notes', on pp. 488–94. The reviews, between 2,000 and 3,000 words in length, are critical; book notes (50–250 words) are mainly descriptive. The majority of the books reviewed and all the reviewers are American. The volume index includes separate lists of book- reviews, essay reviews and special reviews, book notes and reviewers.

Educational studies (American Educational Studies Association, Georgia State University, *and* University of Florida, 1970–. 4 p.a. Circulation: 1,100) subtitled 'a journal in the foundation of education' is self-styled 'a journal of reviews and criticism'. Vol. 15 (3), Fall 1984 (pp. 295–347), carries 27 listed reviews, signed, with affiliations, on pp. 232–329. Arrangement is in six sections: History of education; Philosophy of education; Comparative and international education; Education and the social sciences; Educational policy studies; Educational issues. The reviews, (800–2,000 words in length) are closely analytical, with quotations plus appended notes, and critical, indicating readership. One monograph is praised for its extensive bibliography, another, on a particular school, is reproved: 'But the fact that a school does *something* well is not a warrant for calling it a good school'; a third is faulted for lack of a glossary in a book with a plethora of esoteric terms. An author's rebuttal of a criticism of his book has a reviewer's equally lengthy reply. Bibliographical detail is full. The annual index has entries for reviewers' names.

Educational studies (Abingdon, Oxon., Carfax Publishing, Ltd., 1975–. 3 p.a. Circulation: 2,000) aims to provide a forum for original investigations and theoretical studies in education. Vol. 10 (2), 1984 (pp. 87–152), has six book-reviews, signed, with affiliations, on pp. 145–52, of between 450 and 1,100 words in length. Reviews are descriptive and may indicate readership; for example, 'This book is likely to be particularly useful to those starting personal study in the area and for group work'. There are also strictures on proof-reading: 'My only criticism of an otherwise valuable set of commentaries is the quite apalling number of misprints'. Bibliographical details do not always give prices and ISBNs are only sometimes stated. An annual index is lacking, and contents lists do not include books reviewed.

Educational review (Abingdon, Oxon., Carfax Publishing, Ltd., 1948–. 3 p.a. Circulation: 1,650), edited by members of the Faculty of Education, Birmingham University, publishes general articles and accounts of research of interest to teachers, lecturers, research workers in education and educational psychology, and to students of education. Vol. 37 (1), February 1985 (pp. 1-91), has 18 book-reviews, signed, but without affiliations, on pp. 79-91 — short, clear, practical reviews of British books likely to be of interest to the journal's readership, and averaging about 250 words apiece. Full bibliographical details are given. Book-reviews are omitted from the annual index and cumulative index to vols. 1–30 (1948–78), but covered in *Educa-*

tion index, Social science citation index and *Internationale Bibliographie der Rezensionen.*

Comparative education (Abingdon, Oxon., Carfax Publishing Ltd., 1965–. 3 p.a. Circulation: 1,300) is an international journal of educational studies aiming to present up-to-date information on significant trends throughout the world on comparative education and related disciplines, for professional teachers, researchers, administrators and students. Vol. 20 (2), 1984 (pp. 191–298), has nine book-reviews, signed, but without affiliations, on pp. 287–96. Reviews are mainly, but not wholly, descriptive; for example, 'It is hard in a brief review to do justice to the richness of such a book', and 'The book can be faulted in a number of ways'. Review-length ranges from 500 to 1,000 words, and full bibliographical details are given. The volume index omits book-reviews, for which see *Education index, Social science citation index* and *Internationale Bibliographie der Rezensionen.*

Adult education (Leicester, National Institute of Adult Continuing Education, 1926–. 4 p.a. Circulation: 2,600) provides an opportunity for administrators and practioners, professional and voluntary, to exchange ideas and information about policy and action. It is concerned with the development of all aspects of adult continuing education. Vol. 57 (3), December 1984 (pp. 205–304), has 10 signed book-reviews on pp. 290–304, 7 shorter notices and 13 brief notes on pamphlets and reports. Length of reviews ranges from 400 to 550 words. Reviews are mainly descriptive but can be critical, as shown in excerpts from two juxtaposed reviews: 'This is a somewhat rambling and repetitious collection of jottings...The reader is left to sort out the wood from the trees', and, after a quoted first sentence, 'This crisp, clear and enticing opening sentence is typical of this splendid book'. Full bibliographical details are given. The annual index includes a list of 'Main book reviews'. A revised cumulative index to vols. 1–51 (1926–79) has been published.

Primary education review (London, National Union of Teachers, 1975–. 3 p.a.) is for primary school teachers. No. 22, Spring 1985 (pp. 1–40), has 89 book-reviews, initialled, and followed by 'About our reviewers' (an A–Z list of reviewers' names, with affiliations). The reviews are in two main sections: Fiction, subdivided into Nursery, Infant, Junior and Upper Junior/Middle; and Non-fiction, subdivided by subjects (Poetry, Sport, Music, etc.). Reviews are informative rather than critical, *PER* being more a current-awareness service than a provider of serious reviews. Bibliographical details are full, including ISBNs.

School science (Hatfield, Herts., Association for Science Education, 1919–. 4 p.a. Circulation: 18,500) is the journal of the Association, with articles and reviews covering biology, chemistry, physics,
middle school science and science education. Vol. 65 (232), March
1984 (pp. 425–634), includes 42 book-reviews, signed, but without
affiliations, on pp. 617–34. Reviews are very short (60–100 words)
and are coded to indicate academic level, whether mainly for
teachers or pupils, subjects and type of book (i.e. textbook, reference
book, etc.). Bibliographical details are full, giving ISBNs. The volume
index does not include book-reviews.

The Times educational supplement (London, Times Newspapers,
Ltd., 1910–. Weekly. Circulation: 132,000) is in tabloid form and
includes around 1,000 lively book reviews each year, on education
and related topics. Selection is more orientated towards books on
education than is *The Times higher education supplement*. The
10 May 1985 issue (112pp.) includes 21 signed book-reviews, interspersed with advertisements, in four sections: Books; Books in class;
Arts; Resources (including resources other than books). Bibliographical details include ISBNs but omit pagination. Indexed in
Education index and *Book review index*.

The Times higher education supplement (London, Times Newspapers, Ltd., 1971–. Weekly, Circulation: 21,000) is also in tabloid
form and carries about 1,000 signed reviews each year. The issue for
22 February 1985 (36pp.) has 10 pages devoted to 'Books', with
many advertisements interspersed, containing 26 signed reviews of
varying length. Selection is wide in this issue, including a biography
of Lloyd George, books on drama, on industry and philosophy, as
well as some on perspectives of higher education. Bibliographical
details are full, including ISBNs. Indexed in *Education index*.

Chronicle of higher education (Washington, Gorbin Gwaltnay,
1966–. 46 p.a. Circulation: 70,000) is a similar publication to *The
Times higher education supplement*. In tabloid form, sections titled
'New scholarly books' and 'New books on higher education' have
two- or three-line descriptions. Occasionally two or three signed
reviews figure. Indexed in *Education index*.

Law

Indexes to reviews

The major indexing service for legal periodicals is *Index to legal
periodicals,* which does cover book-reviews, but *Internationale Bib-*

liographie der Rezensionen and *Social science citation index* also have very good coverage. *Current law index,* however, indexes only one of the titles below.

Reviewing journals

The law quarterly review (London, Stevens, 1885–. 4 p.a. Circulation: 4,000) is a major journal covering all aspects of British and international law. Vol. 100, October 1984 (pp. 513–736), has 13 book-reviews, signed, but without affiliations, on pp. 717–36. Reviews range from 200 to 1,700 words in length, are analytical (citing cases) and critical, indicating readership. One book is criticized for failing to appreciate the variedness of American practice; another, for neglecting to cite French and German law sources. There is a book-review editor, and bibliographical details are full. The annual index list includes a list of books reviewed.

The modern law review (London, Stevens, for The Modern Law Review, Ltd., 1937–. 6 p.a. Circulation: 3,000) has articles and commentary on the law. Vol. 47 (3), May 1984 (pp.261–384), has a 'Reviews' section on pp. 359–69. This contains a 10½-page review-article relating to two books on critical law studies, with an extensive appended bibliography, and three reviews, 500, 1,000 and 3,000 words in length, respectively. Reviews are signed, with affiliations, plus full bibliographical details and many footnotes with references to other publications. The volume index has separate listings for review articles and books reviewed.

Harvard law review (Cambridge, Mass., Havard Law Review Association, 1887–. 8 p.a. Circulation: 10,000) is the most prestigious of the American law journals, each issue containing articles by prominent authors on all aspects of law, as well as notes and one or two book-reviews. Vol. 96 (8), June 1981 (pp. 1769–2000), includes two scholarly book-reviews on pp. 1952–90. The reviews resemble review essays, citing titles and having copious footnotes. One, of 9½ pages, adds two pages of chronology, selected writings and cases; the other is eight pages long. Full bibliographical details are given. The annual index lists 'Books reviewed and noted' and 'Book reviews—reviewers'. The cumulative index to vols. 1–86 (1887–1972) is in three volumes.

ABA journal (Chicago, Ill., American Bar Association, 1915–. 12 p.a. Circulation: 290,000), subtitled 'the lawyer's magazine', is the official journal of the Association. Vol. 71, May 1985 (pp. 1–154), includes a section 'Books for lawyers', pp. 92–111 (interspersed with many full and part-page advertisements). Of the seven book-reviews, signed, with affiliations, two (about 600 and about 350 words in length) have the heading 'For the practitioner', and five (about 350 words apiece), the heading 'General interest', but still on legal topics. 'Noted in brief' covers five more books (about 100 words apiece). Bibliographical details are full. The annual book-review index has separate listings under title, author and reviewer.

The Cambridge law journal (Cambridge University Press, for the Faculty of Law at the University of Cambridge, 1921–. 2 p.a. Circulation: 1,700) is a highly respected academic journal, focusing on Commonwealth law. Vol. 43 (2), November 1984 (pp. 209–416), has 24 book-reviews, signed, but without affiliations, on pp. 377–414. Several reviews concern two subject-linked books; for example, 'Crime in seventeenth century England; Criminal justice in colonial America, 1606–1660', The reviews generally are from 300 to 1,500 words in length and include text-books and treaties, plus some foreign titles of interest to the student rather than to the practitioner. Comments are descriptive and mainly favourable, criticism being concise because of restricted space — as claimed in some reviews. There is a book-review editor, and bibliographical details include authors' affiliations. The annual index has a list of books reviewed, and the general index has references to reviews.

American journal of international law (Washington, American Society of International Law, 1907–. 4 p.a. Circulation: 8,500) is published as a forum for lawyers, scholars and jurists to voice opinions and explore matters of international law and relations in depth. Vol. 78 (3), July 1984 (pp. 571–781), has a 'Book-review and notes' section on pp. 684–782, with 19 book-reviews, signed, with affiliations, and six 'Briefer notices', also signed, with affiliations. Review length is between 300 and 1,750 words; that of briefer notices is in the region of 250 words. There is a book-review editor, and reviews are mainly by American lawyers and academics. All reviews are in English but do include some foreign-language items, coverage being international. Reviews are evaluative, with many footnotes, and mainly favourable. The annual index covers book-reviews ('BR') and briefer notices ('BN'). There is a cumulative index to vols. 1–74 (1907–80).

International and comparative law quarterly (London, British Institute of International and Comparative Law, 1952–. 4 p.a. Circulation: 3,000), incorporating the *Quarterly* of the Society of Comparative Legislation and International Law and the *Transactions* of the Grotius Society, is a scholarly journal of high quality, with unique coverage of public and private international law and comparative law. Vol. 33 (4), October 1984 (pp. 777–1128), has 22 book-reviews, signed, but without affiliations, on pp. 1069–96. Review length ranges from 300 to 1,200 words. Some foreign-language items are included. Comments are descriptive rather than critical, such criticism as there is being favourable; for example, 'this timely indispensable tool of reference', and 'produced to a high standard and have excellent indexes'. The annual index includes an 'Index of book reviews and books received'.

Commonwealth law bulletin (London, Commonwealth Secretariat, 1975–. 4 p.a. Circulation: 2,000) includes synopses of significant legislation, judicial decisions, law reform and international developments, book-reviews and abstracts of recent periodical articles. Vol. 10 (3), July 1984 (pp. 1059–1415), carries nine book-reviews, some of them initialled, in a section of 'Reviews and notices' (pp. 1400–9). Length of reviews ranges from 300 to 1,200 words. The reviews are informative rather than critical and usually give recommendations, results, and so on, of publications reviewed *in extenso*. Bibliographical details are full. The annual index is a subject index and omits book reviews.

References

1. Riley, Lawrence E., and Spreitzer, Elmer A. 'Book reviewing in the social sciences, *The American sociologist*, vol. 5, November 1970, p. 158.
2. Snizek, William E., and Fuhrman, E. 'Some factors affecting the evaluative content of book reviews in sociology', *The American sociologist*, vol. 14, May 1979, pp. 108–14.
3. Riley, Lawrence E., and Spreitzer, Elmer A. 'Book reviewing in the social sciences', *The American sociologist*, vol. 5, November 1970, p. 362.
4. Berger, Peter L. *Invitation to sociology: a humanistic perspective.* Garden City, NY, Doubleday, 1966, p. 21.
5. Champion, Dean J., and Morris, Michael F. 'A content analysis of book reviews in the *AJS, ASR* and *Social forces*', *American journal of sociology*, vol. 78 (5), 1973, pp. 1256–7.
6. Snizek, William E.,, Fuhrman, E.R., and Wood, Michael R. 'The effect of theory group association of the evaluative content of book reviews in sociology', *The American sociologist*, vol. 16, August 1981, pp. 185–95.
7. Merton, Robert E. (*ed*). *Sociology of science.* University of Chicago Press, 1973.
8. Hirsch, Walter, and Potter-Efron, Ronald T. 'Book reviews and the status of authors and reviewers', *Contemporary sociology*, vol. 9, July 1980, pp. 520–2.
9. Woodbury, Richard B. 'On book reviewing', *American anthropologist*, vol. 79, Summer 1977, pp. 10 551–4.
10. *Science*, vol. 131, 22 April 1960, p. 1186.

11. *Choice*, vol. 22 (5), January 1985, p. 719.
12. *Choice*, vol. 22 (9), May 1985, p. 1298.
13. *International affairs*, vol. 61 (1), Winter 1984/85, p. 147.
14. *Canadian journal of political science*, vol. 18 (1), March 1985, p. 170.
15. *International affairs*, vol. 61 (1), Winter 1984/85, p. 171.
16. *Political theory*, vol. 12 (4), November 1984, p. 622.
17. Hargrave, Victoria E. 'A comparison of reviews of books in the social sciences in general and in scholarly periodicals', *The library quarterly*, vol. 18 (3), July 1948, pp. 216–17.
18. *International affairs*, vol. 61 (2), Spring 1985, pp. 347–8.

6.   Life and earth sciences

Anthony P. Harvey

The scope of this brief survey omits mathematics, astronomy, physics and chemistry. Instead, it concentrates on science in general (including the historical aspects of science), geology, anthropology, biology, natural history, entomology and zoology — an extensive enough field. The 26 journals selected for analysis vary markedly in the number of reviews they carry, although frequency of publication and review length are important factors here. The quarterly *Systematic zoology* may provide few reviews, but they are in-depth and average 400 words. Chen[1] calculates time-lag in publication of general-science books reviews as 12.2 months, although it could well extend to two years.

The review-essay or article (as favoured by *Isis* and *Journal of the history of science*, for example), in contrast to the normal book-review, allows the reviewer more space to analyse and compare a clutch of recent books on a particular theme (e.g. Halley's comet). It is distinct, again, from the heavily documented 'reviews of progress' to which such scientific serials as *Science progress* and *Reviews of modern physics* are wholly devoted.[2] Zuckerman[3] has maintained that the review article of several thousand words has an important part to play in science communication: 'The reading public deserves to be helped in learning what constitutes science, to appreciate the nature of scientific controversy, and to understand what are scientific facts and concepts, as opposed to speculations and what is just rubbish'.

One expects the science-book reviewer to have an academic background, and his/her review to be clearly written, analytical, balanced, evaluative and comparative, with readership in mind. Science books may, because of their technicality, normally escape weighty criticism.[4] At times, however, reviewers can be abrasive, quoting chapter and verse. Two reviews recently appeared of vol. 1 of the *Oxford illustrated encyclopedia: the physical world*. *British book news*[5] welcomed the book for its many short entries and excellent diagrams and photographs, while asking for more detail on fundamental concepts (e.g., weathering; atomic structure). But the conclusion is warm: 'This encyclopedia ought to find its way onto the reference shelves of every school, university and college library and its value as a home reference tool is without question'. But the *New scientist* reviewer[6] is less contented. He states, in a 400-word assessment, that if the volume 'did not bear the imprint of the Oxford University Press, it would not merit a review in *New scientist*'. Its 'extraordinary Anglophile approach suggests that many of the great achievements in physics made by foreign scientists followed solely from work carried out in Britian'. Examples follow. 'This is very definitely *not* a reliable encyclopedia of "the physical world".' The reviewer concludes that even if the book dropped most of its physics and mathematics, to concentrate on planet earth, it would still 'be faced with very stiff competition from the vastly superior *Cambridge Encyclopedia of Earth Sciences*'.

Indexes to reviews

The general science indexes are: *General science index* (New York, H.W. Wilson, 1978–. 10 p.a.) and *Index to book reviews in the sciences* (Philadelphia, PA., Institute for Scientific Information, 1980–. 12 p.a.). Scientific review-essays or survey articles are covered in *Index to scientific reviews* (Philadelphia, Pa., Institute for Scientific Information, 1974–. 2 p.a., with annual cumulation), paralleling the Institute's *Science citation index* (1981–. 4 p.a., with annual cumulation). Of the more general indexing services, *Internationale Bibliographie der Rezensionen* (Osnabrück, Dietrich, 1971–. 2 p.a.) and *Reference sources* (Ann Arbor, Mich., Pierian Press, 1977–. Annual) have relevance. For specific areas of the life and earth sciences, the following should be consulted: *BioResearch index* (Philadelphia, Pa., Biosciences Information Service, 1967–79, 16 vols.); *Entomology abstracts* (Bethesda, Md., Cambridge Scientific Abstracts, 1969–. 12 p.a.); *Review of applied entomology* (London, Commonwealth Institute of Entomology); and *Zoological record* (Philadelphia, Pa., Biosciences Information Service, and the Zoological Society of London, 1864–. Annual in 20 issues).

Science: general and history

Reviewing journals

American scientist (New Haven, Conn., Sigma XI, The Scientific Research Society, 1913–. 6 p.a. Circulation: 125,000) publishes original and review papers in the broad spectrum of science. Vol. 73 (4), July/August 1985 (pp. 302–401), has 63 reviews, signed, with affiliations (150–850 words apiece), plus a list of over 400 books received. The reviews, pithy, descriptive and generally evaluative, are grouped into physical sciences, earth sciences, life sciences, behavioural sciences, mathematics and computer science, engineering and applied sciences, plus history and philosophy of science. Levels are indicated. *Volcanic hazards: a source-book on the effect of eruptions*, by G.R.I. Blong (London, Academic Press, 1984) is given a 300-word review: 'There is now a comprehensive handbook on the effects of eruptions. This well-written and illustrated sourcebook should be required reading for city planners and engineers, employees of disaster agencies, agriculturists, health officials and even volcanologists...The book is thorough, yet fascinating...It covers everything from the spectrum of types of eruption to economic impact'. Bibliographical details omit illustrations and ISBNs. There is an author-index of books reviewed, the annual index listing these under both authors and titles.

Nature (London, Macmillan Journals, 1869–. 51 p.a. Circulation: 27,000) is the premier science journal. Vol. 316 (6029), 15-21 August 1985 (pp. 565–662), has seven book-reviews, signed, with affiliations (and full addresses), on pp. 583–6. The reviews are analytical and evaluative, average between 600 and 1,000 words apiece, and have illustrations. The reviewers are senior experts in their particular fields. Two works on a common theme are contrasted in a 1,000-word review: *No immediate danger: prognosis for a radio-active earth*, by Rosalie Bertell (London, The Women's Press, 1985) and *Power production: what are the risks?*, by J.H. Fremlin (Bristol, Alan Hilger, 1985). Fremlin has written a scientist's book: for him nuclear power is one of mankind's few bright hopes in our overcrowded planet, whereas for Bertell it is an ultimate evil: 'Both books will fail to persuade unsympathetic readers to change their views...To this reader, at least, the truth seems less likely to dwell among her [Bertell's] passionate advocacies than among Fremlin's cool arithmetic'. Bibliographical details omit details of illustrations, full pagination and ISBNs. Book-reviews are listed in the contents, and the volume-index covers authors and reviewers. Special book-review issues in 1984 were:

Textbook supplement (vol. 308 [5955], 8–14 March 1984, pp. 115–43); 112 book reviews; title index.
Spring books supplement (vol. 308 [5962], 26 April/2 May 1984, pp. 777–808); introductory article on the study of the history of science, followed by 31 book-reviews.
New journals review (vol. 311 [5984], 27 September/3 October 1984, pp. 309–30.
Autumn books supplement (vol. 312 [5991], 15–21 November 1984, pp. 201–26); introductory article on conference proceedings; 30 reviews.
Reference books (vol. 312 [5995], 13–19 December 1984, pp. 667–79); introductory review of best biotechnology reference books of 1984; 34 reviews.

Science (Washington, DC, American Association for the Advancement of Science, 1880–. 51 p.a. Circulation: 160,000) is the Association's official organ. Vol. 228 (4700), 10 May 1985 (pp. 629–774) has four in-depth book-reviews. The length is between 160 and 1,200 words apiece, and reviewers (affiliations given) are experts in their fields. Comments are analytical and evaluative. The 600-word review of *James E. Keeler: a nineteenth-century astronomer*, by D.E. Osterbrook (New York, Cambridge University Press, 1984, notes that Keeler (1857–1900) was widely regarded as 'the leading American astronomical spectroscopist of his generation'. Osterbrook tells his story with charm. He has scoured some twenty-five archives for his material, 'although his interpretation of Keeler's work in terms of the science of his time and larger issues in the politics and sociology of science is weak'. Bibliographical details omit only ISBNs. The reviews are listed in the contents and in volume indexes. Vol. 224 (4650), 18 May 1984, was a special review issue, with reviews of 32 books on pp. 708–43.
Annals of science (London, Taylor and Francis, 1936–. 6 p.a.) is 'an international review of the history of science and technology from the thirteenth century'. Vol. 42 (2), November 1985 (pp. 545–684), has 15 listed reviews, signed, with affiliations, on pp. 617–30, preceded by an essay-review and 'Correspondence' concerning a previous essay-review. The 15 reviews (100–1,700 words in length) are grouped into ten sections: Essays and biographies (2); History of philosophy (1); Philosophical aspects of science (1); Libraries and museums (1); Bibliography and reference (2) Technology and engineering (1); Instruments and measurement (1); Physical sciences (3); Medicine and health (2); Psychology (1). The 1,700-word review of *The tiger and the shark: empirical roots of wave–particle dualism*, by Bruce R. Wheaton (Cambridge University Press, 1983) begins by

explaining the title. With the words 'the tiger and the shark', J.J. Thomson commented in 1925 upon the evidently incompatible properties of light and water, and the reviewer traces the background history of the hypotheses brought forward by physicists. While the last chapter, on quantum mechanics, is criticized as sketchy and some questions remain open, the overall impression of Wheaton's book is considered excellent. 'Notwithstanding its brevity [about 350 pp.], his account fills a long-felt gap in the historiography of 20th-century physics by emphasizing the importance of experimental investigations for the conceptual development of early quantum theory'. Bibliographical details include a note on illustrations but omit ISBNs. The 1985 annual index has a 'Book reviews' section in 21 parts. There is a cumulated index for vols. 1–25.

The British journal for the history of science (Chalfont St. Giles, Bucks., British Society for the History of Science, 1962–. 3 p.a. Circulation: 1,300) is the Society's official journal. Vol. 18 (1), March 1985 (126 pp.), has a 3,750-word essay-review, followed by 34 book reviews (about 130–1,500 words apiece) on pp. 77–121, and a list of 96 books received. Reviews are signed, with affiliations, and although arranged in no particular order, are given a section contents list. Comments are analytical and evaluative, descriptive, but firmly noting errors of fact and poor production. *Death as a social disease: public health and political economy in early industrial France*, by William Coleman (Madison, Wis., University of Wisconsin Press, 1982) examines the relationship between public health and political economy through the writings of Louis René Villermé (1782–1863). Coleman sees Villermé as a sincere medical reformer. But while the authority which medical enquiries commanded is emphasized, there is no discussion of how controversial they were in some quarters. Nevertheless, concludes the reviewer, this is 'a stimulating and innovative book which places medicine where it belongs, in the context of class dynamics, debates about the work and productivity, social policy and politics'. The volume index includes book-reviews by author and title.

Isis (Philadelphia, Pa., History of Science Society, 1913–. 4 p.a. Circulation: 3,500) is an international review devoted to the history of science and its cultural influences. It is the premier periodical in the field. Vol. 76 (282), June 1985 (pp. 145–292), devotes nearly 50 per cent of its text to 73 book-reviews (about 250–1,000 words apiece), with two essay-reviews, averaging 1,500 words. The book-reviews are in sections: History of science; Bibliographical tools; Philosophy of science; Scientific instruments; Scientific education; Social relations of science; Humanistic relations of science; Physical sciences; Earth sciences; Biological sciences; Social and behavioural sciences; Medical sciences; Technology; Classical antiquity; Middle Ages; Renaissance; Seventeenth and eighteenth centuries; Nineteenth and twentieth centuries. The reviews, signed, but without affiliations, are authoritative and analytical, setting a high standard. *Hegel and the sciences*, by Robert S. Cohen and Mark W. Wartofsky (Dordrecht, Reidel, 1984) is an attempt to rehabilitate Hegel as one of the greatest modern philosophers. It is criticized as an uneven collection of papers in which 'the competent but unremarkable are the best...In conclusion, this book is mostly unrewarding and sometimes impossible to read'. Bibliographical data omit only ISBNs. All the books reviewed are listed in the contents, but only essay-reviews are included in the annual index.

Earth sciences

Reviewing journals

Earth science reviews (Amsterdam, Elsevier Science Publishers, 1966–. 4 p.a.) is 'the international geological journal bridging the gap between research articles and textbooks'. Vol. 22 (2), September 1985 (pp. 107–72), has signed reviews of 33 books (about 200–1,700 words apiece) on pp. 141–72, in 11 sections: Economic geology (3); Engineering geology (1); General geology (12); Geochemistry (1); Geomorphology (4); Geophysics (2); Meteorology (2); Oceanography (3); Precumbrian geology (1); Sedimentology (3); Volcanology (1). Non-English-language titles are included. Reviews are mainly descriptive, with an indicating of the books' usefulness and level. *World energy supply*, by Manfred Grathwohl (Berlin, de Gruyter, 1982) deals with almost every aspect of energy, the author being Scientific Director of the Armed Forces Command and General Staff College of West Germany. Most of the book is decribed as factual, but a short final chapter summarizes conclusions. It may 'serve well as a first source of information on most aspects of energy'. Each issue subject-lists the reviews, but there is no volume index.

Geological magazine (Cambridge University Press, 1864–. 6 p.a. Circulation: 1,300) is one of the leading geological periodicals, covering the whole field of the earth sciences. About 10 per cent of the text is devoted to reviews. Vol. 122 (2), March 1985 (pp. 97–221), has 26 book-reviews on pp. 190–220 that include two essay-reviews (about 1,400 words and about 2,600 words). Coverage extends beyond books to parts of monographic serials (e.g. London Research series in geography, and special publication, Geological Society of Zimbabwe) and new periodicals (e.g. *Quaternary science review*). Reviews are not limited to English-language texts and reflect the broad-subject approach of the journal itself. Comments are analytical, evaluative and comparative, noting level of usefulness and type of audience. Though the reviews are only initialled, it is often possible to identify the reviewers, since they are clearly authorities in their field. *Geochemical aspects of radioactive waste disposal*, By D.G. Brookings (Heidelberg, Springer-Verlag, 1984), is considered a very good textbook 'which is readable despite being quite comprehensive'. The reviewer speaks of 'an excellent index', 'a creditable number of key diagrams and tables', and the fully listed 300 (approx.) references. However, the volume is expensive (DM125; $48.50) and 'there are an awful lot of typographical errors'. Bibliographical details are in full, including ISBNs. The annual index covers reviews by broad subject. Consolidated indexes are for 1864–1903 (1905) and 1904–63 (1984).

Geology (Boulder, Colo., Geological Society of America, 1973–. 12 p.a. Circulation: 13,800) publishes short papers on all aspects of the earth sciences on an international scale. Reviews include non-English-language items, parts of monographic serials as well as books. The reviews consist either of brief comments on content and quality of specialized books, or full reviews of books of interest to a wide, interdisciplinary audience. It is policy not to review books costing more than US $100. Vol. 13 (9), September 1985 (pp. 593–671), has seven book-reviews on pp. 669–71 (about 60–600 words). The reviews, signed with affiliations, are basically descriptive, their range reflecting the periodical's subject scope. *Industrial minerals and rocks*, by Milos Kuzvart (New York, Elsevier, 1984), well translated from the Czech, carries a 28-page list of the endogenous and exogenous types of industrial minerals and rocks: 'Kuzvart's book is the most thorough treatment of the subject known to me; it may be read profitably by all economic and general geologists'. Bibliographical details omit ISBNs. The annual subject, author and advertisers' indexes do not include book-reviews.

AAPG bulletin (Tulsa, Okla., American Association of Petroleum Geologists, 1917–. 13 p.a. Circulation: 42,000) is the Association's major publication and covers the whole field of earth sciences in relation to petroleum exploration and development. Vol. 69 (6), June 1985 has five reviews (pp. 1039–410), on items relating to Australia, stratigraphy, sedimentation, salt evaporites and brines, and carbonates. The reviews, signed, with affilations, range in length from about 300 to 1,200 words. Comments tend to be descriptive, although longer reviews are more analytical, and major errors are always noted. The annual index includes reviews.

Anthropology

Reviewing journals

American anthropologist (Washington, DC, American Anthropological Association, 1888–. 4 p.a. Circulation: 12,000) publishes original articles, reports and commentaries, devoting more than one-third of its text to book and film reviews. Vol. 87 (1), March 1985 (238pp.), has 56 reviews, signed, with affiliations, on pp. 152–238, arranged by subject: Applied; Archaeology; General/theoretical; Linguists; Cultural/ethnology; Physical. Review length varies between 250 and 1,500 words. Parts of monographic serials are covered in this, the major reviewing medium for the broad field of anthropology. The reviews are authoritative, analytical and evaluative. *Blood groups of primates: theory, practice, evolutionary meaning*, by W. Wlochyalow and others (New York, Alan R. Liss, Inc., 1983), while considered to have value as an introduction to primate blood-group research and its medical applications, has serious shortcomings (e.g. uneven treatment, errors of fact and confused English). Citations are limited to the European literature and are frequently outdated: 'The book could have benefited from more extensive editing and greater scholarly care'. Bibliographical data omit details of illustrations and ISBNs. Reviews are listed in the contents by title, and the annual index records reviews by titles and authors.

Man (London, Royal Anthropological Institute, 1966–. 4 p.a. Circulation: 3,300) is the Institute's journal. Vol. 20 (3), September 1985, has 46 book reviews on pp. 548–86, plus a list of 100 books received for review. The reviews, signed, with affiliations, range from 300 to 1,600 words in length. Comments are of a high standard, with adequate descriptive detail and analysis, comparative and highlighting strengths and weaknesses. *Reconstructing Quaternary environments*, by J.J. Lowe and M.J.C. Walker (London, Longman, 1984) is written for undergraduate and postgraduate students, paying special attention to the British Isles and to the Upper Quaternary. It is an 'excellent introduction to the subject for undergraduate geologists and geographers'. Bibliographical data omit ISBNs. There is an index to reviews, under authors. The volume index includes entries under authors, titles and reviewers.

Biology

Reviewing journals

The quarterly review of biology (Stony Brook, NY, Stony Brook Foundation, Inc., for State University of New York at Stony Brook, 1926–. 4 p.a. Circulation: 2,900) is the major review-journal in biology, publishing critical reviews of recent research. 'New biological books' forms an integral and important part of the *Quarterly*, reviewing books on an international scale in a comprehensive and critical way. Vol. 60 (2), June 1985 (pp. 145–264), has a review-article, followed by 115 book-reviews. The latter are grouped under 15 headings: History, philosophy and ethics; Palaeontology; Molecular biology; Cellular biology; Genetics and evolution; Reproduction and development; Microbiology; Botanical sciences; Zoological sciences; Aquatic sciences; Environmental sciences; Neural sciences; Human biology and health; Biomedical sciences; De omnibus rebus et quibusdam aliis. The reviews, averaging 400 words in length, are signed, with affiliations. They provide detailed descriptions, with critical and comparative comment, plus an indication of the audience most likely to benefit. The 700-word review of *Animals and why they matter*, by Mary Midgley (Athens, Ga. University of Georgia Press, 1983) provides 'an excellent introduction to the concepts of rights and equality as they have been used to promote or dismiss the notion that animals and other living things should be the subjects of moral concern'. Our avoidance of anthropomorphic terms, argues the author, is metaphysical rather than scientific, since it threatens to commit us to the uncomfortable ethical stance that animals matter more than we have allowed. The reviewer finds Mary Midgley an invigorating advocate of this thesis. Not all the books reviewed are highly specialized; one elicits the following remark: 'This is a wonderful bedtime book and a controversial rewriting of an episode in the history of biology'. Each issue has an index by author/editor and by title of review; this index is cumulated per volume.

Natural history

Reviewing journals

Journal of natural history (London, Taylor and Francis, 1967–. 6 p.a.) is the major journal publishing original research and reviews in evolutionary and general biology, and on the interaction of organisms with their environment as well as classical taxonomic work, cladistics, experimental taxonomy, parasitology, ecology and behaviour. Vol. 19 (3), May/June 1985 (pp. 419–621), has nine book-reviews, signed, but without affiliations, on pp. 613–21. The reviews, all by specialists, including many at the British Musuem (Natural History), are well-written, authoritative, analytical and evaluative, making this the major source of reviews for scholarly books in the broad field of natural history. Length of comment varies from about 500 to 1,450 words. I.L. Mason's *Evolution of domesticated animals* (London, Longman, 1984) is welcomed with an arresting first sentence: 'It is a long time since a book presenting a comprehensive account of *all* domestic animals was published'. It is preceded by F.E. Zeuner's classic *A history of domesticated animals* (London, Hutchinson, 1963) — the first of its kind, with a unifying theme of archaeological discovery: 'Mason's book is quite different and reflects his own interests in the breeding of livestock and the diversity of modern breeds'. Bibliographical details do not always note illustrations, and ISBNs are omitted. Neither parts nor volume list book-reviews.

Natural history book reviews: an international bibliography (Berkhamsted, Herts., AB Academic Publishers, 1976–. 4 p.a. Circulation: 400) is the only book-review periodical in the earth and life sciences. It reviews a wide spectrum of titles for the whole range of natural history, including landscape, architecture and country life. Emphasis is on English-language titles at a variety of levels, and reviewers are specialists in their fields. Vol. 8 (1) 1985 (84pp.), has a lengthy review-article followed by 58 book-reviews of between 100 and 400 words apiece. The 11 sections of reviews (pp. 15–84) cover: General (7); Ecology (5); Evolution (8); Mammals (5); Birds (7); Fish (6); Insects (2); Flowering plants (5); Fungi (1); Topography and travel (6); Young naturalist (6). The 400-word review of *Mammals of Australia*, by J. Mary Taylor (Melbourne, Oxford University Press, 1984) is assessed as a straightforward factual book, providing descriptions of all the genera of Australian mammals and, under each genus, all the species. But nearly half the book is taken up with whales, seals, and so on; better to have concentrated on terrestrial animals, 'and to have used the space so saved to indicate the distinguishing features of the species'. Nevertheless, the book is thoroughly recommended for being full of facts, reasonably priced and fitting easily into the pocket. Bibliographical details are given in full. Individual titles of books reviewed are not listed and the annual index, like the periodical itself, appears sporadically, a pity in the case of such a useful journal.

Botany

Reviewing journals

Economic botany (New York, The New York Botanical Garden, for the Society of Economic Botany, 1947–. 4 p.a. Circulation: 2,000) publishes primary research and review-articles dealing with plants useful to man. Vol. 38 (4), October/December 1984 (pp. 377–520), has 16 book-reviews, signed, with affiliations, on pp. 406, 416, 432, 438, 451, 463, 490–6), about 200 to 1,000 words apiece. Reviews are descriptive, with critical comment to help the potential user. *The diversity of crop plants*, by J.G. Hawkes (Cambridge, Mass., Harvard University Press, 1983) consists of Hawkes' Prather Lectures in published form. It 'will provide a most valuable stimulus to the teaching of economic botany and ethnobotany, branches of the plant sciences that are currently experiencing rapid expansion in our universities'. Books reviewed are not listed per issue, but the annual index includes a separate section, an author/title listing and an A–Z list of reviewers.

Journal of ecology Oxford, Blackwell Scientific Publications, for the British Ecological Society, 1913–. 3 p.a. Circulation: 3,900) publishes original research papers on any aspect of plant ecology, provided that they contain elements of general interest. Vol. 73 (1), March 1985 (379pp.), has 21 signed reviews, plus a list of 13 publications received. Items are arranged A–Z under author/editor and length varies from about 325 to 1,100 words. Comments are authoritative, critical and evaluative (e.g. 'don't be put off or misled by the pretentious title of this volume. Much of it is worth reading'). A second edition of M. Allaby's *Dictionary of the environment* (London, Macmillan, 1985) shows some timely rewriting and modification, states the reviewer. Subjects most extensively covered are geology, botany, zoology and ecology, with lesser contributions from geomorphology, soil science, geography, climatology and chemistry, but 'At £25...the environmental scientist may find better value in a collection of specialist dictionaries covering the same area more adequately. These would be more reliable in supplying technical terms'. Book-reviews are not listed per issue, but the annual index carries a heading 'Reviews'.

The new phytologist (London, etc., Academic Press, 1902–. 12 p.a.) publishes papers in the broad field of botanical science and teaching. Vol. 101 (2), October 1985 (pp. 233–350), has eight signed reviews, between 250 and 750 words in length. Comments briefly describe contents and are analytical and critical, paying attention not only to scientific text but also to standard of presentation and book production. C.S. Reynolds' *The ecology of freshwater phytoplankton* (Cambridge University Press, 1984) is termed a 'highly factual book, with numerous equations and passages of numerical data' — a valuable contribution. While the author considers it 'primarily intended for use by students', more experienced workers will also find it of value. Bibliographic details omit ISBNs. The items reviewed (which include non-English titles) are not listed per issue or annually indexed.

Taxon (Utrecht, International Bureau for Plant Taxonomy and Nomenclature, 1951–. 4 p.a. Circulation: 2,300) is devoted to systematic and evolutionary biology, with an emphasis on botany. Vol. 34 (2), May 1985, has a section 'Reviews and announcements' (pp. 374–85) covering 60 publications, including books and periodical parts and arranged by author/editor A–Z. Most reviews are short (about 150–250 words) and signed, with affiliations. Although concise, the book-reviews convey the essence of the text concerned, drawing attention to production (printing, binding, etc.) as well. Full bibliographical details include ISBNs and, often, addresses for less well-known publishers. *Taxon* does not list reviews in each issue but does include them in the annual index.

Entomology

Reviewing journals

Antenna (London, Royal Entomological Society of London, 1977–. 4 p.a.) is the Society's bulletin and contains news, comments and reports, aiming to provide entomologists in general with a news forum. Vol. 9 (2), April 1985, has 11 book reviews on pp. 87–91, ranging in length from about 100 to 1,300 words. Four of the reviews are signed, and although no affiliations are given, reviewers include authorities in the field. Titles include non-English works, as well as parts of monographic serials. All the reviews are descriptive, with analytical and evaluative comment when they are longer. Bibliographical details omit ISBNs. The reviews are not listed per issue, nor is there an annual index.

Entomologia generalis (Stuttgart, E. Schweizerbart'sche Verlagsbuchhandlung, 1974–. 4 p.a. Circulation: 450) is an international journal for general and applied entomology, concerned with experimental, comparative and descriptive problems in all fields of research on insects and other terrestrial arthropods. Vol. 10 (2),

1985, has 38 book-reviews, signed (without affiliations), about 100 to 500 words in length, on pp. 75–6, 85–6, 96, 120, 124, 142, 148, 149–60. Some of the books reviewed are in German, and some reviews are in German. Comments, essentially descriptive, make recommendations as to their value to specialist users (e.g. 'the limnologist and freshwater entomologist'). Issue contents do not list reviews, but the annual index has a 'Reviews' heading, with page references.

Entomological Society of America. Bulletin (College Park, Md., the Society, 1955. 4 p.a. Circulation: 8,500) publishes papers and commentaries in the broad field of entomology. Vol. 31 (2), Summer 1985 (68pp.) has 25 book-reviews, signed, with affiliations, on pp. 37–58, plus a list of 20 publications received for review. Not all books are in English and some parts of monographic serials are included. The reviews, between about 70 and 1,600 words in length, are authoritative, providing adequate description, together with analysis of coverage and level, and an appreciation of relationship to the literature as a whole. *A new ecology: novel approaches to interactive systems*, by Peter W. Price (New York, Wiley, 1984) is reviewed analytically, in the main. 'The final chapter...was particularly interesting in illustrating the naiveté of ecologists regarding the role of the physical environment and historic and prehistoric human influence in organizing communities.' Bibliographical details lack only ISBNs. Reviews are neither listed nor systematically arranged, and there is no annual index.

Zoology

Reviewing journals

The Auk (Washington, DC, The American Ornithologists' Union, 1884–. 4 p.a. Circulation: 4,500) publishes original papers dealing with the biology of birds. Vol. 102 (1), January 1985 (244pp.), has 29 book-reviews (about 200–1,700 words apiece) on pp. 212–41, with shorter notes on six other items. Lengthy reviews, signed (but without affiliations), adequately describe content, noting errors and omissions in both text and production. Analytical and evaluative comments relate the books to the corpus of the literature and make recommendations as to areas of usefulness (e.g. as a field guide, a reference source). Ian Wallace's *Birds of prey of Britain and Europe* (Oxford University Press, 1983) is regarded as 'simply a vehicle to present the colour plates from Cramp and Simmons (Eds.) "Handbook of the Birds of Europe, the Middle East and North Africa. The Birds of the Western Palearctic" (1980), without the encumbrance of the text'. As a field guide for the identification of European birds of prey, the review recommends buying instead *Flight identification of European raptors* by R.F. Porter (3rd edn. Calton Poyser, 1981) — deficient only in colour plates (which appropriate illustrations from the Wallace could have rectified!). Bibliographical data include ISBNs. The reviews are not listed or grouped, but annual indexes enter books reviewed under original author and reviewer.

Ibis (London, etc., Academic Press, 1859–. 4 p.a. Circulation: 2,600) is the journal of the British Ornithologists' Union and publishes original full length papers and short communications covering the whole field of ornithology. Vol. 127 (3), July 1985, has 28 book-reviews (pp. 395–408), and short notices on a further 13 books. Reviews form part of the section 'Recent ornithological publications', subdivided into books (two sequences: books and 'also received', each under authors/editors A–Z); and sound recordings. The reviews average between 400 and 500 words, are signed (without affiliations) and include some non-English-language titles. Comments are adequately descriptive and critical, aimed at pricing, scientific content and illustrations. C.J. Fear's *The starling* (Oxford University Press, 1984) is considered excellent 'for anyone interested in obtaining an overview of the natural history of the starling, but the overview of the biology is selective and 'the author does not pretend to cover the literature comprehensively'. The full bibliographical details include ISBNs. The reviews are not listed per issue or in the annual index.

The journal of animal ecology (Oxford, Blackwell Scientific Publications, 1932. 3 p.a. Circulation: 3,500) is published for the British Ecological Society and includes original research papers on any aspect of animal ecology. Vol. 54 (3), October 1985 (pp. 685–1038), has 17 book-reviews (about 100–600 words apiece) on pp. 1029–38, plus short notices (less than 50 words each) on a further four. The books reviewed include non-English-language titles and the succinct comments adequately describe, analyse and evaluate. R.J. O'Connor's *The growth and development of birds* (Chichester and London, Wiley, 1984) collates and synthesizes the current state of knowledge on the subject, satisfying a growing need. Importance or otherwise of climate on the survival of eggs and chicks and the section bringing together the effects of age upon first breeding and subsequent reproduction are inadequately handled. 'Overall, the book is to be recommended to the serious ornithological student', but the price (£20) 'will put it beyond the reach of many purses'. Bibliographical details omit ISBNs. A list of reviews is not included per issue, but it does appear in the volume contents.

Systematic zoology (Washington, DC, Society for Systematic Zoology, 1952–. 4 p.a. Circulation: 2,800) furthers the objectives of the Society by publishing original papers in the theory, principles and methods of systematics, as well as evolution, morphology, zoogeography, palaeontology, genetics and classification. Vol. 34 (1), March 1985, has four book-reviews averaging 400 words apiece), signed, with affiliations, on pp. 102–5. The reviews are closely analytical, fully evaluative of scientific content and carry references. Comments can reflect strong opinions (e.g., 'one of the best general essays on plant evolution I have ever encountered'), but other reviewers tend to rewrite the book concerned. A list of 19 books and parts of monographic serials has short descriptive annotations. Bibliographical details lack details of illustrative matter and ISBNs. Books reviewed appear in the contents list under abbreviated titles, while the annual index includes original authors but not reviewers.

Acknowledgements

The author would like to thank his colleagues in the Department of Library Services, British Museum (Natural History), for their help in the preparation of this chapter.

References

1. Chen, Ching-chih. 'Reviews and reviewing of scientific and technical materials', in *Encyclopedia of library and information science*, vol. 25, p. 366.
2. Lambert, Jill. *Scientific and technical journals* London, Bingley, 1985, p. 26.
3. Zuckerman, Sir Solly. 'The reviewing of scientific books', *Veterinary record*, 23 May 1970, p. 611.
4. Lincoln, Tim. 'The book review business', *Nature*, vol. 302, 28 April 1985, p.1757.
5. *British book news*, October 1985, pp. 589–90.
6. *New scientist*, 5 September 1985, p. 57.

7. Medicine

A.J. Walford

'Periodicals are the most important part of a live medical library', states L.T. Morton,[1] and this applies both to the current medical information they provide and to the role as a forum for the exchange of views. Medicine being the science of healing, its structure is extensive, covering surgery, obstetrics, pediatrics, nursing, psychiatry, biomedical engineering and much besides. Each branch has its periodical literature and reviewing apparatus. This survey is largely restricted to five general-interest medical journals (plus *American journal of psychiatry*) that have a wide professional audience and also rank high on Chen's graded quantitative list of biomedical journals carrying reviews.[2] They are, in Chen order: *British medical journal, The lancet, Annals of internal medicine, JAMA, The New England journal of medicine*; also *American journal of psychiatry*. To these are added the *Bulletin of the history of medicine* and *Medical history*.

What differentiates the medical reviewer from others? Like other scientific and technical reviewers, he or she has to pay much more attention to the accuracy of information presented and the validity of ideas or methods discussed than does his or her literary counterpart. Whereas the librarian-reviewer may be regarded as a general professional, the medical reviewer must be a highly specialized professional. *British medical journal*, 15 December 1984, carried eight book-reviews, the reviewers comprising a professor of surgery, a professor of medicine, four consultants, a university reader in neurology and a general practitioner. These will have had academic/professional training, have practised and have themselves produced books or presented papers in their fields.

One feature of the medical book-review is its relative brevity: 'A well written essay of 250 well-chosen words may constitute a superb book review and rarely, in medical journals, need a review exceed 500 words'.[3] Another feature is its relative promptness. The time-lag for reviews appearing in *The lancet* in 1970, according to Chen,[4] was 5.8 months. A third feature is the correspondence column, staging the reactions of authors to the reviews of their books.

While description of a book's contents may require only reporting skill, evaluation calls for subject expertise. Nor is it enough to spot errors in spelling, construction and debatable conclusions, worthy as these are of criticism. For Dr Koch,[5] 'a good review should define the scope and plan of the work in question, set forth its major premises, and point out if possible its importance and significance to the medical world. If one cannot add something of praise as to originality, careful presentation, good writing, and so forth, I think the reviewer has an obligation to do so'.

The level of treatment of a book needs to be clearly stated by the reviewer. What purports to be a definitive study may prove to be only an introduction, whereas a monograph will assume a certain acquaintance with its subject by the reader. One role of evaluation is to indicate level of readership — whether the book is for the beginner, undergraduate, general practitioner or specialist/researcher. The slant may be theoretical or practical (citing case histories); it may be parochial or national. Comparative treatment is less common, although 'clustering'[6] of two, three or more books on a topic does enable the reviewer to contrast them. This also applies to volumes in a series or to essays in a collection. The librarian/book selector, however, needs also to know whether a new book X updates or displaces book Y or simply supplements Z. Is the volume really a 'revised and updated' edition?

It might be argued that the bibliographical details of a work, its imprint, full pagination, date, price, illustrative matter, index, bibliography and ISBN, are of slight concern to the reviewer, but these data are necessary and should complete the picture. Sometimes the reviewer notes these points in his comments, deploring their absence or deficiency, or else praising their quality.

Book-reviews can be ranked as poor or bad when they give no clear idea of what a book is about. They may be perfunctory or indifferent when they describe but do not evaluate, leaving the reader in doubt as to depth of treatment or usefulness for his/her purpose. The mini-review has its own limitations, as shown in a 78-word vague effusion on a 1014-page treatise, *Clinical roentgenology of the digestive tract*:[7]

it is difficult to be too laudatory of this book, which is well-balanced throughout, well written and splendidly illustrated and has a comprehensive bibliography. Every roentgenologist should own it. Indeed, it would seem to be a necessity for any internist. It does not unduly stress the advantages of roentgenological studies but candidly states their limitations as well. It is well documented with statistics from the medical literature as well as from the author's broad personal experience.

The foregoing review was awarded grades by Julia E. Wilson:[8] author, purpose, subject presentation and reliability, 1; physical characteristics, 2; form and comparison, 0 (grade 5 being the top grade).

In about 200 words the following review,[9] also anonymous, succeeds in being inclusive, informative, evaluative, critical and comparative, providing compulsive reading:

A Traveller's Guide to Health. James M. Adams, B.Sc., M.B., Lieut.-colonel, Royal Army Medical Corps. London, Hodder & Stoughton (for the Royal Geographical Society), 1966. pp. 189...This admirable and low-priced little book exactly fits its function, replacing the medical chapters of the Royal Geographical Society's *Hints to travellers*, long out of date. It is primarily designed for the small scientific expedition, without a doctor, which will be visiting remote areas in increasing numbers as the International Biological Programme gets into its stride in 1967. But the explorer, the mountaineer, and even the tourist will find much of value in it. It covers preparatory planning (including training and immunization), general principles, diseases peculiar to the tropics, and medical problems in cold regions. Appendices contain suggestions for further reading and a list of dental equipment for use in trained hands. While this volume is very difficult to fault, it is a pity to see 'natural resistance', in the sense of physical fitness, lingering on in the section on infectious diseases, and there is no reference to smallpox modified by vaccination — that bugbear of diagnosis. The advice on the prevention of the diarrhoeal diseases from infected food might have been summarised as 'peel it, cook it, forget it'.

Indexes to reviews

Although *Index medicus* has a separate listing for review articles — 'Bibliography of medical reviews' — it does not include book-reviews: 'Nor does MEDLINE or any other bibliographic tool from the National Library of Medicine', reports Patricia Y. Morton in 1983.[10] *Science citation index* records only the medical-book reviews appearing in *Science* and *Nature*, but *Arts and humanities citation index* covers four of the five general-interest medical journals dealt with here. The half-yearly *Internationale Bibliographie der Rezen-*

sionen indexes reviews in *The lancet, American journal of psychiatry, Bulletin of the history of medicine* and *Medical history*.

Reviewing journals

British medical journal (London, British Medical Association, 1857–. Weekly. Circulation: 96,000) is international in scope, dealing with all aspects of medicine. Vol. 290 (6479), 11 May 1985 (pp. 1369–1448), has a section 'Medicine and books': seven signed reviews on pp. 1425–8, and an appended note on the contributors' posts held. The reviews have headings and range from 200 to 2,000 words in length. Comments are analytical and critical. The review on R.D. Mann's *Modern drug abuse: an enquiry on historical principles* (Lancaster, MTP Press, 1984) begins arrestingly: 'If you expect to find an account of modern drug abuse you will have to wait until the final two chapters in a scholarly and encyclopaedic work of over 750 pages and 2,500 footnotes and references, and containing 150 illustrations of people, plants, texts and anatomical drawings'. Ronald Mann, a principal medical officer in the medicines division of the Department of Health and Social Security, has in reality written a detailed history of Western medicine. Bibliographical data omit place of publication, ISBNs and full pagination. The half-yearly index has entries for reviewers' names, citing review heading and page.

The lancet (London, The Lancet, 1823–. Weekly. Circulation: 27,000) offers a current stimulus of fresh ideas and information to general practitioner and specialist. No. 8416, 15 December 1984 (pp. 1353–1410), has seven book-reveiws, signed, with affiliations, on pp. 1373–4. All but one of the reviewers are in hospital units. Headings preface reviews, which average between 500 and 700 words and are analytical and critical, indicating readership. One monograph, on infection and disinfection, is faulted for not being abreast of advances in that field; the author of a book on health and safety is advised to provide 'a more detailed treatment of the very important subject of stress' in the next edition. Among the 29 letters is an author's reactions to a criticism of his book on South Africa. Bibliographical details omit ISBNs. The half-yearly name-index includes books reviewed, and the subject-index cites reviewers.

Annals of internal medicine (Philadelphia, Pa., American College of Physicians, 1922–. 12 p.a. Circulation: 96,000) has a section 'The literature of medicine' that includes audiovisual and software items. Vol. 101 (5), November 1984 (pp. 581–732), has 31 reviews on pp. 723–32, signed, with affiliations, and between 50 and 500 words in length. Seven sections make for easy reference: Pulmonary disease;

Cardiovascular disease; General internal medicine; Geriatrics; Clinical pharmacology; Rheumatology, Oncology. Reviews are analytical and critical, indicating readership. One monograph is faulted for an inadequate index; another, for omissions; a third, for arguable advocacy of certain drugs in hypertension; a fourth, for underestimating the role of the patient's family in discussing hospital patients. The 'Letters and corrections' section refers normally to articles. The half-yearly 'Author list' includes reviewers; the subject-index has a 'Book-reviews' heading.

JAMA: the journal of the American Medical Association (Chicago, Ill., the Association, 1848–. 4 per month. Circulation: 279,000) is 'a forum for open and responsible discussion of matters relevant to the field of medicine'. Vol. 253 (23), 21 June 1985 (pp. 3360–3496), has a 'Books' section: nine listed reviews, signed, with affiliations, on pp. 3467–70, with boxed quotations. Headings preface the reviews, which average around 600 words and are analytical, indicating readership. The text of *The unborn patient: prenatal diagnosis and treatment*, by Michael R. Harrison and others (Orlando, Fla., Grune and Stratton, 1984) is largely a detailed discussion of conditions considered to lend themselves to prenatal surgical correction: 'some parts of the text are repetitious, perhaps because the authors intended each chapter to be able to stand on its own feet...While the authors' own data are invariably presented in simple detail, their analysis of the experience of other investigations is occasionally cursory'. Diagrams, photographs and tables are voted excellent. 'The book will be of interest to practitioners of obstetrics, neonatology and pediatric surgery, as well as to researchers in those fields'. Bibliographical data omit price, full pagination and ISBNs. The half-yearly subject-index has a heading 'Books', while the author-index includes reviewers.

The New England journal of medicine (Boston, Mass, Massachusetts Medical Society, 1812–. Weekly. Circulation: 207,000) is among the oldest continuous medical journal in the U S. Vol. 312 (25), 20 June 1985 (pp. 1589–652) has seven book-reviews, signed, with locations, on pp. 1646–8. The reviews average between 400 and 800 words, are briefly analytical and critical, and indicate readership. Comments on *Principles of geriatric medicine*, edited by Reuben Andres and others (New York, McGraw-Hill, 1985) begin, 'There is no doubt that this one of the current major books in geriatrics'. The three editors have all made major contributions on biologic ageing. A summary analysis of the chapters follows. Chapters on health-care environments are lacking. 'There should have been a more clinically oriented, practical approach to the care of the dying. There is no coverage of ethic issues and decision making or of the values associated with decisions regarding the elderly'. However, the review concludes that the book is 'clearly important for physicians who care for elderly persons'. Bibliographical details omit only ISBNs. The half-yearly A–Z index has a heading 'Book-reviews [and reviewers]', subdivided by subject.

American journal of psychiatry (Washington, DC, American Psychiatric Association, 1844–. 12 p.a. Circulation: 35,000) is primarily a professional journal for practising psychiatrists. Vol. 140 (11), November 1983 (pp. 1413–1542), includes a 'Book forum', with an editor, on pp. 1530–6. The 10 book-reviews are signed, with locations, and form four subject groups: Neuroses and character disorders (3); Psychosis (1); Substance abuse (e.g. alcoholism)(3); Neurology and psychiatry (3). Reviews range in length from 500 to 1,250 words and are analytical and critical, particularly noting readership. One monograph is faulted for a misleading title; another (on borderline and narcissistic disorders), for lack of organization. 'Letters to the editor' refer to articles, not reviews. Bibliographical details omit prices and ISBNs. The half-yearly subject-index includes entries for reviewers but not authors of books reviewed; the subject-index contains a heading 'Book-reviews'.

Bulletin of the history of medicine (Baltimore, Md., Johns Hopkins University Press, for the American Association for the History of Medicine and Johns Hopkins Institute of the History of Medicine, 1933–. 4 p.a. Circulation: 1,700) is a leading scholarly journal in its field. Vol. 59 (1), Spring 1985 (153pp.), carries 32 book-reviews on pp. 117–50. signed, with affiliations, and averaging 650 words apiece. Reviews are analytical and fairly critical. *The history of medicine in Ireland,* by John F. Fleetwood (2nd edn. Blackrock, Dublin, Skellig Press, 1983) had a first edition in 1951—mainly a listing of notable doctors and a chronology of hospitals, professional bodies and corporations, similar to J.D. Comrie's *History of Scottish medicine* (London, Baillière, Tindall and Cox, for the Wellcome Historical Medical Museum, 1950), but not illustrated. The second edition updates it, adding a chapter on Belfast and 'an unfortunate essay on the future of Irish medicine, with a defense of nepotism'. The text, with its numerous short sentences and paragraphs, is considered not easy to read. There is little attempt at analysis of great events and their repercussion, and text references (listed by themes, not chapters) omit page numbers, 'leaving the entire year to be searched'. Bibliographical data lack only ISBNs. The annual 'subject' index has entries for reviewers as well as authors.

Medical history: a quarterly journal devoted to the history of medicine and related sciences (London, Wellcome Institute for the History of Medicine, 1957–. 4 p.a.) is primarily concerned 'with the evolution of scientific and social concepts in medicine'. Vol. 29 (2), April 1985 (pp. 115–236), has an essay-review on pp. 210–17 and 23 book-reviews, signed, with affiliations, on pp. 218–33, averaging about 450 words apiece. The reviews are analytical and critical. *Sources in the history of American pharmacology*, by John Parascandola and Elizabeth Keeney (Madison, Wis., Institute of the History of Pharmacology, 1983) has three parts: on the beginnings of American pharmacology; a bibliographical essay; and 26 biographies. This is an 'admirable source of information...Apart from an occasional misprint, it shows all the signs of meticulous preparation and careful recording. The biographies are also most helpful in adding to the picture of an evolving subject. One could wish there were more of them'. Bibliographical details lack only ISBNs. The annual index has a 'Book-reviews and notices' section and also entries for authors and reviewers.

References

1. Morton, L.T. *How to use a medical library*, 6th edn. London, Heinemann Medical Books, 1979, p. 11.
2. Chen, Cheng-chih. 'Current studies of biomedical book reviewing. Part 1', *Bulletin of the Medical Library Association*, vol. 62 (2), April 1974, p. 112.
3. King, Lester S. 'The book review', *JAMA*, vol. 203 (6), 5 August 1968, pp. 343–4.
4. Chen, Cheng-chih. 'Biomedical book reviewing', *Nature*, vol. 242, 27 April 1973, pp. 577–8.
5. Koch, Sumner L. 'Medical book reviewing from the specialist's standpoint', *Bulletin of the Medical Library Association*, vol. 41 (2), April 1953, pp. 148–50.
6. Moore, Francis D. 'Review of reviews', *New England journal of medicine*, vol. 309 (17), 27 October 1983, pp. 1067–70.
7. *New England journal of medicine*, vol. 219, 1938, p. 546.
8. Wilson, Julia E. 'An evaluation of medical book reviews', *Bulletin of the Medical Library Association*, vol. 33 (5), July 1945, pp. 309–14.
9. *The lancet*, no. 7464, 17 September 1966, p. 624.
10. Morton, |Patricia Y. \ 'Medical book reviewing', \ *Bulletin of the Medical Library Association*, April 1983, p. 205.

8. Technology

D.J. Grogan

Books are only secondary sources of information for the scientist and technologist, as is well known. Their primary tools are research reports, conference papers, patents, standards and, above all, journals. It is therefore not surprising that book-reviews appearing in their journals are not accorded the degree of prominence that one takes for granted in the humanities and the social sciences. This comparative neglect is even more marked if one looks particularly at technological journals.

Firstly, the great majority of such journals publish no book-reviews at all. This is true even of many of the most substantial, highly regarded and widely circulated titles; for example, *AIAA journal* (American Institute of Aeronautics and Astronautics), *Aviation week, Chemical and engineering news, Drapers' record,* Institution of Mechanical Engineers *Proceedings, Journal of chemical technology and biotechnology, Radio and electronic engineer, Textile research journal.* Book-reviewing journals tend to be found among the secondary journals — those that digest, comment on and interpret the original work reported in the primary research journals.

Secondly, those journals which do review books deal with very few, even compared to the scientific and medical journals. It is rare to find any title which devotes to the task more than two or three pages of each issue. Commonly a single page is thought to suffice. Neither can one rely on reviews appearing regularly in every issue: *Physics in technology* (see below) had no book-reviews in the May 1984 issue; the usual reviews were missing from the May 1984 issue of *AIChE journal* (see below); they were also lacking from the March and July 1985 numbers of *Electronics and power* (see below); half of the 1984 issues of *Fuel* (see below) were without reviews; *New civil engineer* (see below) has reviewed books in only three or four of its last six months' weekly issues.

Thirdly, the reviews that do appear are usually briefer than those in science and medicine and far briefer than is normal in the humanities and the social sciences. Those over 600 words are unusual; most are far less.

On the credit side, it is generally agreed that reviews of technological books do their job better than those in some other fields. It is worth remembering that a short review is more likely to be read than a long one. Their comparative rarity means that duplication of reviews among technological journals is negligible. (Though in this context it is worth noticing the policy of deliberate duplication adopted by the *Proceedings of the IEEE* (Institute of Electrical and Electronics Engineers), which includes half-a-dozen book-reviews each month 'Selected from those recently published in the various IEEE Transactions, Magazines and Newsletters. They are reprinted here to make them conveniently available'.

By the nature of the subjects they treat, books in technology are much concerned with practical matters, factual details, and theories that can be validated by empirical testing. It follows therefore that good reviewers pay particularly close attention to the practicality of the methods described, to factual accuracy and to the validity of the theories expounded. Compared to book reviewers in the humanities, for instance, reviewers of technological books usually take pains to describe content at some length. Rarely do they take advantage of their position to air their own views on a subject.

To write such a review requires a subject specialist; generalist reviewers able to range with confidence beyond their own specialties, are rare birds in technology. This often means, as in other fields, that the reviewer is a friend or colleague of the author of the book. In contrast to some of these other fields, however, there is ample evidence that technological reviewers are quite willing to criticize severely the work of friends and colleagues. Perhaps they find it easier because such criticism tends to focus on methods, facts, and theories rather than views or opinions. While in literature or politics one person's opinion may be as valid as another's, those who are capable of evaluating the merits of a specialized book in science or technology are usually few in number. The authority with which the reviewer writes is crucial, and it is for this reason that it is particularly important that reviews in this field should be signed. Some would argue that without a reviewer's name a judgement on a book in the field of science and technology is virtually worthless.

One advantage claimed for the journal as a form of literature derives from the fact that it is a *current* publication. It can therefore respond quickly to changes in the nature of its subject, or in its readers, or the market, or the economic, political and social climate. Such response to stimulus is particularly noticeable in the area of technology, by its character more rapidly advancing than most other subject fields. Journals in technology — especially those in the technical/ trade category, dependent so much on advertising revenue — frequently change their appearance (typography, layout of contents, size, etc.); for example, *Microelectronics journal* (see below) underwent a complete physical transformation between 1982 and 1983. Frequency, too, can alter: in 1985 *AIChE journal* became a monthly, thus doubling the number of issues a year — and also doubling its output of book-reviews. More of a problem from the point of view of this chapter are the not uncommon changes in the *character* of journals, especially when this occurs without notice, or even in some cases with no editorial comment. Sometimes such changes will have no effect on their book-review columns (see *Chemical engineer,* below), but often it will. Output of reviews can vary substantially from year to year, doubling or halving in some instances. Change can be even more drastic; for example, for many years *Computer journal,* the research quarterly of the British Computer Society, published between 8 and 10 book-reviews in each issue. Between 1984 and 1985, coincidentally with a change of publisher from Wiley to Cambridge University Press, that pattern was interrupted, and the 1985 issues have no book-reviews. The standing instruction to publishers on where to send books for review has also been dropped. By way of compensation, its companion journal, the Society's professional quarterly, *Computer bulletin* (see below), stepped up the number of reviews in its 1985 issues.

To keep abreast of such changes in so far as they affect book-reviewing policies, there is obviously no substitute for close and continuing acquaintance with the journals themselves.

Other sources of book-reviews

Though there are no journals consisting entirely of technological book-reviews (as opposed to descriptive annotations; see below), there are a number of general reviewing serials that include substantial sections on technology. Often compiled by librarians for librarians, they usually confine themselves to a particular category of book. Two useful examples are the monthly *Choice,* concentrating on books considered appropriate for US undergraduate libraries (30 to 40 technological titles per issue), and *American reference books annual* (up to 70 technological titles per year). Both use signed reviews of up to 300 words that are evaluative as well as descriptive.

Where abstracting services include books in their coverage, they often provide what is in effect a brief descriptive (and sometimes evaluative) review to accompany the bibliographical citation. In the technological field two good examples are *Engineering index* and *Applied mechanics reviews*, both abstracting services despite their titles. Similar reviews can be found in the appropriate technological sections of *Science abstracts*.

There are also two long-established journals that are devoted to science and technology books but confine themselves to what are better described as descriptive annotations rather than book-reviews:

Aslib book list (London, Aslib, 1935–. 12 p.a. Circulation: 600), subtitled 'a monthly list of selected books published in the fields of science, technology, medicine and the social sciences', includes about 50 unsigned annotations per issue, mainly descriptive and very brief (50 words), written by subject specialists. Books are rated A (elementary level: general readership), B (intermediate level: university textbook), C (advanced level: specialist readership), D (reference book). A degree of evaluation is implied by inclusion; all books are 'recommended'. It confines itself to English-language books, and is arranged by Universal Decimal Classification. There is an annual author-index and classification-index.

New technical books (New York Public Library, Science and Technology Research Center, 1915–. 10 p.a. Circulation: 1,700), subtitled 'a selective list with descriptive annotations', covers physical sciences, mathematics, engineering, industrial technology. There are approximately 150 signed annotations per issue, written by NYPL staff. Issues commonly include an abbreviated contents list. Books reviewed range from technician to advanced-research level, and almost all are in English. A degree of evaluation is implied by the fact of inclusion. It is arranged by Dewey Decimal Classification. There is an annual author-index and subject-index.

Indexes to reviews

So far as locating reviews of individual books is concerned, there are certain difficulties. As a class, technological journals are not as public-spirited as they might be in providing indexes to their own contents; tracking down such book-reviews as they do publish can be a hit-and-miss affair. Neither do the periodical indexing services furnish as much help as one would hope. *Current technology index, Engineering index,* and *Science abstracts* do not index book-reviews at all. *Science citation index* provides an apt illustration of the low priority given to book-reviews as a form of literature in science and technology compared with the social sciences and the humanities. All book-reviews are ignored except those in *Science* and *Nature,* with the result that out of 569,277 source-items indexed in 1984 only 763 were book-reviews. In the companion works *Social sciences citation index* and *Arts and humanities citation index* the corresponding figures were 121,428 source-items of which 36,416 were book-reviews, and 698,447 source-items of which 89,127 were book-reviews (or reviews of performances, etc.). A welcome exception here is *Applied science and technology index* which lists book-reviews A–Z by author (together with the reviewer's name) at the end of each monthly issue and annual cumulation.

The searcher is further handicapped by the virtual exclusion of technology from the general English-language book-review indexing services, such as *Book review digest* and *Book review index.* Fortunately, there is one well-established specialized book-review index that covers technology. It is more akin to *Book review digest* than to the simple indexes, in as much as it includes quotations from the reviews it indexes: *Technical book review index* (Pittsburgh, Pa., JAAD Publishing Co., 1935–. 10 p.a. Circulation: 1,400). 'Compiled in co-operation with the Science and Technology Division, Carnegie Library of Pittsburgh, and the Maurice and Laura Falk Library of the Health Professions, University of Pittsburgh', published up to 1976 by the Special Libraries Association, its purpose is 'to identify reviews in current scientific, technical, medical and trade journals and to quote from those reviews'. In five sections (pure sciences, life sciences, medicine, agriculture, technology) it has books arranged A–Z by author within each. For each excerpt quoted, the full citation of the original review is given, with approximate length and name of reviewer. Normally only one review is quoted, but the book may reappear in a later issue with another review quoted. Technology is the largest section, with 90 to 100 books per issue. Titles are almost entirely US publications. There is no list of journals indexed, but there is an annual index of authors only.

Reviewing journals

The 20 titles which follow have been selected on the basis of their value as *book-reviewing journals,* which does not necessarily match their general standing as journals. And in a list as restricted as this it has not been possible to choose a title to represent each area of technology — even assuming one could be found. Nevertheless, collectively they do span much of the field, and as well as being book-reviewing tools, they are all significant journals in their own right.

Each of the main categories of technological journal is represented, both primary and secondary — research journals, professional journals, and technical and trade journals — and some hybrids. In the case of two or three of the titles it could be argued that their 'reviews' are descriptive annotations rather than critical assessments, particularly where they are anonymous. Nevertheless, it has been decided to include these journals as representing important sources of information about new books in certain areas of technology otherwise sparsely provided for. Virtually all of them are covered by *Applied science and technology index*, which, as has already been mentioned, does analyse book-reviews. All of them are also indexed (though not their book reviews) in one or more — and in many cases several — of the other major technological indexing and abstracting services, notably *Engineering index, Applied mechanics reviews*, the *Science abstracts* series and (in the case of the British titles) *Current technology index*.

AIChE journal (New York, American Institute of Chemical Engineers, 1955–. 12 p.a. Circulation: 6,100) is the central publication of the Institute, 'devoted to fundamental research and developments having immediate or potential value in chemical engineering'. Each issue mainly consists of a dozen or more original research papers, with perhaps half that number of research and development notes, and occasional letters to the editor. 'Books' is a regular feature with two or three reviews of 350 to 500 words (and an occasional example of 1,000 words), signed, with affiliations, but not stating positions held. Description of books is thorough, sometimes with detailed chapter-by-chapter analysis. Level is carefully specified: 'designed to be a research monograph rather than a text', 'a bachelor's level engineer or chemist should be able to follow anything, there is little math', 'for practical engineers a short refresher treatment'. Recommendations are sometimes negative: 'I cannot see a role for it in the undergraduate curriculum — it fails to cover too many of the basics'; 'I would not recommend any novice to try to learn the basics from this book'. Criticism is pointed: 'the breadth of the book is narrow'; 'the title is rather misleading'; 'odd choice of English vocabulary by European authors'. There are annual indexes by author, subject and title, but omitting book-reviews.

Aeronautical journal (London, Royal Aeronautical Society, 1897–.

10 p.a. Circulation: 2,000) incorporates *Aeronautical quarterly* and the journals of the Institution of Aeronautical Engineers and the Helicopter Association of Great Britain. The world's oldest journal in the field, it combines original research papers with occasional articles accessible to the non-specialist. 'Library reviews' (preceding 'Library additions' and 'Library reports') is the regular book-review section, treating two or three books per issue. Signed, though without affiliations, the reviews are detailed, informative and helpful, combining both description and evaluation, and averaging 500 words in length. Praise is not stinted: 'the best book of its kind I know'; 'a mathematically rigorous text'. Possibly even more helpfully, neither is censure restrained: 'could have wished for more diagrams'; 'author has not been ruthless enough in discarding material which is no longer in current use'. Comment is not confined to content: 'indices could be improved'; 'high price per page'. Particularly valuable are the careful and specific recommendations as to use: 'my feeling is that the person who might gain most...is the mathematician and not the engineer'; 'a useful book for the library, but I would not recommend it to students as a reading text'.

Automotive engineer (Bury St Edmunds, Suffolk, Mechanical Engineering Publications, Ltd., 1962–. 6 p.a. Circulation: 7,500) describes itself as 'the international journal of the Automobile Division of the Institution of Mechanical Engineers'. Formed by merger of *Automotive design* and *Journal of automotive engineering,* it is a technical journal for designers of cars, vans, trucks, and so on. 'Books reviewed' pages consist of about 10 descriptive annotations per issue. Mostly unsigned (though some have initials), they are concise (around 100 words), but informative and helpful. No evaluation is given.

Chartered mechanical engineer (Bury St Edmunds, Suffolk, Mechanical Engineering Publications, Ltd, 1954–. 11 p.a. Circulation: 55,200) is the professional journal, as opposed to the research journal (*Proceedings*), of the Institution of Mechanical Engineers, with short, appealing, illustrated articles on a wide range of topics in the fields of management, design, production, and research and development, and including news, professional announcements, and so on. 'Books' is the regular book-review page (occasionally two pages), treating anything from 4 to 10 titles per issue. Sometimes a new journal is reviewed. Ranging in length from 50 words up to 600, only the longer reviews are signed, some just with initials. Occasionally illustrated, usually by a coloured or black-and-white reproduction of the book's dust-jacket or front board, sometimes by a diagram taken from the book. Emphasis is on description rather than evaluation, but this is clearly and concisely done: 'it assumes no knowledge or experience in this area'; 'there is very little theory in this book'. Books are regularly placed in context and compared with other books and earlier editions: 'in large scale use both as a teaching and as a site handbook since 1977'; 'this is an American book published for an American readership'. Sometimes author's qualifications are mentioned: 'an Arabic scholar as well as a working engineer'; 'over twenty years of practical expertise'. Audience is indicated: 'directed at university and polytechnic students'; 'the industrial user is kept very much in mind'. Recommendations are frequent: 'an essential reference work'; 'a worthwhile purchase for engineers and managers'. Evaluation is not avoided: 'first-class'; 'disappointing'; 'long-overdue'; 'somewhat high in price, even by today's standards'.

Chemical engineer (Rugby, Warwickshire, Institution of Chemical Engineers, 1923–. 11 p.a. Circulation: 25,600), describing itself as 'the chemical and process industries journal', used to be the professional magazine of the Institution, and earlier still had been published as part of the *Transactions*. 'At the beginning of 1983 its role and style changed. It now reaches a wider audience, and sets out to provide a service to the profession...in a broader and more accessible form than before.' It is now a technical/trade journal with news items, letters, obituaries, announcements, and well-illustrated articles of a practical rather than research kind. 'Book reviews' feature usually comprises three reviews of 350 to 500 words each, occasionally illustrated with diagrams and photographic reproductions. All are signed, with affiliations, and usually give positions held: 'Consultant Engineer', 'Ex-Director of Safety Services', 'Head of Oil Pollution Division', 'Occupational Hygienist'. Reviews are thorough and detailed, with particularly helpful recommendations: 'a useful reference book to have in a University, Polytechnic or Industrial Library'; should be obligatory reading for all teachers'; 'I would suggest that a library copy be reviewed first to assess its usefulness to an individual'. Occasionally the reader is referred to another, better book. Reviews do not hesitate to condemn: 'of limited value in the UK'; 'too superficial to be helpful'; 'general lack of cohesiveness in the presentation'; 'could even prove misleading'.

Chemical engineering (New York, McGraw-Hill, 1902–. 26 p.a. Circulation: 73,000) is a technical-trade journal for the chemical-process industry, incorporating news items, comment and short, well-illustrated feature articles appealing to a wide audience. 'Bookshelf' feature in each issue consists of two or three reviews of 400 to 500 words, with occasional 1,000-word examples. All are signed, with affiliations and positions held: 'Professor Emeritus', 'Process Consultant', 'Materials Engineering Supervisor', 'Librarian (Physical Sciences and Engineering)'. An irregular supplementary feature, 'In rapid review', consists of one or two short descriptive annotations, sometimes signed, sometimes not. There are occasional special surveys of books on a specific topic; for example, biotechnology — two dozen 250-word reviews by a subject expert. The regular fortnightly reviews are thorough, combining detailed description with careful evaluation. Efforts are made to place books in context and to compare with similar works: 'the subject is better covered in other books such as ...'. Potential audiences are identified: 'for someone not having a great deal of experience'; 'a handy reference for nontechnical personnel'; 'written for senior undergraduates'; 'more for the research and development engineer that for the process design or project engineer'. Adverse comment is often highly critical: 'glaring omissions'; 'It lacks the strong sense of organization, continuity, completeness and treatment of fundamentals that one would expect to find in a book'; 'written in a pedantic style that requires a great deal of concentration'. There is an annual index, listing book reviews A–Z by title only under 'Book reviews'.

Computer bulletin (Cambridge University Press, 1957–. 4 p.a. circulation: 27,000) is the professional journal of the British Computer Society (its research counterpart is *Computer journal*). It includes news items, obituaries, professional announcements, student matters and feature articles with a wide general appeal. From 1985, in view of the fact that 'reviews are to appear primarily in *Computer Bulletin*', the number was increased from a previous average of around 12 and coverage was extended to include software and video material. Ranging from 100 words to 500 words or more, all are signed, but instead of the normal affiliation, all that is given is place (town or city). Detailed and informative, they occasionally draw comparisons with other books, and usually make a firm recommendation as to the appropriate audience, though this is sometimes negative: 'hard to identify the type of reader who would benefit from it'; 'would not expect many of my students or staff to buy their personal copies'; 'Alas, the book cannot be recommended except to someone desperate'. Adverse criticism is quite specific: 'fails to demonstrate the principles and methods convincingly'; 'the title is extremely misleading'; 'the translation from French is very poorly done'.

Electronics and power (London, Institution of Electrical

Engineers, 1955–. 11 p.a. Circulation: 43,500) is the professional as opposed to the research journal of the IEE *(Proceedings;* see below), with a line going back as far as 1871. It includes news, letters, interviews, editorials and well-illustrated feature articles. Some 8 to 10 titles per month are treated in 'Book reviews', though this is not always found in every issue. Ranging from 200 up to 400 words and signed, but without affiliations, they are very detailed, with care taken to place the book in context and provide maximum information: 'devoid of mathematics'; 'written with the USA in mind'. A judgement on level is regularly given: '*not* a handbook for the practising electronics engineer'; 'could form the basic reference to engineers concerned with plant performance'; 'I would recommend this as supplementary reading in undergraduate engineering courses'. Adverse criticism is rare, most reviews being favourable. When it is found it is unusually mild: 'there are omissions', 'for the price one would have expected a more comprehensive work', 'very little reference to European work'. The annual index includes the separate section 'Books', arranged A–Z by author.

Food trade review (Orpington, Kent, Food Trade Press, Ltd, 1931–. 12 p.a. Circulation: 5,000), the standard trade journal for food manufacturers, processors and packers, provides news items, trade information, personalia and technical articles. 'New books for your libraries' reviews some 8 to 10 titles per month. Unsigned, 200 to 300 words in length, they are fully descriptive, often listing contents. There is occasional evaluation or recommendation. An order form is supplied for those wishing to purchase the books, and 'prices quoted include packing and despatch'.

Fuel (Guildford, Surrey, Butterworth Scientific, Ltd, 1922–. 12 p.a. Circulation not stated), is subtitled 'science and technology of fuel and energy'. It is one of the oldest journals in the field, with an international editorial board from 20 countries, publishing two dozen original research papers and three or four 'Short communications' each month. By no means to be found in every issue, the 'Book review' pages usually have two or three signed reviews (no affiliations) of around 450 words (occasionally over 600), and an occasional foreign-language title. Thorough, detailed and taking care to place the books in context and relate them to other books, they provide very positive evaluations: 'a wealth of information not available elsewhere in compact form'; 'the most wide-ranging guide that I have seen'; 'hard to find a subject which has been ignored'. Especially valuable is adverse criticism: 'occasionally opinions are given as statements of fact'; 'offers no technical depth for those working in the field'; 'prejudiced book with a very parochial view'; 'considerable overlap between the chapters'; 'prejudices are apparent in attempts to substantiate errors'. Welcome also are comments on documentation and physical format: 'a comprehensive index'; 'adequately referenced'; 'well bound'; 'some sacrifice of paper quality has clearly been made'. There is an annual author-index and 'Classified contents' but book-reviews are excluded.

IEE proceedings (London, Institution of Electrical Engineers, 1871–. 6 p.a. Circulation: 2,500 to 4,500 according to part), now comprising 10 parts (A–J), is the Institution's primary research journal, devoted pricipally to publishing original papers. Each of the 10 parts contains a 'Book reviews' column, though only irregularly. Treating two or three books per issue, the reviews are signed but with no affiliations, and are usually around 400 to 500 words in length, though some may approach 1,000. Combining description with evaluation, they usually begin by placing the work in context: 'in this field there is a great need of textbooks which aim to bridge the gap between...'; 'only recently have most engineering curricula given space to...'. Other books are compared: 'the author has wisely avoided the temptation to rewrite the epic treatises of the past [specified]'; 'the reader interested in these topics will find N's new book much more useful'. Potential readership is usually identified: 'for graduate students who are already employed in industry'; 'may be more highly appreciated by lecturers than by students'; 'persons setting up a measurement laboratory will therefore be well advised to buy a copy to get them started'. As often, adverse criticism is very helpful: 'as a basic undergraduate text, it lacks worked problems'; 'little attempt has been made to integrate the new material with the old'; 'will quickly seem to be dated'. Annual author- and subject-indexes cover all 10 parts together, with book-reviews (a total of 38 in 1984) listed separately, A–Z by title.

IEEE spectrum (New York, Institute of Electrical and Electronics Engineers, 1964–. 12 p.a. Circulation: 198,000), formerly *Electrical engineering*, with a line going back to 1905, is the general journal received by all IEEE members. Each issue contains five or six well-illustrated articles designed to appeal to a wide professional audience, together with editorials, regular columns, new items, notes, announcements, tables of contents of other IEEE journals, and so on. A 'Book reviews' section comprises about four largely descriptive reviews, well written and presented and highly readable. Up to 700 or 800 words in length, each is signed and furnished with four or five informal lines on the reviewer's affiliation, present position, background and experience, books written, and so on. Books are placed in their subject context, and compared with other books, which are sometimes recommended as a preferred alternative. Though primarily informative ('this popular-style...treatment', 'fully documented'), evaluation is not avoided: 'uniformly excellent'; 'well researched, well written'; 'this one is a bust'; 'nowhere does he state clearly his definition of...'.

Journal of metals (Warrendale, Pa., Metallurgical Society of American Institute of Mining, Metallurgical and Petroleum Engineers, 1949–. 12 p.a. Circulation: 13,300), the membership journal of the Society, with research papers, offers technical articles and various 'Departments' including 'Book reviews'. There are usually two or three reviews per issue, averaging 400 words, signed, with affiliations but not positions held. Reviews combine detailed description with thoughtful evaluation: 'the diagrams and photographs are remarkably clear'; 'would be of particular interest to graduate students and researchers'; 'an excellent alternative to the existing books'.

Journal of the American Oil Chemists Society (Champaign, Ill., 1917–. 12 p.a. Circulation: 6,800). This is a highly specialized professional journal publishing technical articles on fats and oils from animal and vegetable sources for the food, soap, cosmetics and fatty-chemicals industries. There are between two and five reviews in each issue, around 300 words long, but occasionally over 500 words. Reviews are signed, with affiliations, but without indication of positions held. Certain reviewers' names appear regularly. Reviews are fully descriptive, often with considerable detail: 'references to research literature are not included'; 'it brings together all the important syntheses reported since 1979'. Reviews regularly include a recommendation: 'mainly of interest to academic and industrial chemists'; 'not for the specialist and therefore of limited interest to readers of JAOCS'; 'a resource for graduate students as well as professors'. Reviews do not hesitate to criticize sharply: 'at $96, it is doubtful that this book will appear on many private bookshelves'; 'a severe lack of documentation'; 'this chapter was a mistake and perhaps reflects the author's lack of recent experience'.

Journal of applied mechanics (New York, American Society of Mechanical Engineers, 1935–. 4 p.a. Circulation: 5,000) is one of the series of *Transactions of the ASME*; its purpose is 'to disseminate technical information of permanent interest to the field of mechanical engineering'. It is obviously a journal of record, consisting almost entirely of original research papers. 'Book-reviews' deals with six to eight titles per issue. Averaging about 600 words, all reviews are signed, with affiliations and positions held. Virtually all the reviewers are academics and their views are noticeably magisterial in tone. Very full and thorough, often with a chapter-by-chapter analysis. An effort is usually made to give subject background, to place topic in context, and reference to and comparison with other books or earlier editions is frequent: 'one of the most interesting developing fields in applied mechanics research'; 'most books in this field tend to be "recipe" books'; 'significantly revised and updated version of the first edition'; 'there are only minor differences between this third new edition and the previous second edition'. Likely audience is usually assessed: 'designed as a text for graduate students'; 'an ideal book for self-study'; 'will appeal mostly to specialists'; 'engineers will probably have the most difficult time with the books'. Most reviews are favourable (perhaps reflecting some editorial weeding of books to be reviewed), and praise can be lavish: 'this is a *superb* book'; 'a splendid book'; 'an outstanding contribution to the literature of the subject'; 'a major contribution...by one of the subject's best expositors'. There is an annual author-index, which includes book-reviews under author of review.

Mechanical engineering (New York, American Society of Mechanical Engineers, 1906–. 12 p.a. Circulation: 80,000) is the general-membership journal, with news items, regular columns, letters, well-illustrated feature articles designed to be 'interesting', ASME announcements, and so on. 'Current books: book reviews' includes no more than two per issue, but can be up to 700 words long. Reviews are signed, with affiliations and positions held: 'President', 'Mechanical Engineer', 'Senior Research Scientist', 'Manager, Special Projects'. Two reviews of the same book appear side by side in the May 1985 issue. Reviews are bright and highly informative as well as evaluative: 'a good text for those in commercial operations'; 'an excellent choice for addition to the libraries of engineers'; 'Happiness is...a book like this'. In addition, reviews are sharply critical where judged appropriate: 'will not assist buyers, sellers, designers, or manufacturers'; 'a grossly unfair, unjustified book'. A separate section, 'Recent additions to the Library', consists of shorter (up to 250 words) non-critical descriptions of two to four books per month.

Microelectronics journal (Luton, Bedfordshire, Benn Electronics Publications, Ltd, 1967–. 6 p.a. Circulation: 700) is a technical and research journal for 'scientists and engineers concerned in the various fields of silicon and hybrid device technology and design'. It includes original research papers, state-of-the-art reviews, notes, statistics, announcements and abstracts. 'Book reviews' offers on average two reviews per issue (though occasionally an issue is missed), signed, but without affiliations. Most are around 200 words in length, but some extend to 700; they are largely descriptive, with considerable pains taken to place topics in context. There are only occasional evaluations, though specific recommendations are often found: 'serves well people with experience'; 'should certainly be in college and other libraries'; 'an essential reference work for researchers'; 'a very good text for students'. 'Classified index to articles' appears every two years, but book-reviews are excluded.

Mining magazine (London, Mining Journal, Ltd, 1909–. 12 p.a. Circulation: 9,700) is a technical/trade journal for 'minerals industry personnel worldwide'. It offers news items, editorial comment, personalia, general technical articles of broad appeal, and abstracts. 'Book reviews' feature usually contains two unsigned reviews of between 350 and 800 words in length, mainly descriptive and often elaborating in some detail on contents. There is some evaluation: 'very readable'; 'some excellent photographs'; 'more for general information than the engineering specialist'.

New civil engineer (London, Thomas Telford, Ltd, 1972–. Weekly. Circulation: 49,000) describes itself as the 'Magazine of the Institution of Civil Engineers'. It is a typical professional 'organ', with news items, editorials, a letters page, Institution announcements and illustrated feature articles. The 'Books' column appears only irregularly (three or four weekly issues in six months) and comprises three or four reviews of up to 300 words in length, some signed (no affiliation), some not. They are highly informative, placing the book in context and comparing with other books: 'he based the contents on lectures given to engineering undergraduates'; 'a worthy sequel'; 'a substantial increase in the number of worked examples'. Evaluation is positive and helpful: 'one of the most useful and comprehensive publications yet produced on the subject'; 'it is not really up to date'; 'supplementary reading will be needed'; 'undergraduates may require a book in which principles are more simply explained'.

Physics in technology (Bristol, Institute of Physics, 1970–. 6 p.a. Circulation: 1,200) covers 'the whole spectrum of the application of physics to technology' and 'discusses developments wherever physics is relevant: in innovation, in technical change and in society at large'. Aimed at a wide readership, it offers original review-articles, accessible to the non-specialist, editorials, news items, conference reports, and so on. 'Book reviews', signed but with no affiliations and ranging from 4 to 10 in each issue, with an average length of around 300 words, are descriptive and evaluative, with care taken to place topics in context and occasional references to other books. Recommendations are usually quite specific: 'aimed at, and should be useful for, the technician'; 'obligatory for any technical library'; 'could not easily be used as an introduction to the field'; 'if you can't afford it try to persuade your library to do so'. Most books are praised: 'a very informative report; 'an easily read book'; 'could hardly be more topical'; 'an authoritative review of trends'. Criticism is gentle: 'no clear perceptions appear to emerge'; 'difficult to avoid a feeling of disappointment at the lack of real content'; 'a general bibliography would have helped'. Even criticism of physical form is mildly expressed: 'the poor reproductions of photographs are unfortunate'; 'it is a pity, though, that the physical structure of the book is not up to the usual standard'. There is an annual author-index and subject-index, but book reviews are omitted.

Bibliography

Brightman, R. 'The art and technique of book reviewing. 2: The reviewing of scientific and technical books', *Aslib proceedings*, vol. 1 (2), August 1949, pp. 125–7.

Chen, Ching-chih. *Biomedical, scientific and technical book reviewing.* Metuchen, NJ, Scarecrow Press, 1976.

Chen, Ching-chih. 'Reviews and reviewing of scientific and technical materials', in *Encyclopedia of library and information science*, vol. 25, pp. 350–72.

Clegg, Hugh A. 'The art and technique of book reviewing. 1: Signing book reviews'. *Aslib proceedings*, vol. 1 (2), August 1949, pp. 119–24.

Collison, R.L. 'The art and technique of book reviewing. 3: Book reviews and the librarian', *Aslib proceedings*, vol. 1 (2), August 1949, pp. 128–32.

Culver, Marguerite R., and Long, Frank R. 'Too much time lag in technical book reviews', *Library journal*, vol. 74, 15 May 1949, pp. 805–6.

Field, Margaret M. 'A study of reviewing mediums for technical books', *Special libraries*, vol. 37 (10), December 1946, pp. 324–6.

McClellan, E.H. 'Reviewing of technical books — the minimum requirements', *Journal of chemical education*, vol. 25, 1948, pp. 380–2.

Sadow, Arnold. 'Book reviewing media for technical libraries', *Special libraries*, vol. 61 (4), April 1970, pp. 194–8.

Vickers, Tom. 'Reviews...and reviewers', *Computer bulletin*, 3rd series, vol. 1 (1), March 1985, pp. 31–2.

Walford, A.J. 'The reviewing of scientific books', *TBR/Technical book review*, no. 40, February 1967, pp. 4–6.

9. Fine arts

Margaret Girvan

The field of the fine arts and related subject-areas such as architecture and the various decorative arts, is vast, both in terms of books published — nearly 2,000 in Great Britain alone in 1981[1] — and in the number of serial titles available, estimated in 1979 to be 6,000-odd worldwide,[2] a figure that may vary with the demise of short-term titles, but remains a daunting total.

The annotated list of art serials included in Arntzen and Rainwater's *Guide to the literature of art history*[3] gives some indication of the subject coverage and the relative importance of book-reviews as a feature of a particular journal, but the *Guide* is already sufficiently out of date to be misleading about some titles, notably *The connoisseur*, formerly a major British art journal with excellent concise book-reviews until the transfer of its editorial office to New York in 1982, when a drastic change of policy effectively terminated its usefulness as an art periodical. Further to evaluative listings of art periodicals, work is in progress on two Greenwood Press publications which should appear shortly: Winberta Yao's *International art periodicals*,[4] to comprise substantial essays on 100 major art periodicals, and Deborah Shorley's annotated bibliography of current English-language serials.[5]

Having identified a periodical likely to have reviewed a specific book, the reader may then have difficulty in finding the book-review section , since book-reviews tend not be itemized on the contents page or even adequately identified in the annual index. The reader having recourse to the various general art indexes discussed in detail below, will discover that the delay before a substantial review can appear in print is compounded by a further delay before a reference to the review can reach one of the art-indexing services. There is less pressure in the arts field for a review to appear quickly than there would be in more technical subjects. Several magazines list basic details of a new publication as it is received, with the promise of a more detailed critique at a later date. The proliferation of special subject-areas within the arts field, and corresponding specialist journals appearing no more than once or twice a year, may produce quality reviews by subject experts, but also adds to the delays in publication.

Having identified and traced a particular book-review, one needs to consider the qualifications of a reviewer to write the review, and probably those of a particular journal to print it. Information supplied by an art journal on its reviewers is generally confined to scholarly or institutional affiliations. Even those journals which supply notes on contributors of articles rarely extend the courtesy to more than one major reviewer. Investigating the credentials of a reviewer for the purposes of evaluating a review can be an arduous task in the arts field, in which biographical sources concentrate on practising artists, with the honourable exception of *Who's who in American art*, which includes scholars, museum curators, art historians, journalists, educators, and so on, in its pages. Unless the reviewer is already well-known, it will be necessary to make use of general biographical and scholarly directories, or library catalogues and bibliographies, in connection with an author.

The craft of reviewing art books is as varied as the nature of art books themselves. One expert reviewing another's *magnum opus* on their mutual pet subject could produce a carefully balanced critique or a raging argument on paper. An eminent writer on eighteenth-century French painting produced a competent description but very lopsided evaluation of a major pioneering study of seventeenth-century interiors and furniture; half the limited review space was taken up with minor corrections and additions by the reviewer, and the resulting review totally failed to convey the importance and interest of the book. The ideal compromise would seem to be a reviewer with sufficient specialist knowledge to appreciate the finer points of the book, but without so much knowledge of the subject that he feels compelled to rewrite the book in the course of his review. This ideal review should state clearly what the book is about, whether the author succeeds in his intentions and whether he communicates them to the reader, place the book in the context of existing studies of its subject, note the degree of original research, comment on the quality and choice of illustrations and accuracy of the bibliography, index and any other ancillary critical apparatus; the inclusion of a full bibliographical description should go without saying — and is in fact becoming more common — also a comment on the physical make-up of the book and the state of the binding would not come amiss, since many expensive art books are quite inadequately bound.

Since the best of the analytical and critical scholarly reviews which I have scanned are too long to quote in this context, I offer instead the following concise 300 words from *Country Life* of 1 February 1979, which conveys the salient points — that the book will be significant and influential in its own subject field, contains the results of original research into unfamiliar sources, is well illustrated and documented and extremely readable — summarized by a reviewer who is also an authority on historic interiors:

Seventeenth-century interior decoration in England, France and Holland. By Peter Thornton (Yale University Press, [1978], £30).

Last year was certainly a bumper one for books throwing light on English houses, and one of three that made it so was Peter Thornton's important study. Compared with the 18th century, the 17th century is a much more difficult period for historians and restorers, with a much greater need to reply and speculate on documents because the objects themselves have disappeared. Mr. Thornton has met this challenge with a felicitous combination of ideas, documented evidence and a fascinating variety of plates, including many French and Dutch paintings, engravings and drawings. He complements and elaborates aspects of Mark Girouard's book on country-house life, but he approaches the subject from a most unusual angle, as someone trained in the difficult world of textiles who has gone on to furniture, and this background makes him uniquely suited to deal with the 17th century, where upholstery provides the key, albeit, alas, often now missing.

So much of the material is new and culled from sources unfamiliar in England that lengthy notes are often required, and over 60 pages of these are provided. Much in the book is grand and splendid, state beds, canopies and illustrated French royal inventories, but what is fascinating is to find almost as much attention paid to the simpler things, rugs and fledges, morters and *bakermats*. Thus there are great rewards for the social as well as the furniture historian, and signs of the book's influence will be seen not only in the footnotes of a generation of writers but probably in the look of much 17th century furniture as well.

Indexes to reviews

There are two major art-periodical indexes that include clearly indentifiable references to book-reviews. One is *Art index* (H.W. Wilson, 1929–. 4 p.a., cumulated annually), which indexed reviews by subject, author and reviewer in its main index until 1973, after which, beginning with vol. 22 (1973/74), an appended 'Book-reviews' section provided entries under authors of books reviewed. The other major source is *RILA: Répertoire international de la littér-ature de l'art* (1973–. 4 p.a.). It is a bibliographical abstracting ser-vice that lists book-reviews with the books reviewed, noting the exis-tence of a review in the author-index.

ARTbibliographies MODERN (Oxford, Clio Press, 1973–) includes book-reviews as periodical articles — only identifiable by checking all the references under authors' names in the author-index. Of the general indexing services, *Book review index*, *Arts and humanities citation index* and *Internationale Bibliographie der Rezensionen* have relevance.

Reviewing journals

The art journals listed below can be no more than an indication of major titles, and some of the more specialized ones offering high quality in their subject fields.

Apollo: the magazine of the arts (London, Apollo Magazine, Ltd, 1925–. 12 p.a. Circulation: uncertified) is a quality journal of equal interest to art historians and to collectors and connoisseurs, since it covers both fine and decorative arts. Vol. 121 (no. 278, n.s.), April 1985 (pp. 217–88), contains two substantial critical signed reviews of between 1,000 and 2,000 words (pp. 280–3), followed by 'Further book-reviews' (pp. 283–6) — six signed reviews covering eight titles of about 500 words each, which offer a more summary description and evaluation. Bibliographical details are confined to publisher, date of publication and price. Only the authors of the two major reviews are included in 'Notes on contributors' at the end of the issue, which supplies rather more than the bare note on affiliations found in many art journals, giving details of former posts held and fields of expertise, as well as of publications. Major book-reviews are included in the contents lists, but only under title of the review and name of the reviewer; there is no mention of the author and title of the book reviewed. Shorter reviews are indicated simply as 'Further book-reviews' and a page reference, followed by a list of reviewers — hardly a helpful practice. Reviews are indexed in *Art index*, *RILA*, *Répertoire d'art et d'archéologie* and *ARTbibliographies MODERN*.

Art book review (London, Art Book Review Co., March 1982– 4 p.a. [irregular; at present in abeyance]. Circulation: about 1,000) should be mentioned briefly as the only journal devoted exclusively to original reviews of art books. The first editorial noted the expansion of art-book publishing since the 1950s, and that over 2,000 titles appeared in Britain alone in 1981, many of which would be unlikely to receive the briefest of notices. *Art book review* was founded to redress the balance, but regrettably was unable to maintain its original impetus and standards. The first issue of March 1982 offered, in addition to an author/title/keyword listing of the previous six months' art titles from information supplied by Whitaker's, 25 susbstantial signed reviews (1,000–4,000 words) and 36 brief notices (50–100 words). The list of contributors, with affiliations, and including some well-known names — art historians, curators, art dealers and so on — substantiated the author's intention to use leading writers to provide a balanced evaluation of the literature of art. By the sixth (and, to date, final) edition of January 1984, the number of 'name' contributors had decreased, and there were more and shorter reviews by unaffiliated writers, or survey articles covering a number of titles by staff reviewers, all varying considerably in quality. The editor states that it has not ceased publication, and hopes to resume publication in late 1985 or 1986. Reviews are indexed in *RILA*.

Art bulletin (New York, College Art Association of America, 1913–. 4 p.a. Circulation: about 8,500) is the major American academic journal of art history, covering a diversity of topics in long scholarly articles. Vol. 67 (1), March 1985 (pp. 1–176), includes eight substantial reviews (pp. 137–72), of between 1,000 and 4,000 words, of books on subjects as varied as American Gothic architecture and Chinese painting, including two with French texts. The reviews are thorough, detailed, analytical and critical studies, all signed by scholars — four American, three British, one French — affiliated to institutions as eminent as the Victoria and Albert Museum or the Folger Shakespeare Library. Bibliographical details include pagination and price but not format or ISBNs. Books reviewed and reviewers are given in the contents list and indexed by author and reviewer in the annual index. A cumulative index to vols. 1–30 (1913–48) was published in 1950. The journal is also indexed in *Art index*, *RILA* and *Arts and humanities citation index*.

Art documentation: bulletin of the Art Libraries Society of North America (New York, ARLIS N/A, 1982–. 4 p.a. Circulation: 1,200), the American equivalent of *Art libraries journal* (see below) and successor to the *ARLIS N/A Newsletter*, tends to have more and shorter reviews, somewhat variable in quality and generally descriptive and evaluative rather than analytical and critical. Vol. 4 (2), Summer 1985 (pp. 37–98), has an eight-page, two-column review section that offers 16 fairly short reviews (300–1,200 words). Some art-reference works are reviewed, but many more general monographs are covered than in *Art libraries journal*. All reviews are signed, mainly by professional librarians, with affiliations given. Full bibliographical details are given, including ISBN and Library of Congress numbers. The book-reviews are not itemized in the contents list, and there has not been any index published to date, but *Art documentation* is in *RILA*.

Art history: journal of the Association of Art Historians (London, Routledge and Kegan Paul, for the Association of Art Historians of Great Britain, 1977–. 4 p.a. Circulation: uncertified), the most recently published of the scholarly art journals, is sponsored by an association with membership 'open to those who are art historians by profession or avocation or otherwise directly concerned in the advancement of the study of the history of art'. The standing of the journal is enhanced by an editorial board of academics and museum staff, and an impressive international advisory board of scholars of world repute. Vol. 8 (2), June 1985 (pp. 139–270), devotes pp. 228–70, or 30 per cent of its text, to reviews in the form of seven lengthy (2,000–10,000 words) comparative surveys of two, three or four works on related topics, plus an annotated list of 15 volumes on Islamic art. While a critical comparison of several volumes allows the reviewer to set each book more clearly in context, it can also allow him to stray from his proper place into an exposition of his own views on the subject under review. The scope of the journal is art history in a fairly wide sense: the reviews consider both ancient Chinese art and the Victorian nude. Each review is signed, with affiliations. Bibliographical details quoted include pagination and price, but not format or ISBN. Although the contents list for each itemizes individual titles reviewed, the annual index is quite inadequate for a scholarly journal: the name-index includes reviewers among the contributors, but not authors of books reviewed; and the title-index includes the topical headings used for the comparative reviews, but not individual book titles. It is indexed in *RILA* and *Répertoire d'art et d'archéologie*.

Art libraries journal (London, Art Libraries Society UK, Spring 1976–. 4 p.a. Circulation: about 600) is published by and for professional art librarians and others concerned with art documentation, and the two to four reviews of varying length that appear in each issue concentrate on the kind of art reference tools — bibliographies, indexes, encyclopaedias and the like — which are too specialized to be of interest to general art-history journals, as well as on books of professional library practice. Vol. 9 (1), Spring 1984 (pp. 1-80), includes four reviews (pp. 68–78) of between 600 and 1,000 words, covering one general and one special art bibliography, a periodical issue on art librarianship and a database of information on art-sale results. The thorough analysis and criticism offered by these reviews of moderate length illustrates the value of specialist reviewers familiar on a working basis with the type of material they are asked to review; the reviews are all signed by professional librarians, with current affiliations. It is surprising in the circumstances that full bibliographical details were not given in every case, although an ISBN for a database might present a problem. The contents list gives author, title and name of reviewer; the annual index in the fourth quarterly issue indexes books reviewed under author, title and reviewer. *Art libraries journal* does not yet appear in any standard index to art journals.

The British journal of aesthetics (London, Oxford University Press, for the British Society of Aesthetics, 1960–. 4 p.a. Circulation: 1,500) is a leading scholarly and interdisciplinary journal in its field. The Society aims 'to promote study, research and discussion of the fine arts and selected types of experience from a philosophical, psychological, sociological, scientific, historical, critical and educational standpoint'. Vol. 23 (4), Autumn 1983 (pp. 294–381) has 13 book-reviews (around 1,200 words each) on pp. 360—81. The reviews are signed, with affiliations; 'Notes on contributors' adds 'brief details of reviewers' specializations and publications (if any). The 1,600-word analytical and critical review of J.G. Davies's *Temples, churches and mosques: a guide to the appreciation of religious architecture* (Blackwell, 1982) values the book as an excellent all-round history of Western religious architecture viewed in the light of well-thought-out principles. 'It is equally good on the analysis of design for specific ritual and the description of structural evolution. While the religious significance of the dome and apse are emphasized, more could perhaps be made of the apse as the half dome.' The book production also merits praise. Bibliographical details lack full pagination and ISBNs. The annual index has a 'Reviews' section.

Burlington magazine (London, Burlington Magazine Publications, Ltd, 1903?. 12 p.a. Circulation: uncertified), the leading old-established British art-historical journal, is aimed at art scholars and researchers, but enjoys a wide and varied international readership, two-thirds of its circulation being abroad. It is devoted primarily to the history of the fine arts in the Western tradition, with marginal coverage of other fields such as the decorative arts and contemporary painting. Vol. 127 (no. 985), April 1985 (pp. 199–272), has a book-review section (pp. 232–44) comprising 16 substantial signed reviews (500–1,500 words) and a 'Publications received' section of 15 shorter notices (40–400 words), which reflects the journal's international scope and bias towards the 'fine' arts. More than half the reviews are of foreign-language (French, German, Italian, Spanish) publications or of English-language titles published abroad. Full bibliographical details include pagination and ISBNs. Although well-known names in the field of art scholarship appear among the reviewers, no affiliations are stated for reviewers or contributors; it seems to be assumed that the journal's own high reputation, backed by an editorial board of eminent art historians, is sufficient guarantee of the authority of its reviews, which are analytical, well-balanced, critical and frequently comparative. Cumulative indexes — vols. 1-106 (1901–62); vols, 105–14 (1963–72); and vols. 115–24 (1973–82, projected) — cover book-reviews by authors A to Z, and classified by title. The annual index lists reviews by author only, and monthly and annual title-pages, by book title, with author's name in brackets. There is no index or list of reviewers. It is also indexed in *Art index* and *RILA*.

Costume: the journal of the Costume Society (London, the Society, 1967–. Annual. Circulation: 2,000) aims 'to promote the study and presentation of significant examples of historic and contemporary costume. This involves the documentation of surviving examples and the study of decorative arts allied to the study of dress, as well as literary and historical sources'. No. 19, 1984 (176 pp.) carries 21 signed book-reviews (150–1,300 words) on pp. 153–67. Reviews are descriptive and evaluative. Thus *Jewellery*, by Diana Scarisbrick (London, Batsford, 1984), is found to concentrate 'almost entirely on the jewels worn by Royalty and the upper classes', while being very good on the developments of diamond-cutting and setting, and on engraved gems and cameos. The book is criticized for lack of balance and failure to cross-refer to plate numbers. Joan Evans's *A history of jewellery, 1100–1870* and Vivienne Barker's *Costume and 20th century jewellery* (1980) are much preferred. Books reviewed are not confined to costume and its trappings. Ann Saunders's *The art and architecture of London: an illustrated guide* (Oxford, Phaidon Press, 1984) is commended for the special relevance of its description of monumental brasses, sculptured figures and the like. Bibliographical details do not give full pagination or ISBNs, but do note illustrations and size.

Gazette des beaux-arts (Paris, Imprimerie Louis Jean, 1859–. 10

p.a.), 'la doyenne des revues d'art', is an esteemed journal of long standing. No. 1401, October 1985 (pp. 99–140 + 32 pp.) has authoritative articles and, under 'La Chronique des arts', a section 'Livres et travaux' (pp. 16–30), comprising mostly very brief notices of books, periodical articles, theses, exhibitions, gallery acquisitions, and so on, the whole enlivened by small photographs. This section has seven period subheadings, ranging from 'Antiquité' to 'XX siècle' (this last occupying pp. 22–30 and covering architecture, art and literature, aesthetics, and art in general). A few of the book notices do qualify as brief (100–200 words) reviews, largely descriptive and hardly allowing for evaluative analysis. Richard Cork's *Art beyond the gallery in early 20th century England* (New Haven, Conn., Yale University Press) is praised for fulfilling its title and for the quality of its illustrations; Cork himself is mentioned as an art historian who has published on Vorticism and Henri Gaudier. Bibliographical details are minimal. Reviews are indexed in *Art index*, *RILA*, *Arts and humanities citation index*, *ARTbibliographies MODERN* and *Internationale Bibliographie der Rezensionen*.

Journal of the Society of Architectural Historians (Philadelphia, Pa., the Society, 1940–. 4 p.a. Circulation: 4,500) is one of the few scholarly architectural periodicals with substantial book-reviews. Vol. 44 (1), March 1955 (85 p.), has 10 reviews, pp. 75–84, under three headings: Architectural records, American architecture and urbanism, and Architecture and burial. Analytical and critical comments stress illustrative matter, noting paucity of plans, omission of dates on photographs and inadequacy of cross-references. *A field guide to American houses*, by Virginia and Lee McAlister (New York, Knopf, 1984) is, however, praised for giving as much attention to ordinary post Second World War housing developments as to 'the noblest of nineteenth-century Greek Revival homes'. Bibliographical details include full pagination and data on illustrations, but omit ISBNs. The 'Letters' section is concerned with an author's reactions to a previous review. Reviews are covered in *Art index* and *America: history and life* as well as in the annual index.

Oxford art journal (Oxford, Oxford Microform Publications, 1978–. 2 p.a.) has devoted each number to a particular theme in art history, although as from 1985 the *Journal* will regularly publish issues of a non-thematic nature. Vol. 7 (2), 1984 (72 pp.), highlights 'photography', but the nine signed reviews (pp. 60–72), averaging 1,000 words, deal with books in a broad range of art history. Two monographs on seventeenth-century Dutch painting are treated together, both being 'illustrated with a breadth of images which is impressive' and 'invaluable additions to any library'. Four books on art history are compared, including two in the 'Cambridge Introduction to the History of Art' series — regarded as 'more attractive and less forbidding'. *Reviews of Soviet photography: Grigory Shudakov, Olga Suslova and Lilya Ukhtomskaya* (London, Thames and Hudson, 1985) is described as 'written and selected in line with a revisionist view of Soviet history', emphasizing 'both the strength and weaknesses of Soviet visual sensitiveness'.

Simiolus: Netherlands quarterly for the history of art (Amsterdam, Foundation for Dutch Art Historical Publications, in association with Uitgeverij Gary Schwarz, Maarsen, 1966/67–. 4 p.a., since 1971. Circulation: about 1,600) covers material on the history of art with some relevance to the Netherlands. It is included in this survey partly because of the high quality of its book-reviews, and partly as an outstanding example of a journal national in scope and international in outlook. Contributions appear in Dutch as well as English, French and German, but vol. 15 (3) contains a single 2,000-word Dutch review (translated into English) of a Dutch-language book. Vol. 15 (1) 1985 of this small publication includes a meticulously detailed comparative 3,000-word review of *Répertoire d'art et d'archéologie* and *RILA: Répertoire international de la littérature de l'art* which emphasizes the scholarly accuracy for which this journal is known. Reviews are indexed in *RILA* and *Répertoire d'art et d'archéologie*.

Zeitschrift für Kunstgeschichte (Munich, Deutscher Kunstverlag, 1932–. 4 p.a., since 1956. Circulation: about 900), edited by art historians from the Institut für Kunstgeschichte, University of Munich, is one of the world's major academic art journals, not only for German art history but for the whole subject-field. It includes articles and sometimes reviews in languages other than German. Vol. 47 (3), 1984 (pp. 293–420) devotes about 20 per cent of its text (pp. 400–20) to five long (1,500–5,000 words) scholarly, analytical and critical reviews, written very much by experts for experts with considerable awareness of other literature in the field. Reviews are signed, but without affiliations; if the reviewer happens to be on the editorial board (composed mainly of German art-historians, with one American representative), the university or art institution to which he is attached will be given at the front of the issue. One review is in English, of an English publication. Bibliographical details include pagination and illustrations but not ISBNs or prices. There is no index in vol. 46 (1983), only a detailed contents list that includes book-reviews — a total of eight for the year. From 1984 each issue has been increased in size by 20 per cent and more reviews and articles are included. Reviews are indexed in *Art index*, *RILA* and *Répertoire d'art et d'archéologie.*

References

1. Freitag, Wolfgang. 'Tapping a serviceable reservoir: the selection of periodicals for art librarians', *Art libraries journal*, vol. 1 (2), Summer 1976, p. 10.
2. Editorial, *Art book review,* vol. 1 (1), March 1982.
3. Arntzen, Etta, and Rainwater, Robert. *Guide to the literature of art history.* Chicago, Ill., ALA, and London, Art Book Company, 1980.
4. 'Bibliographies update', *Art libraries journal*, vol. 8 (4), Winter 1983, pp. 30–1.
5. 'Bibliographies update', *Art libraries journal*, vol. 8 (3), Autumn 1983, p. 50.

10. Music

A.J. Walford

There are two major aspects of music: the music itself (its performance and recording) and musicology (the scholarly study of music). This brief survey is confined to book reviewing in the field of musicology. The sub-discipline is defined in *The new Grove dictionary of music and musicians*[1] as 'the collecting and study of musical instruments, the science of acoustics, the performing of early music (with the allied practices of textual criticism and editing of folksong). The development of music history as a scholarly discipline came, in a sense, rather later, although it has its roots extending back to the 17th century'.

The reviewer in this area would be expected to have had academic training and/or professional qualifications, to be a musicologist ('chiefly a historian')[2] and, possibly, a teacher of music. His or her reviews should be comparative, providing a balanced assessment and indicating level and readership. The use of quotations and, where appropriate, music examples, would also help analysis.

Ian Woodfield's *The early history of the viol* (Cambridge University Press, 1984) is welcomed, with a few reservations, in *The musical times*.[3] Most of the book concerns the spread of the viol throughout Western Europe and discusses many of the leading aspects of its use and techniques during the seventeenth century. However, the 800-word review criticizes the work as 'lumping together playing techniques and performing practices from separate periods and countries where quite different aesthetics applied'. (Examples are given.) Two smaller discrepancies regarding the *lira* and the *lirone* are pointed out. The review concludes, 'This book makes a valuable contribution to the literature on the instrument, especially for its presentation of more than 100 important plates. It should be read, albeit with caution, by anyone seriously interested in the viol'.

The daunting task of reviewing *The new Grove dictionary* (London, Macmillan, 1980. 20 vols.) can be tackled variously. Rosen gives prominence in the *New York review of books*[4] to its biographical entries. In *Music and letters*[5] Dahlaus favours more general sampling and comparison. He questions whether the status of an encyclopaedia is decided by the large-scale articles on Mozart and Verdi, Baroque and Romantic. To do this would be to overlook the value of *The new Grove* for quick-reference purposes, while to resort to compiling lists of errors is 'tedious pedantry'. Dahlaus elects to concentrate on the treatment of 'Opera' and 'Aesthetics', plus aspects of Bach and Beethoven, having ascertained that the detail in selected small-scale articles is 'unusually good'. Selection of entries, he concludes, has been made with discrimination; 'there are bound to be omissions'. The plan adopted by *The musical times*[6] is to invite ten people, each with different musical interests, to write on two volumes apiece of *The new Grove*, 'and to consider it from their standpoint in the musical world'. The result is more extensive and specialized sampling, spread over four consecutive issues of *The musical times*. Even finer-tuned sampling is apportioned by the book-review editor of *Ethnomusicology*.[7] It consists of a 17-part review of ethnomusicological articles in *The new Grove* by 19 contributors, spread over two issues of the journal. Many of the contributions concern specific ethnic regions, such as Oceania and Sub-Saharan Africa. The review-article, 'Grove and the long-suffering Celtic composers', in *Musical opinion*,[8] focuses its criticism on *The new Grove*'s selective treatment of Scottish and Welsh musicians, noting omitted names. The comments make no attempt at a balanced appraisal of the work; in fact, the reviewer confessed that he had not consulted *The new Grove dictionary* in any detail while composing his article: 'Indeed, I am relying almost entirely on the opinions of others'.

Indexes to reviews

One of the two main sources is *Music index: the key to current music periodical literature* (Detroit, Mich., Information Coordinators, Inc., 1949–), a monthly guide, with annual cumulations, to about 300 periodicals from 34 countries. It has a 'Book reviews' section, with some 250 entries per month. The other main source is *RILM abstracts*, the basic international service for musicological documentation (New York, International RILM Center, 1967–. 4 p.a., the 4th issue being the annual index, and cumulated 5-yearly). The abstracts include music reviews in scholarly journals from 43 countries. The reviews are listed by 13 types (1a. Review of an article; 1b. Review of a book, magazine or pamphlet...;1t. Review of a translation).

A non-serial source is *Speculum: an index of musically related articles and book reviews* (compiled by Arthur S. Wolfe, Ann Arbor, Mich., Music Library Association, 1970). *Arts and humanities citation index* has references to some 70 music journals. *Internationale Bibliographie der Rezensionen* records reviews in at least five of the major music journals dealt with below; *Combined retrospective index to book reviews in humanities journals, 1802–1974* covers four journals; *Humanities index*, three journals. Joan M. Meggett's *Musical periodical literature: an annotated bibliography of indexes and bibliographies* (Metuchen, NJ, Scarecrow Press, 1978) provides a further source, *Index to religious periodical literature*, 1949–1976 (Chicago, Ill., American Theological Library Association, 1953–77), under the heading 'Music', and continued in *Religious index one: Periodicals* ATLA, 1977–. 2 p.a., cumulated 2-yearly and on COM-fiche), which has a book-reviews section.

Reviewing journals

Music and letters (Oxford University Press, 1920–. 4 p.a.) is the leading journal of English musicology. 'Its title stresses the relation between music and literature and between word and note — as in song, opera and oratorio.'[9] Vol. 66 (2), April 1985 (pp. 93–200), has 41 book-reviews, signed, but without affiliations, on pp. 127–95. The reviews are analytical, some with quotations, and critical. The reviewer of *A history of English opera*, by Eric Walter White (London, Faber, 1983) notes that there is a distinct need 'for a substantial and scholarly work on the post-war achievements of opera in Britain'. White's book lacks two essentials — 'In the first place there is little effort to analyse the various types of entertainment that has passed at different times under the title of "opera"'; and: 'He says a great deal about the theatrical background, including financial and social conditions, and sometimes about librettos, but almost nothing, apart from a few generalities about the music'. The absence of a bibliography, too, is a major defect in a book of this kind. 'The book is a vast concatenation of facts — and facts are important when they are correct; it is not a history of English opera for which we might have hoped.' Bibliographical details lack only ISBNs. The annual index of books reviewed is under authors (with mention of reviewers). There is a cumulative index to vol. 1-40: 1920-59 (1962).

The musical times (Sevenoaks, Kent, Novello, 1844–. 12 p.a. Circulation: 8,000), oldest of all music journals with a continuous record of publication, 'seeks to inform professional musicians of all kinds who are not musicologists as well as the interested layman, and it contains a certain amount of journalism'.[10] Vol. 126 (1705), March 1985 (pp. 129–92), 'Bach tercentenary issue', has 13 headed book-reviews on pp. 156–61. The reviews, signed, without affiliations, are between 250 and 800 words in length, analytical and critical. *The concertgoer's companion. 1: Bach to Hadyn*, by Anthony Hopkins (London, Dent, 1984), is faulted for the misleading subtitle, the 14 composers covered being in A–Z, not chronological, order (vol. 2 is to deal with composers Holst to Wagner.). The engaging style would have benefited from more music examples. 'Yet for its intended readership [the intelligent music lover] this is a book worth having.' Bibliographical details omit price and full pagination. The annual index has entries for book-reviews under both authors and reviewers.

Musica (Kassel, Barenreiter, 1946–. 6 p.a.) is a well-respected journal on classical music. Vol. 39, March/April 1985 (pp. 97–232), has 12 signed book-reviews in German on pp. 194–201, plus 23 shorter notices and appended lists of new editions and reprints. The signed reviews, between 400 and 1,000 words in length, are analytical and briefly critical. Karl Hochreither's *Zur Aufführungspraxis der Vokalinstrumentalwerke Johann Sebastian Bachs* (Kassel, Merseberger, 1983) discusses Bach's own scoring of vocal and instrumental parts in his cantatas, in contrast to later elaborations. The role of vocal trios, use of contemporary instruments, dotted notes, triplets and figured bass have been the subject of polemics, and Hochreither cites sources. But the reviewer concludes by asking: might not Bach himself have changed his earlier more generous attitude and insisted on the exact notation of his scores? Bibliographical details omit full pagination and ISBNs. The annual index has entries for books reviewed, with reviewers' names in parentheses.

Notes: the quarterly journal of the Music Library Association (Washington, DC, the Association, 1931–. 4 p.a. Circulation: 3,000) devotes 25 per cent of its contents to book-reviews — noted for their authority and forthrightness. Vol. 41 (2), December 1984 (pp. 233–460), has 19 listed reviews, with editor, on pp. 268–94. The reviews, signed, with affiliations, are between 800 and 1,200 words in length, analytical and critical. Paul Griffiths' *The string quartet* (London, Thames and Hudson, 1983) is described as comprising 'brief program-notish descriptions of most of the basic quartet repertoire, filled out with some of the author's personal choices and connected by brief references to those whom he evidently thinks to be the, as it were, major minor figures'. The reviewer concludes, 'For history, properly so-called, *The new Grove* article, compact as it is, is much better and remains the best treatment of the subject we have'. Bibliographical details omit ISBNs and full pagination. The annual index has entries under reviewers, authors and titles of books reviewed.

The music review (Cambridge, Heffers, 1940–. 4 p.a. Circulation: 1,000), comparable to *Music and letters*, has authoritative contributions on Western music. Vol. 44 (2), May 1983 (pp. 83–160), has 16 initialled book-reviews on pp. 136–52. The reviews range from 500 to 1,300 words in length, being analytical, with quotations, and critical, indicating readership. One monograph is blamed for lack of balance between sacred and secular music; another, for a misleading title. Bibliographical details omit ISBNs. Reviews of recent issues of other periodicals are included in alternate issues. The annual contents-list covers book-reviews, reviews of other journals, and so on.

Early music (Oxford University Press, 1973–. 4 p.a. Circulation: 7,000) not a learned journal in any exclusive sense,[9] concerns all aspects of pre-classical music. Vol. 13 (2), May 1985 (pp. 161–336), the Bach tercentenary issue, has eight book-reviews, signed, but without affiliations, on pp. 275–91, plus six items 'briefly noted'. The book-reviews average about 700 words, being analytical and briefly critical. The 500-word review of *Domenico Scarlatti*, by Ralph Kirkpatrick (rev. edn. Princeton, NJ, Princeton University Press, 1983) notes that few facts have come to light since the first edition (1953). These are now listed at the end of the book, with minor corrigenda and adjustments to the original text. The main text and illustrations remain unaltered. 'Those wanting a general book on Scarlatti have only Kirkpatrick, for Sheveloff's is for the keyboard specialist.' The review concludes, 'Scarlatti remains an obstinately shadowy figure despite Kirkpatrick's supreme efforts to bring him to life'. Bibliographical details lack full pagination (if any) and ISBNs. Some issues of *Early music* carry letters relating to reviews. The annual index has entries for authors, titles and reviewers of books reviewed.

Brio: journal of the United Kingdom Branch of the International Association of Music Libraries, Archives and Documentation Centres (Editor: Clifford Bartlett, 36 Tudor Road, Godmanchester, Huntingdon, Cambs.) (1964–. 2 p.a. Circulation: 500) carries articles and reviews on all aspects of music. Vol. 21 (1), Spring/Summer 1984 (38 pp.) has 17 book-reviews, signed, without affiliations, on pp. 17–28. The reviews, between 200 and 1,000 words in length, are analytical, with quotations and critical. Richard Traubner's

Operetta: a theatrical history (London, Gollancz, 1984) is given almost unqualified approval: 'Perhaps one day Mr. Traubner might consider giving us the equivalent to the revised edition of Kobbe's "Complete Opera" by bringing his dedicated enthusiasm to updating and enlarging the long out of print "Complete Book of Light Opera", by Mark Lubbock'. Percival Price's *Bells and men* (Oxford University Press, 1983) is welcomed for having 'garnered so much in one place...in clear and vivid English', although a discrepancy is noted in the date of the casting of Big Ben. ISBNs, but not full pagination, are given in the bibliographical details. The cumulative index to vols. 1–12: 1964-75 (1076) has one sequence that includes entries for authors and titles of books reviewed.

Tempo: a quarterly review of modern music (London, Boosey and Hawkes, 1939–. 4 p.a. Circulation: 33,000) is a basic journal on twentieth-century music. No. 151, December 1984 (55 pp.) has 10 reviews in all on pp. 37–53 — of books (5), recordings (1) and first performances (4). The book-reviews, signed, but without affiliations, are between 1,000 and 1,500 words in length, being analytical and critical. The need for *The Britten companion*, edited by Christopher Palmer (London, Faber, 1984) is queried. (The first *Companion* appeared in 1952.) To justify itself, 'this new book should not merely add accounts of works composed since 1952 but should attempt a thorough, fresh look at Britten in the light of all available biographical knowledge. On the whole it does not'. Bibliographical details omit place of publication, pagination and ISBNs. Lively letters concerning reviews are included. Reviews are included in *Music index*.

Popular music (Cambridge University Press, 1981–. Annual) devotes each issue to a particular theme. Vol. 4 ('Performers and audiences') includes two undocumented essay-reviews, 13 lengthy book-reviews, signed, with affiliations, on pp. 312–43, plus 14 'Shorter notices', pp. 344–65, and 'An annotated bibliography of books on popular music published in 1982/3'. The main book-reviews, between 1,200 and 2,500 words in length, are closely evaluative. *Music in the mix: the story of South African popular music*, by Muff Anderson (Johannesburg, Raven, 1981) is given qualified praise. while the author is 'to be congratulated for writing a wide, well-illustrated conspectus of the variety of South African music,...the specific ideological support provided by apartheid doctrine also needs separate place and a more sustained analysis than this book provides'. Bibliographical details lack prices and ISBNs. The detailed contents list compensates to some extent for lack of an index.

References

1. *The new Grove dictionary of music and musicians*. London, Macmillan, 1980, vol. 12, p.850.
2. Samuel, Harold E. 'Musicology and the music library', *Library trends*, vol. 25 (4), p. 833.
3. *The Musical times*, vol. 126 (1707), May 1985, p. 286.
4. *New York review of books*, vol. 28, 28 May 1981, pp. 26–38.
5. *Music and letters*, vol. 62, July/October 1981, pp. 249–60.
6. *The musical times*, March, April, May, June 1981.
7. *Ethnomusicology*, vol. 29 (1), Winter 1985, pp. 138–75; vol. 29 (2), Spring/Summer 1983, pp. 314–51.
8. *Musical opinion*, vol. 106, October 1982, pp. 30–1.
9. *The new Grove dictionary*, vol. 14, p. 420.
10. *TLS*, no. 4211, 16 December 1983, p. 1398.

11. Literature and language

A.J. Walford

Literature

The term 'literary criticism' implies the critical appraisal of belles lettres (poetry, plays, novels and literary essays). George Watson's *The literary critics: a study of English descriptive criticism* traces the course of literary criticism from Dryden to Leavis, i.e. through the leading critics of the time rather than as a steady evolution of doctrine. Personal preference and conviction were certainly involved in F.R. Leavis's admiration for Stuart Mill, George Eliot, Henry James, Conrad and D.H. Lawrence, Ezra Pound and Manley Hopkins.[1] Again, few would wholly approve of Anthony Burgess's *Ninety-nine novels: the best in English since 1939* (London, Allison and Busby, 1984) as a personal choice. Anatole France[2] declared that objective criticism was foreign to his nature; 'the truth is that one never gets outside oneself'. The subjective approach to literary reviewing, while possibly making for more lively reading, has its drawbacks. Today there is no accepted canon but a variety of critical schools, labelled by Watson as the Moralists, the New Critics and the Historians.

T.S. Eliot advises moderation:[3] 'Comparison and analysis are the chief tools of the critic, but they are tools to be handled with care'. Interpretation, he insists, is only legitimate when it is not interpretative at all, 'but merely putting the reader in possession of facts which he would otherwise have missed'. The critic should try to discipline his prejudices and cranks (tastes to which we are all subject) 'and compose his differences with as many of his fellows as possible, in the common pursuit of true judgement'. The ideal literary critic, then, must not only have professional competence in the field under review

— by being himself a writer who has read widely and probably possesses an academic background — but must also be able to offer balanced approval. As Baird[4] has it, his aim should be to state the author's case almost as well as author himself could do. Authors look to being judged by recognised specialists, by their peers, nor do they wish their work to be dismissed in a sentence or two.

The captious tone of some literary reviews is reflected in a *TLS* appraisal[5] of the quarterly *Essays in criticism*, for being less enthusiastic or missionary than it once was. 'The book pages — in which long detailed reviews are given to academic works — are often dull with the sound of sledgehammers missing nuts.' Dorothy Parker was equally dismissive; 'This is not a novel to be lightly tossed aside; it should be flung with great force'. Again, the periodical, *The use of English* notes[6] 'an ill-tempered outburst against Philip Larkin in *The Gadfly* (no. 3)' and concludes, 'Let's have wit, then, which is the sharp end of thought, but not abuse — nor the tedious irony which flogs a dead horse'. Finally, Bateson quotes a Lytton Strachey epigrammatic comment[7] on Dr. Johnson, in his review of the Birkbeck Hill edition of *The lives of the poets:*

> Johnson's aesthetic judgements are almost invariably subtle, or solid, or bold; they have always some good quality to recommend them — except one: they are never right.

Bateson comments[8] that a scholar-critic would never at any time have written as Strachey did: 'Not only are the facts wrong, the contradiction between what is censured is just clever journalism; implicit too in the censure is the vulgar assumption that literature progresses by revolutions...In reality, as a scholar critic soon discovers, a gradual, almost imperceptible evolution is occurring all the time. That is literary history. The rest is propaganda — or self-advertisement'.

One genre of the novel that has not been given the rigorous analysis by critics, reviewers and academics it deserves is the short story.[9] This is in part due to the promiscuous company which it keeps — the romantic magazine as well as the serious novel. The short story is thought to lack profundity because of its brevity, to be a by-product that a novelist turns out in intervals between novels, and associated with the pot-boiler industry in which monetary rewards are uppermost: 'The dilemma of combining entertainment appeal with serious art form remains. Let us hope that a more substantial body of literary criticism will emerge in the next decade that can come to grips with short fiction on its own terms'.[10] It strikes a reassuring note for the future that a reviewer can give the analytical and critical attention to short stories by Douglas Dunn and Ronald Frame as that shown in a recent issue of *Books in Scotland*.[11]

A dictionary of English literature offers ready opportunities for critical analysis, in the detection of omissions, uneven treatment, adequacy of documentation and cross-references, and comparison with other such dictionaries. *The Cambridge guide to English literature*, edited by Michael Stapleton (Cambridge University Press/ Newnes, 1983) was uncritically reviewed in *Library journal* thus:[12]

> This handbook serves as a guide to literature in the English-speaking world...The more than 3100 alphabetically arranged entries provide factual information about authors, major works, prominent characters and literary terms, subjects and periods. Since editor Stapleton feels that 'a guide who never makes a comment makes a dull companion', some entries reflect his own opinions. The handbook is nicely illustrated with a smattering of black-and-white portraits, drawings, and other reproductions. It complements the Oxford Companion and is likely to become another standard reference tool.

The *Cambridge guide*'s treatment is, in fact, uneven. Stapleton makes a feature of providing lengthy digests of novels, plays, and so on (e.g. 2½ columns each on *Vanity fair*, *Huckleberry Finn* and *The ambassadors*, but nothing on the *Fellowship of the ring* and its parts). Yeats and Tennyson are each allotted over 10 pages of text, but entries are lacking on John Wain, Babel, Malmud and Singer (Nobel Prize for Literature, 1977). What is particularly serious is the slighting of comment on literary criticism. 'The critical writings of Coleridge and Arnold are skimped here, and those of T.S. Eliot fare little better, There are no entries for I.A. Richards or F.R. Leavis', observes *British book news* reviewer.[13] Editions of authors' works are cited, but not critical monographs on them. The *BBN* review concludes, 'Serious students of the subject will approach its judgement with caution and its presuppositions with resignation'.

The Oxford history of Hungarian literature, by Lóránt Gigány (Oxford, Clarendon Press, 1984) — the author being lecturer in Hungarian literature at the University of California, Berkeley, 1969–73 — is well reviewed in *The incorporated linguist*.[14] The 25 footnoted chapters contain accounts of many individual works, sometimes with translated extracts. Supporting ⁺he text is an extensive bibliography, two glossaries and a detailed index. 'Also to be welcomed is an account of the work of writers now living outside Hungary, this being a subject unlikely to receive due consideration in histories of literature produced in Hungary in recent years.'

Indexes to reviews

The *Wellesley index to Victorian periodicals, 1824–1900* (University of Toronto Press, 1966–) includes indexes to book-reviews; vols. 1-3 (1966–78) cover 8, 12 and 15 periodicals respectively. General indexes provide keys to book-reviews in twentieth-century literary journals: *Arts and humanities citation index* (Philadelphia, Pa., Institute for Scientific Information, 1978-. 3 p.a.); *Book review index* (Detroit, Mich., Gale, 1965–. 6 p.a., with annual cumulation and for 1969–79); *Humanities index* (New York, H.W. Wilson, 1974–. 4 p.a., cumulated annually); *References sources* (Ann Arbor, Mich., Pierian Press, 1977–. Annual); *An index to book reviews in the humanities* (Williamston, Mich., Thomson, 1960–. Annual); *Current book review citations* (New York, H.W. Wilson, 1976–82) and *Internationale Bibliographie der Rezensionen* (Osnabrück, Dietrich, 1971–. 2 p.a.). *Index to reviews of bibliographical publications* (Boston, Mass., G.K. Hall, 1976–. vol. 1–. (vol. 6: 1981. 1984) covers over 300 journals in English and American literature and language, and so on. For reviews in 'little magazines', see Marion Sader's *Comprehensive index to English-language little magazines, 1890–1970* (Millwood, NY, Kraus-Thomson, 1976, 8 vols.) and B.C. Bloomfield's *An author index to selected British 'Little magazines', 1930–1939* (London, Mansell, 1976).

Reviewing journals

TLS/The Times literary supplement (London, Times Newspapers, Ltd, 1902–. 52 p.a. Circulation: 30,000) is an authoritative review of the international literary scene. No. 4290, 21 June 1985 (pp. 681–708) consists mainly of signed, analytical and critical reviews of 48 books. Reviews range from 600 to 5,000 words. Subject scope is extensive: architecture; bibliography; biography; children's literature; china; economics; fiction; French literature; history; literature; philosophy; Russian history; science; social studies. Details are given of 26 reviewers' affiliations or publications. Barry Menikoff's *Robert Louis Stevenson and 'The beach of Falesá': a study in Victorian publishing, with the original text* (Edinburgh University Press, 1984) concerns the bowdlerized text of Stevenson's novel. 'For reasons he does not explain, Menikoff disdains all conventional textual apparatus. He gives no clear account of the transmission of *Falesá* and its published versions, nor any full description of the manuscript he is transcribing.' Menikoff's informality 'diminishes the scholarly authority of an otherwise usefully regenerated text'. 'Letters' includes authors' reactions to reviews and reviewers' replies. Bibliographical details do not give full pagination or (infuriately) date of publication. The weekly index of books reviewed is cumulated annually and for 1902–39, 1940–80. Current issues of scholarly journals are reviewed at intervals. *TLS* 'Special numbers' (about 20 p.a.) highlight particular subjects (e.g. Reference books, April 1984). Reviews are indexed in the monthly *Times index* (cumulated annually), 1974–.

World literature today: a literary quarterly (Norman, University of Oklahoma Press, 1927–. 4 p.a. Circulation: 2,500), formerly *Books abroad*, aims to keep abreast of foreign literature and interpret it for American readers. Vol. 58 (3), Summer 1984 (pp. 385–483) has 250 reviews, subdivided: French; Spanish, Italian; Other Romance languages; German; Other Germanic languages; Russian; Other Slavic languages; Finno-Ugric and Baltic languages; Greek; Other European and American languages; Africa & West Indies; Near East; Asia and the Pacific; Perspectives on world literature. The signed reviews embrace literature, criticism, fiction, theatre, and so on, and are brief (200–600 words), analytical and critical. The review of *World poetry in English: essays and interviews*, by Syed Amanuddin (New Delhi, Sterling, 1981) has an arresting opening: 'Some of the best writings in English these days are being produced outside England by writers who are not English'. The collection comprises 18 essays and three interviews, all on recent writing from Commonwealth countries, plus the US. Bibliographical details omit ISBNs. The annual index includes a list of reviews (entries asterisked are titles considered by reviewers to be worthy of translation).

London review of books (London, Dept. LRB, 1979–. 24 p.a. Circulation: 15,000) is published with assistance from the Arts Council. Vol. 6 (24) 20 December 1984/24 January 1985, has 21 lengthy reviews (3,000–7,000 words), signed, with notes on contributors. The reviews are analytical, with quotations, and broadly critical. Items reviewed concern autobiography, biography, essays, history, novels and such topical themes as espionage and gardening. Batching of reviews is a feature, and comments are in an easy style. The letters section includes authors' reactions to reviews. Bibliographical data include exact dates of publication. An annual review index is lacking, but the *Book review index* covers *LRB* items.

Modern fiction studies: a critical quarterly (West Lafayette, Ind., Purdue University Department of English, 1955–. 4 p.a. Circulation:

4,000) is devoted to criticism, scholarship and bibliography of American, English and European fiction since about 1880. Vol. 30 (2), Summer 1984 (pp. 173–433) features 'Recent books on modern fiction', pp. 291–432. The 133 reviews are sectionalized: The Americas (59); British and Irish (36); Continental (9); Miscellaneous (29). Batching of analytical, critical and comparative reviews is not unusual (e.g. eight reviews, totalling 3,000 words, on Conan Doyle and Sherlock Holmes books). Reviews normally average 750 words in length. Bibliographical details are confined to author, title, publisher and ja,price. The annual index only states pagination of the review sections of the four quarterly issues, but individual reviews are listed in *Humanities index* and *Internationale Bibliographie der Rezensionen*.

Modern language review (London, Modern Humanities Research Association, c/o King's College, 1905–. 4 p.a. Circulation: 3,000), despite its title, systematically covers European literatures. Vol. 79 (4), October 1984 (pp. xxxv, 769-1008), has 98 reviews, signed, with affiliations, on pp. 877–1008. Seven sections, each with a book-review editor, respectively cover: General; English and American; French; Italian; Hispanic; German, Dutch and Scandinavian; Slavonic and East European literatures. The reviews, closely analytical, with quotations, and critical, are listed and run to between 250 and 2,00 words. One review records 34 lines of omissions and errata. Another review observes that 'cut by half or more, this book could have been enlightening; as it is, it is enervating'. Bibliographical details lacks ISBNs. The annual index, cumulated 10-yearly, has a review section, with author entries.

French studies: a quarterly review (Oxford, Blackwell, for the Society for French Studies, 1947–. 4 p.a. Circulation: 1,900) devotes 50 per cent of its text to listed reviews. Vol. 38 (4), October 1984 (pp. 355–512) carries 80 shortish reviews (150–1,000 words apiece), signed, with locations. Coverage extends to French texts, monographs and bibliographies. Comments are analytical, with quotations, and critical. A volume of *Transactions* and a biography of Benjamin Constant are faulted for lacking indexes; a book of feminist writing in France is challenged for stopping short at the 1950s; an author is advised to seek a wider readership by publishing 'in some of the established journals'; and a monograph is criticized for failing to draw any firm conclusion. Bibliographical details omit full pagination and ISBNs. The annual index has a heading 'Review', the author entries adding reviewers' names.

Books in Scotland (Edinburgh, Ramsay Head Press, 1976–. 4 p.a.

Circulation: 3,000), a valuable source for Scottish writing, has Scottish Arts Council financial aid. No. 17, Winter/Spring 1985 (40 pp.), has 76 book-reviews (including 'Recent fiction') on pp. 8–38, plus two pages of 'Books in brief'. The signed reviews, analytical and critical, are grouped under headings and run on between 250 and 1,200 words in length. *The literature of Scotland*, by Roderick Watson (London, Macmillan, 1984) is acclaimed as the first book to give adequate space to writing in Gaelic as well as Scots and English. Some reservations (e.g. oversimplification of Scott's attitude to the Union of 1801) do not diminish the reviewer's admiration of Watson's work. *The languages of Britain*, by Glanville Price (London, Edward Arnold, 1984) has, states the reviewer, been overtaken by events, but this does not detract from its overall value as scholarly, and as showing the writer's interest and concern for the threatened tongues. Bibliographical details omit pagination and ISBNs.

Zeitschrift für romanische Philologie (Tübingen, Niemeyer, 1877–. 6 p.a.) is a scholarly journal devoted to Romance literatures and languages. Vol. 100 (5/6), 1984 (pp. 513–791) has 74 reviews, signed, with locations, and mostly in German, on pp. 527–689. The six main sections comprise: Collected works (13); Transactions of congresses (16); Festschriften (12); Commemorative works (4); Serials (19); Bibliographies (10). Short notices and literature guides follow on pp. 689–787. Longer reviews, averaging 1,000 words, are analytical and critical. *Arthurian literature II* edited by Richard Barber (Cambridge, D.S. Brewer, 1982) contains articles of varying importance for the study of medieval Arthurian literature. One paper, on Gildas' *De excidio Britanniae*, disposes once and for all of the problems raised by Geoffrey of Monmouth's debt to Gildas. Another contribution is marred by excessive misprints in the texts cited. The collection 'epitomises what is best in Arthurian scholarship today'. Bibliographical details omit prices and ISBNs. The annual index cumulates reviews into the sections provided.

Canadian literature/Littérature canadienne: a quarterly of criticism and review (Vancouver, University of British Columbia, 1959–. 4 p.a. Circulation: 2,300) is a leading scholarly literary journal. No. 104, Spring 1985 (187 pp.) has 39 'Books in review', signed, with affiliations, on pp. 109–75. Reviews, averaging 1,200 words, are analytical, with quotations, critical and comparative (thanks to batching). Comments on *The Oxford companion to Candian literature*, edited by Wm. Toye (Oxford University Press, 1983) begins, 'What is an *Oxford companion* and what should we expect of it?' We expect it to be 'a tool, a resource text where one expects concise, accurate information', and the editor has done a creditable job, on the whole. Entries for regional, category, children's literature, and so on, are certainly helpful. This said, authors are omitted, and why are manuscript sources identified for some and not others? Also, 'serious failures of tone and the biased generalizations have eluded editorial vigilance'. However, shortcomings aside, the reviewer feels pride and satisfaction regarding the volume. Bibliographical details lack place of publication, pagination and ISBNs. Reviews are listed per issue only, but are indexed in *Combined retrospective index to periodicals in the humanities*, 1802–1974, *Humanities index*, and so on.

The literary review, incorporating *Quarto* (London, Literary Review Quarto, Ltd, 1979–. 12 p.a. Circulation: 7,000) was founded 'to fill a gap left by the absence of *The Times Literary Supplement* during the prolonged Times strike...and now with an identity of its own'. No. 75 September 1984 (48 pp.) carries 24 analytical reviews (signed, with 'Notes on some contributors') mainly of fiction, essays, poetry, biography, autobiography and letters. Appended is 'Pick of the paperbacks' (19 titles). The reviews range from 750 to 2,500 words in length. Presentation is attractive and makes use of illustrations, headings, batching for contrast, and the whole is entertainingly written. Reviewers include authors, academics, newspaper and magazine editors and freelance contributors. Bibliographical details omit full pagination and ISBNs.

German quarterly (Cherry Hill, NJ, American Association of Teachers of German, 1928–. 4 p.a. Circulation: 9,000) concerns German literature, literary texts and the teaching of German. Vol. 56 (4), November 1983 (pp. 539–727), has 66 book-reviews, signed, with affiliations, on pp. 624–714. There are four main sections: Literary theory and collections (9); Older literature (9); Modern literature (47); Intellectual and social history (1). Reviews, many in German and between 300 and 1,500 words in length, are closely analytical, with quotations and critical. *Marcel Proust und Deutschland: eine Bibliographie*, by Georg Pistorius (Heidelberg, Winter, 1981) is faulted for its omissions (mentioned in detail) but finally assessed as 'a generally valuable contribution'. A monograph on Arthur Schnitzler is praised for breaking new ground. Bibliographical details omit pagination, prices and ISBNs. The annual index has sections for 'Book reviews' (under authors) and reviewers' names.

The Slavonic and East European review (London, Modern Humanities Research Association, for the School of Slavonic and East European Studies, University of London, 1922–. 4 p.a. Circulation: 1,300) is interdisciplinary and covers the languages, literatures and history of all countries in the region. Vol. 62 (4), October 1984 (pp. 481–640) contains 62 book-reviews, listed and signed, with locations, and between 600 and 1,500 words in length. Comments are analytical and critical, faulting a bibliography for stopping at 1958, and a monograph for being 'cobbled up rather than clearly thought out'. On the other hand, a work is complimented for its engaging style, and another, as 'a welcome addition to the literature'. Bibliographical details omit prices and ISBNs. The annual index has a book-review section that includes review-articles and shorter notices.

The review of English studies: a quarterly journal of English literature and the English language (Oxford, Clarendon Press, 1925. 4 p.a. Circulation: 2,000) emphasizes historical scholarship rather than criticism, being directed at university teachers and students. New series, vol. 35 (140), November 1984 (pp. 449–609), has 58 listed and signed reviews on pp. 517–93, plus two short notices. Comments average 700 words, two books being sometimes taken together. The prose style of a monograph on William Faulkner is criticized for its 'impenetrability'; another book, on T.S. Eliot, for lacking quicker insight and for a style 'burdened with italics'. Bibliographical details omit ISBNs. The annual index enters reviewed books under authors and includes a list of reviewers.

Revue d'histoire littéraire de la France (Paris, Colin, 1894–. 6 p.a. Circulation: 2,500) covers all periods of French literature. Vol. 85 (2) March/April 1985 (pp. 195–382), contains 37 signed reviews, all in French, on pp. 283–334. The reviews (averaging 1,000 words) are analytical, with quotations, and critical. *Le théâtre religieux en France*, by Michel Liouvre (Paris, Presses Universitaires de France, 1983) is commended as filling a gap in a relatively neglected field, but it pays insufficient attention to social and historical conditions influencing the stage at the time. Bibliographical details omit prices and ISBNs. Each issue of the *Revue* lists its reviews. Reviews are indexed in *Internationale Bibliographie der Rezensionen*.

Bulletin of the School of Oriental and African Studies (London, the School, University of London, 1917–. 3 p.a.) is an interdisciplinary journal, with special reference to languages, history and culture. Vol. 47 (3), 1984 (pp. 425–618), has 58 signed reviews (450–3,000 words) on pp. 549–609. Reviews are analytical, with quotations, and generally favourable, while critical of minor blemishes. Readership is sometimes indicated. Seventeen short notices follow (pp. 609–15). Bibliographical details omit ISBNs. Reviews are indexed in *Internationale Bibliographie der Rezensionen*.

Études anglaises: Grande Bretagne. États Unis (Paris, Didier, 1946–. 4 p.a. Circulation: 1,500), sponsored by Centre National de la Recherche Scientifique, is largely concerned with British and American language and literatures. Vol. 38 (1), January/March 1985 (126 pp.), has 45 book-reviews, signed, some with affiliations, (pp. 72–108). Reviews, mostly in French, average 500 words and are briefly analytical and critical. *Politics and the novel in Africa*, by Abderrahmane Arab (Algiers, Office des Publications Universitaires, 1982) covers both English- and French-speaking Africa, but is restricted to the period 1950–70. The book reveals affinities between Sub-Saharan and Maghreb writers, in a well-written study. It is only a pity, states the reviewer, that the 1970s could not have been covered. Following the main reviews are 21 book-notices. Bibliographical details omit ISBNs. The annual index has a reviews section.

British journal for eighteenth-century studies: the offical journal of the British Society for Eighteenth-Century Studies (Liverpool, the Society, c/o Department of French, Liverpool University, 1978–. 4 p.a.) deals with history, art, literature and philosophy in the Age of Enlightenment. Vol. 8 (10), Spring 1985 (iii, 127 p.) has 30 book-reviews, signed, with affiliations, on pp. 97–124. Reviews vary in length from 350 to 2,000 words and are analytical and critical. the 350-word review of *Diderot*, by Peter France (Oxford University Press, 1983) is commended as being 'comprehensive, clear and judicious'. If the book has a fault, it is that the author's very fluency and logical unfolding of complex ideas 'renders Diderot's views almost too intelligble and coherent and suggest that his works make easier reading than is the case'. One item is added to the select bibliography. Bibliographical details lack ISBNs. Six shorter notices, initialled, follow the main reviews. There is no general index, but review-articles and reviews are listed per issue.

Nineteenth-century fiction (Berkeley, Calif., University of California Press, 1945–. 4 p.a. Circulation: 2,500), formerly *The Trollopian*, deals with both British and American novels. Vol. 39 (1), March 1985 (pp. 379–581), has eight lengthy reviews on pp. 459–85, plus 'Recent books. American fiction' (running commentary) and 28 brief notices. The major reviews average 2,000 words, signed, with affiliations. Comments are analytical and closely critical. The review of Karen B. Mann's *The language that makes George Eliot's fiction* (Baltimore, Md., John Hopkins Press, 1983) begins cautiously: 'Karen Mann sets out to defend Eliot's style and Mann's book certainly adds something to our knowledge and perception'. But it is inadequate as a study of Eliot's fiction; 'it is not the book that answers the most important questions we can ask about Eliot's figurative language'. Bibliographical details omit ISBNs. The annual index has a 'Book review' section under authors, plus cross-references from reviewers' names.

Notes and queries, for readers and writers, collectors and librarians (London, Oxford University Press, 1849–. 4 p.a.) is 'devoted principally to English language and literature, lexicography, history and scholarly antiquarianism'. New series vol. 32 (2), June 1985 (pp. 145-258)m has 38 listed and signed reviews, with about 88 words apiece. *Restoration and eighteenth-century prose (excluding drama and the novel* (London, Macmillan, 1983) is the result of redistribution of 'Great writers of the English language' series, edited by James Vinson. For each writer it provides brief biographical data, a selection of bibliographies (if any) and of secondary criticism, and a signed critical essay on the author's work, It scores in clarity of layout and matter not given in standard bibliographies. Where it fails is in frequently neglecting to mention the edition or the most recent and best edition. Bibliographical details omit ISBNs. The annual index has a 'Reviews' heading.

Renaissance quarterly (New York, The Renaissance Society of America, 1948–. 4 p.a. Circulation: 3,725). Vol. 37 (3), Autumn 1984 (pp. 351–520), has 29 book-reviews, signed, with affiliations, on pp. 421–504. Reviews (800–1,500 words) are analytical, with quotations, and critical. One monograph is faulted for reliance on printed editions and secondary sources rather than manuscript material; another is awarded 'high marks for accuracy'; a third is approved for its beautiful and copious illustrations 'helpfully arranged within the text'. Bibliographical details lack ISBNs. The annual index has entries for both authors and reviewers of items reviewed.

MLN/Modern language notes (Baltimore, Md., Johns Hopkins University Press, 1888–. 5 p.a. Circulation: 5,000) devotes each issue to one language and its literature (e.g. Italian, Spanish, French, German). Vol. 100 (3) April 1985 (pp. 461–714), is a 'German issue', with 22 listed and signed reviews, with affiliations, on pp. 665–704. There is a book-review editor, and reviews are analytical and critical. *German baroque literature: the European perspective*, edited by Gerhart Hoffmeister (New York, Ungar, 1983), consists of 20 essays by American, Canadian and British scholars. The collection, designed for both advanced researcher and student, well meets its aim, states the reviewer. The essays are complementary, providing a balanced view: 'This anthology deserves to become a standard reference work because of its breadth and the authors' ability to present lucid and incisive perspectives on the complexities of German baroque literature'. Bibliographical details lack prices, full pagination and ISBNs. The annual index has sections for review-articles, and reviews.

Eighteenth-century studies (Berkeley, Calif., University of California Press, 1967–. 4 p.a. Circulation: 3,000) is a scholarly interdisciplinary journal. Vol. 18 (1), Fall 1984 (146 pp.), carries lengthy reviews (2,000–3,000 words) on pp. 76–144. The reviews, signed, with affiliations and notes on contributors (including reviewers) are closely analytical, providing quotations and footnotes. There is a book-review editor and nearly all the reviewers are American. Items include French and German monographs and concern history and politics, as well as literature. Bibliographical details lack full pagination and ISBNs. Reviews are listed only on the quarterly contents pages, but they are indexed in *Humanities index* and *Internationale Bibliographie der Rezensionen*.

American literature; a journal of literary history, criticism, and bibliography (Durham, NC, Duke University Press, with co-operation of the American Literature Section of the Modern Language Association, 1929–. 4 p.a. Circulation: 4,390) is an authoritative, scholarly periodical in its field. Vol. 56 (3), October 1984 (pp. 311–478), contains 19 listed book-reviews, signed, with affiliations, on pp. 427–53. The reviews (500–1,000 words) are analytical, with quotations, and critical, indicating readership. Two works on Saul Bellow are helpfully contrasted, and a book on Hemingway's achievement is faulted for failing to see it 'within a broader social, historical, literary or historical context'. Bibliographical details give full pagination but omit ISBNs, 'Brief mention' (pp. 454–60) gives short annotations on some 90 further items. The annual index, cumulated for vols. 1–30, lists books reviewed under authors and titles, citing reviewers' names.

Hispanic review (Philadelphia, Pa., University of Pennsylvania, 1933–. 4 p.a. Circulation: 1,500) is devoted to research in the Hispanic languages and literatures. Vol. 53 (1), Winter 1985 (125 pp.), has 17 book-reviews, signed, with affiliations, on pp. 91–119. The reviews average 2,000 words in length, and are analytical and critical. *Ideologia y teatro en España, 1890–1900*, by Jesús Rubio Jimenez (Zaragoza, Portico, 1983), is considered to break new ground by offering a comparative study of the period. 'A glance at the seven chapter titles of the book gives one an idea of the complexity that has often escaped literary historians.' Bibliographical details lack prices, full pagination and ISBNs. The annual index has a reviews section.

Revue de littérature comparée (Paris, Didier, 1921–. 4 p.a.) is a scholarly journal on comparative literature. Vol. 58 (232), October/December 1984 (pp. 389–502), has 14 book-reviews on pp. 477–97. Reviews are signed, average 900 words and may be in the native language of the reviewer. Treatment is analytical and critical. *Sweden and European drama, 1772–1796: a survey of translations and adaptations*, by Marie Skuncke (Stockholm, Acta Universitatis Upsaliensis: Historia literarum 10, 1981) is thought to promise more than it delivers. The 'Swedish' of the title is virtually 'Stockholm'; 'European' is basically 'French' and 'English'; and 'drama' excludes opera and opéra comique: 'Despite these quite severe self-denying ordnances...the painstaking and controlled collection...of this extensive material, with its particularly valuable and informative appendices, constitute the chief merit of the book'. Bibliographical details lack prices, full pagination and ISBNs. The annual index has author entries for books reviewed, plus cross-references from reviewers' names.

Scandinavica: an international journal of Scandinavian studies (London, Academic Press, 1962–. 2 p.a.) is published with the support of Danish, Norwegian and Swedish learned bodies, plus the British Academy. Vol. 24 (1), May 1985 (125 pp.), has a review-article and 22 book-reviews, signed, with affiliations, on pp. 65–105. The reviews average about 1,500 words and are analytical and critical. *Feud in the Icelandic sagas*, by Jesse L. Byock (Berkeley, Calif., University of California Press, 1983) is given an introductory background: 'Feud is a key concept of this literature, providing a traditional structure for the narrative. It is also closely related to the social and legal organisation of medieval Iceland'. The reviewer concludes, 'To me this seems a sound and convincingly motivated statement of the unique character of the Icelandic saga'. Bibliographical details lack prices, full pagination and ISBNs. There is no annual index, but each issue lists reviews, and reviews are indexed in *Internationale Bibliographie der Rezensionen*.

AEB/Analytical and enumerative bibliography (De Kalb, Ill., Bibliographical Society of Northern Illinois, 1977–. 4 p.a. Circulation: 250) devotes 50 per cent of its scholarly pages to reviews. Vol. 6 (4), 1982 (pp. 207–89), contains 12 lengthy reviews (1,750–3,000 words apiece), on pp. 247–87, signed, and with affiliations. Reviews are of bibliographies of literary criticism, individual author bibliographies and works on manuscripts. There is a book-review editor and an index-of-reviews associate editor. Reviews are closely analytical and critical, some with quotations or appended notes. They query the arrangement of one bibliography, fault the cumbersome cross-reference systems of another, and the deficiences in final proofing and editing of a third work. Bibliographical details include full pagination, but omit a mention of illustrations, facsimiles and ISBNs.

Comparative literature (Eugene, University of Oregon, 1947–. 4 p.a. Circulation: 3,500) takes a more traditional line than *Comparative literature studies* (Urbana, Ill., University of Illinois Press, 1963–. 4 p.a.), carries more reviews and has an annual index. Vol. 37 (1), Winter 1985 (92 pp.), has 10 listed book-reviews on pp. 67–96. Reviews, averaging about 1,200 words, are analytical and critical. *Cervantes and the humanist vision: a study of four 'Exemplary' novels* (Princeton, NJ, Princeton University Press, 1984) is praised for establishing the cultural context, both 'the social structure in which Cervantes's characters move and the religious beliefs and mythology that sustain them'. The reviewer finds that Spanish is translated, but German and Latin (mostly in the notes) are not; also, that while 'genre' is well discussed, it is not indexed. 'However, it is a superbly controlled and subtle study that makes many other writings on Cervantes look thin, or arbitrary, or merely ingenious.' Bibliographical details omit prices and ISBNs. The annual index has sections for reviews and review-articles.

Poetry review: the journal of the Poetry Society (London, the Society, 1909–. 4 p.a. Circulation: 3,000) aims to present and assess the best in contemporary poetry. Vol. 75 (1), April 1985 (63 pp.), has nine signed reviews (500–1,100 words). The reviews are analytical, with numerous quotations from poems, and critical. *The non-aligned storyteller*, by Thomas McCarthy (London, Anvil Press Poetry, 1984), comprising both political and love poems, is praised for extending still further 'the wide variety of this Irish poet's range...It is writing of a kind that English poetry can least afford to ignore'. The 'Letters' section includes a reviewer's objection to unauthorized additions to his review. Bibliographical details give author, title and price only. Reviews are listed in each issue, but an annual index is lacking.

Medium Aevum (Oxford, Blackwell, for the Society for the Study of Medieval Languages and Literature, 1952–. 2 p.a. Circulation: 1,100) is the Society's official organ. Vol. 54 (1), 1985 (157 pp.), has 15 book-reviews on pp. 132–51, averaging 600 words each. The reviews, signed, with locations, are analytical and critical. *Late Latin and early Romance in Spain and Carolingian France*, by Roger Wright (Liverpool, ARCA Classical and Medieval Texts. Papers and monographs, 8. 1982) is introduced thus: 'Mr. Wright's primary concern is to refute the opinion that alongside the developing Romance vernaculars spoken Latin survived among the more educated with no break in continuity'. While the author is at his best and most ingeni÷ ous on phonetics, 'on the more abstract, morphological–syntactical– lexical side his touch seems sometimes less sure'. Notes on 25 'Books received' follow. Bibliographical details omit ISBNs. The annual index has a 'Reviews' section.

Italian studies: an annual review (London, Society for Italian Studies, c/o Department of Italian, University College, 1937–. Annual) devotes 30 per cent of its space to closely analytical and critical reviews. Vol. 39, 1984 (153 pp.), has two review-articles and 22 listed and signed reviews. Italian literature, art, history, language dictionaries and linguistics are the main subjects covered. Comments are largely favourable, paying tribute, in one case, to a 'clear and unencumbered prose'; in another, to a 'high standard of production'; and in a third, to its excellent index. Bibliographical details omit ISBNs. The annual index, cumulated for vols. 1–15, 16–30, 1937– 75, has an entry 'Reviews', with page numbers only.

English: the journal of the English Association (Oxford University Press, 1935–. 4 p.a.) 'aims to provide the knowledge and appreciation of English language and literature'. Vol. 33 (147), Autumn 1984 (pp. 197–290) carries five lengthy book-reviews (2,500–6,000 words) on pp. 247–74. Reviews are listed, headed and signed, being closely analytical, with quotations, and critical. Double reviews (e.g. of George Orwell's *1984*) give opportunity for comparison. The reviewer of *The ambassadors,* by Alan W. Bellringer (London, Allen and Unwin, 1984 — a close analysis, with profuse quotations from Henry James's novel) — asks: why was the work undertaken? 'The very scope, length and comparative simplicity of Dr. Bellringer's book makes it a possible rival to James's own. One hopes such a fear is groundless.' Bibliographical details lack pagination and ISBNs. Reviews are indexed in *Combined retrospective index to book reviews in humanities journals 1802–1974, Arts and humanities citation index,* and *Internationale Bibliographie der Rezensionen.*

Language

Many of the books reviewed in the leading scholarly journals in this field concern linguistics, language dictionaries, grammars and courses, and edited texts. The reviewers are normally academics, language teachers and translators.

The reviewing and selection of foreign-language dictionaries often raise problems. The main points to be considered can be enumerated:[15]

1. Authority of issuing body; reputation of publisher.
2. Aim, as stated by publisher and compiler(s). How far are these met in practice? Are types of intended user stated?
3. Scope. If the dictionary is a technical one, how far are common words with non-technical meanings included? Are roots and derivatives, colloquialisms and country variants covered? How many headwords are there, assuming sub-entries are not counted? How detailed are entries? (Mini-dictionaries usually have only cheapness and portability to recommend them; they are less legible, have a more restricted vocabulary and tend to give one equivalent or a string of undifferentiated equivalents. Polyglot dictionaries, because of the need for compression, are also prone to this weakness.)
4. Arrangement, balance. Is the dictionary primarily for home-country consumption?
5. Consistency (e.g.) a qualifying adjective and its noun should be entered under either adjective or noun (or both) — not varied.
6. Up-to-dateness (particularly applicable to technical dictionaries); in line with current official rulings in orthography. Is a so-called later 'edition' a substantial, reset revision, or the previous edition plus a small (often overlooked) supplement, or merely a reprint?
7. Aids to pronunciation: use of international phonetic symbols (IPA): indication of stress and syllabification; noting of quality of vowels and sibilants.
8. Indication of gender (omitted in many technical dictionaries), genitive singular and/or nominative plural of nouns, basic verb forms, and so on.
9. Appendices: verb and other tables; abbreviations and proper names; conversion tables of weights and measures.
10. Illustrations, especially if keyed parts are shown.
11. Legibility and ease of reference (e.g. use of bold and italic type); avoidance of too many symbols and other abbreviations. Whiteness and opaqueness of paper; stoutness of binding; portability.
12. Price.

The following 150-word review[16] of *Cassell's Colloquial German*, by B. Anderson and M. North (rev. edn. London, Cassell, 1980) categorizes the book as for 'A' level students and beyond, plus adults. It gives evaluation first, then analysis. Not a word is wasted:

Formerly *Beyond the Dictionary in German*. A handbook for 'those who travel to Germany on business or for pleasure and those who study the language for its own sake'. A knowledge of basic German grammar is assumed, as is a fairly advanced vocabularly. The book aims 'to guard against misinterpretations' and to give some information on current usage. It contains: miscellaneous notes on pronunciation, contemporary trends, etc.; a German–English vocabulary of over 1,000 words, with detailed explanations, specialised vocabularies, e.g. Travelling, Motoring, Journalese, False Friends, Food, Courtesy etc; English-German cross-reference index as a guide to the use of the main section.

The 600-word review of *Norsk–Engelsk ordbog*, edited by Einar Haugen (3rd edn. Bergen, Universitetsforlaget, 1984) in *The incorporated linguist*,[17] is commendably analytical, critical, informative and comparative. As a medium-sized dictionary, 'Haugen' was the first to give prominence to both *Bokmål* (book language) and *Nynorsk* (new Norwegian), we are told. This third edition is not markedly different from the first edition of 1965; only about 1,500 new words have been added. 'Haugen' is considered 'more useful to the translator into English than, for instance, W. Kirkeby's admirable Norsk–Engelsk ordbog' (4th fully rev.edn.Oslo, Gyldendal, 1978). The latter, limited to *Bokmål*, also lacks Haugen's illustrative quotations, but is superior in providing data on titles of public bodies.   'Meanwhile, Haugen is indispensable', being intended in this edition (the result of work carried out at the universities of Wisconsin and Harvard) primarily as a book for the learning of Norwegian by American students.

Indexes to reviews

Bibliographie linguistique de l'année, 1939/47–. (Utrecht and Antwerp, Spectrum, 1949–. Annual) and two abstracting services — *LLBA/Language and language behaviour abstracts*, 1967– (San Diego, Calif., Sociological Abstracts, Inc., 1967–. 4 p.a.) and *Language teaching*, 1908– (Cambridge University Press, 1908–. 4 p.a.) — cite reviews. *Reviews of use to teachers of modern languages*, by C. Asher and others (University of Leeds, School of Education, 1979) indexed all reviews appearing in *Audio-visual language journal* (now *British journal of language teaching*), *Modern languages*, 1972 to September 1978, and *Modern languages in Scotland*, 1973 to 1978.

More general indexing sources include: *Arts and humanities citation index* (Philadelphia, Pa., Institute for Scientific Information, 1978–. 3 p.a.), *Reference sources* (Ann Arbor, Mich., Pierian Press, 1977–. Annual), *Book review index* (Detroit, Mich., Gale, 1963–. 6 p.a., cumulated annually), *Book review digest* (New York, H.W. Wilson, 1905–. 10 p.a., with quarterly and annual cumulations), *Humanities index* (H.W. Wilson, 1974–. 10 p.a., also with quarterly and annual cumulations), *Combined retrospective index to book reviews in humanities journals 1802–1974* (Woodbridge, Conn., RP/ Research Publications, Inc., 1982–84, 9 vols.) and *Internationale Bibliographie der Rezensionen* (Osnabrück, Dietrich, 1971–. 2 p.a.)

Reviewing journals

The modern language journal (Madison, University of Wisconsin Press, 1916–. 4 p.a. Circulation: 10,000) is 'devoted primarily to methods, pedagogical research, and topics of professional interest to all language teachers', including second-language teaching. Vol. 68 (3), Autumn 1984 (pp. 201–313), has 60 book reviews, signed, with affiliations, on pp. 268–313, in 13 sections: Pedagogy; Bilingual; Bulgarian; Chinese; Czech; French; German; Greek; Hebrew; Italian; Linguistics; Rumanian; Spanish. The reviews (500–1,000 words each) are sometimes judged for their suitability for US programmes. *A reference grammar of modern French*, by A. Judge and F.G. Healey (London, Edward Arnold, 1983) welcomed as a new reference tool for teachers rather than for their classes, is queried for 'the amount of linguistic knowledge that is presupposed, and the logical organization of the material presented'. Bibliographical details omit ISBNs. The annual index has sections for 'Reviewers and titles reviewed' and 'Authors and editors of books reviewed'.

Anglia: Zeitschrift für englische Philologie (Tübingen, Niemeyer, 1878–. 4 p.a. Circulation: 1,250) is devoted to the study of the English language and of English and American literature. Vol. 103 (1/ 2), 1985 (270 pp.), has 44 listed and signed book-reviews, with affiliations, on pp. 109–261. The reviews (800–2,000 words apiece) are analytical and closely critical; most of them are in German. *Preverbal adverbs and auxiliaries: a study of word order change*, by Sven Jacobson (Stockholm, Almqvist and Wiksell 1983) aims to add a historical dimension to his previous systematic research, but is criticized for overrating the validity of his samples. 'It deepens our understanding of linguistic change in this field in various respects, while raising a number of empirical and theoretical questions'. Bibliographical details omit ISBNs. The annual index of books reviewed is listed under author–title, with reviewers' names added.

Language monthly: the international journal for the language professions (Nottingham, Praetorius Ltd, 1983–. 12 p.a. Circulation: 1,200) reports activities and developments in language teaching, translation and interpreting. No. 10, July 1984 (20pp.), contains eight headed and signed reviews (60–300 words each), as well as a 1,500-word essay, 'Medical dictionaries: a personal choice' and a full-page review of *Cambridge–Eichborn German dictionary: English–German* (Cambridge University University Press, 1983, vol. 1). One book is criticized for paying insufficient attention to language organizations in the UK; another, a dictionary, for a lack of a source list or bibliography; a third, for the demands it makes of pupils in Book 4 of a graded French course. Pagination and ISBNs of items reviewed are omitted. *The incorporated linguist*'s 'Some recent library accessions' spells out much of the contents, including titles of books reviewed, of each issue of *Language monthly.*

Archiv für das Studium der neueren Sprachen und Literaturen (Berlin, Erich Schmidt, 1846–. 2 p.a.) is mainly concerned with Teutonic and Romance languages and literatures. Vol. 221 (240pp.) has 42 listed reviews, signed, with locations, on pp. 145–237. The reviews, analytical and critical, are mostly in German and average about 1,500 words in length. The four sections are: General (2); Germanic and German (3); English and American (19); Romance (18). *Shakespeare's works and Elizabethan pronunciation*, by Fausto Cercignani (Oxford, Clarendon Press, 1981) accepts the view that only standard English is worth describing and that the best guides to its development are the grammarians of the sixteenth and seventeenth centuries. This fails to indicate the different levels of speech either among Shakespeare's characters or within an individual speaker. 'The investigations of the last fifteen years by sociologists have evidently had no influence upon Cercignani's thinking.' The result is an old-fashioned book 'not likely to be read by literary critics or to have much impact upon historical linguists'. Bibliographical details lack full pagination and ISBNs. Indexes are half-yearly. Reviews are also indexed in *Internationale Bibliographie der Rezensionen.*

Modern languages: journal of the Modern Language Association (London, the Association, 1919–. 4 p.a. Circulation: 3,400) covers language teaching at all levels in the UK. Vol. 65 (1), March 1985 (72pp.), has a section, 'Recent books and courses' on pp. 67–72 — 15 reviews, signed, with locations. A cluster of four French texts is included. The analytical and critical reviews average about 450 words. The 1,000-word appraisal of *A concise Spanish grammar*, by R.N. de Leathes (London, Murray, 1984) identifies the book as a reference grammar of written Spanish. The item is recommended as 'an attraction for many teachers, who will see it as a helpful reference book for the learner who has progressed beyond course books. For the Sixth-Former, or beginner in higher education, it can be a useful aid'. Bibliographical details omit ISBNs.

Les Langues modernes: bulletin de l'Association des Professeurs de Langues Vivantes (Paris, the Association, 1906–. 6 p.a. Circulation: 8,000) covers the main Western European and Middle East languages. Vol. 79 (2), 1985 (112p.), has nine reviews ('Bibliographies'), signed, and sometimes with affiliations, on pp. 83–101. Reviews average about 900 words in length and are analytical and critical. *Les noirs américains d'aujourd'hui*, by Sophie Body-Gendrot (Paris, Colin, 1984) reviewed in 700 words, is considered to offer no new approach, but it does provide recent figures and has a good supporting bibliography, a 'Chronologie de l'histoire afro-américaine' and a helpful index, showing the advances made in research since Michel Fabre's *Les noirs américains* (1970). Bibliographical details lack place of publication, prices and ISBNs. Reviews are not indexed.

The incorporated linguist: journal of the Institute of Linguists (London, the Institute, 1962–. 4 p.a. Circulation: 6,000) is addressed to professional linguists, translators, interpreters, teachers, librarians and information officers. Vol. 2 (4), Autumn 1984 (pp. 209–96), has nine longer reviews (350–700 words in length) signed, but without affiliations. The reviews are analytical, with quotations, and critical, noting readership. *Linguistics today*, by Keith Brown (London, Fontana, 1984), is criticized for a title that promises more than the text delivers: it is confined to a study of syntax. The author does not always cite his sources in the text, and the final five-page 'Further reading' would have been better distributed under chapters concerned. Bibliographical details sometimes include ISBNs. 'Some recent library accessions' (pp. 257–66) has mini-reviews of 27 books and recent periodical issues. The annual index includes reviewers; the subject-index has a heading 'Book reviews'.

Language: journal of the Linguistic Society of America (Baltimore, Md., the Society, 1925–. 4 p.a. Circulation: 6,000) is worldwide in scope. Vol. 61 (1), March 1985 (258 pp.), has 11 major reviews, signed, with affiliations, on pp. 175–211, plus appended references and date of receipt of review. These reviews are closely analytical, with quotations, critical and comparative, averaging 1,500 words each. *Perspectives on historical linguistics: a collection of essays*, edited by Winifred P. Lehmann and Yakob Maikel (Amsterdam, Benjamins, 1982) is compared by the reviewer with its predecessor by the same authors (1968) — a classic of historical linguistics: 'This volume offers several valuable contributions. Even if it cannot match the status of L & M 1968, it can hold its own in comparison with most of the recent collections on historical linguistics'. Forty-eight book notices follow the longer reviews and are signed, with affiliations, averaging 750 words. Bibliographical details lack only ISBNs. The annual index comprises an author-index (authors and reviewers) and a title-index (including books reviewed).

Journal of linguistics (Cambridge University Press, for the Linguistics Association of Great Britain, 1965–. 2 p.a. Circulation: 2,000) is a scholarly periodical on all branches of linguistics, including phonetics. Vol. 20 (2), September 1984 (pp. 205–425), has a review-article and 10 lengthy reviews, signed, with affiliations, on pp. 361–412. The reviews average 2,500 words apiece, are closely analytical and critical, and carry references. *Understanding language: towards a post-Chomskyan linguistics,* by Terence Moore and Christine Carling (London, Macmillan, 1982) is found to be 'far less radical both in theory and practice than many of Chomsky's critics. The index is very sparse and the range of references is limited. There are also a fair number of errors, many of which look like the result of computer rather than native speaker performance'. Bibliographical details lack only ISBNs. The annual index has sections 'Review-articles' and 'Reviews, shorter notices and brief mentions'.

References

1. Watson, George. *The literary critics,* 2nd edn. London, Woburn Press, 1973, p. 205.
2. France, Anatole. *La vie littéraire.* Paris, Calmann-Lévy, 1888, p. iv.
3. Eliot, T.S. *Selected prose.* Harmondsworth, Middlesex, Penguin Books, 1953, pp. 18–20.
4. Baird, A.B. 'What we expect of a review', *The quarterly journal of speech,* vol. 37, 1951, pp. 81–6.
5. *TLS* no. 4198, 16 September 1983, p. 989.
6. *The use of English,* vol. 36 (3), Summer 1983, pp. 67–8.
7. Strachey, Lytton. *Books and characters.* London, Chatto and Windus, 1922, p. 68.
8. Bateson, Frederick. *The scholar critic.* London, Routledge and Kegan Paul, 1972, p. 183.
9. Caless, Bryn. 'The short story: state of the art 1980–85', *British book news,* July 1985, p. 392.
10. *Ibid,* p. 393.
11. *Books in Scotland,* no. 18, Summer 1985, pp. 7–8.
12. *Library journal,* vol. 108 (19), 1 November 1983, p. 2073
13. *British book news,* August 1983, p. 509.
14. *The incorporated linguist,* vol. 23 (4), Autumn 1984, p. 255.
15. Walford, A.J., and Screen, J.E.O. (eds.) *A guide to foreign language courses and dictionaries.* 3rd edn. London, Library association, 1977, pp. 9–10.

16. Brown, E.W. (comp. and ed.) *Teaching materials for German: supplementary materials*. London, Centre for Information on Language Teaching and Research, 1983, p. 2.
17. *The incorporated linguist*, vol. 23 (4), Autumn 1984, p. 256.

12. History, archaeology and geography

A.J. Walford

History

The 1970s saw a remarkable increase in the number and size of learned journals devoted to history and archaeology,[1] encouraging researchers to explore new and broader areas of historical experience; for example, the release of primary source material, following application of the thirty years' rule. The study of history is interdisciplinary, spanning social and political spheres, regional and local as well as national areas, periods, persons and events. Bibliographical control of these diverse publication-outlets comprises not only bibliographies, indexing and abstracting services, but also reviews, for the evaluative approach. 'Historical criticism found in book-reviews is of considerable importance to the historical scholar', asserts Kenney.[2] Hay[3] adds a personal note: 'I often find that the only portion of the *E.H.R.* [*English historical review*] which I can appreciate *is* the reviews'.

A reviewer's qualifications in this field are normally an academic background, book or article publication, teaching and/or research experience, and an objective approach. The American journal, *The historian*, invites applications for reviewers, indicating degrees received, areas of qualifications, and publications'. A show of self-ostentation by a reviewer — to parade his own erudition instead of addressing himself to the book in hand — is not, of course, confined to history-book reviewing, but the temptation is there. The then editor of the *American historical review* stated,[4] 'We hope the reviewers will review the book and save his own essays for his own work'. Beyond this, the *AHR* policy is to give the reviewer 'complete freedom (except as to length, grammar and the laws of libel) to write his own estimate as he thinks fit'. The *English historical review,* however, insisted that 'it reserved the right to alter a review and to print it without consulting the reviewer'.[5]

The *Harvard guide to American history*[6] considered the chief vice of historical reviewing to be 'softness', the lack of critical appraisal. This raises the issue: should a reviewer be chosen who is known to be opposed to the author's views? The *EHR* editor took a firm line:[7] 'I should not shrink from offering a book to a reviewer known to be unsympathetic to the author's views, but I should shrink from sending it to a reviewer who was known to dislike the author personally'.

An article in *History*[8] considers that history-book reviewing in British dailies and weeklies is hedged about by the need for speedy copy and limited space. Serious history books were often reviewed by 'writers who were not historians themselves and who bring to their task a bright style and not much else'. And the same book tended to be dealt with in several of the media at the same time. As to weeklies, the *TLS* was conspicuous for reviewing a considerable number of historical works, giving its reviewers plenty of time in which to submit copy.

Sir G.N. Clark has laid out guide-lines for the history-book reviewer:[9]

> The review of a book should above all indicate its place in the literature of the subject — an historical source or study is to be regarded not as an isolated body of information, true or false, but as occupying its own place in the corpus of what is known on the person or subject in question. Has the author used new materials or made new and more correct interpretations of old materials? If there is nothing new in the book, it is of no historical value.

The review editor of *The local historian*[10] claims that its reviews are one of the journal's most popular and widely read features: 'Many writers of local history regard it as a source for comparative studies, as well as a place where they may one day see their own work commended'.

The heading of *The Times* 700-word review[11] of *The Cambridge encyclopedia of Russia and the Soviet Union* (Cambridge University press, 1982) reads: 'Russia from Abakumov to Syzin' — giving the impression, coupled with the word 'Encyclopedia', that here is an encyclopaedic dictionary of the USSR, with entries in A–Z order. This is not Cambridge University Press practice. Here is a survey in 12 sections, covering major aspects of Soviet history, culture, economy, and so on. The fluently written *Times* review disregards the 45 maps, the list of further reading and a select glossary. The detailed index indeed runs from Abakumov to Syzin. A comparison with CUP's *Companion to Russian studies* (vols. 1–2. 1976–80), also arranged by chapters, was clearly called for.

The presidency of Lyndon B. Johnson, by V.D. Bornet (Lawrence, Kans., University of Kansas, 1984) was slated by an anonymous reviewer in *Choice*, May 1984[12] 'This latest volume in a distinguished series is the largest and weakest...Here...is a bowdlerized LBJ, shorn of narcissisms, paranoia and deep hatreds'. In his protest the author[13] claimed that he had made considerable use of manuscript sources for his appraisal of a very controversial presidency. He found the review 'unbalanced, pedantic' and adds, 'Disagreement over Vietnam, the Dominican Republic episode, the Cold War, and LBJ's style of leadership should not preclude access to readership — at least, in my view'.

North Carolina: the history of a Southern State, by H.T. Leflen and A.R. Newsome (Chapel Hill, University of North Carolina Press, 1954), was highly recommended in *The journal of Southern history*[14] for its scholarship, comprehensiveness, balance and willingness to pass judgements, plus good maps, chapter bibliographies, appendices and an excellent index. Although quotations are used with great skill, a caution follows: 'It is noticeable that the weakest section of the book — that part on the twentieth-century developments — has fewer and less apt quotations than any other part of the work'.

The Oxford illustrated history of Britain, by Kenneth O. Morgan (Oxford University Press, 1984) is praised in a *Books in Scotland*[15] 800-word review for containing excellent material: 'less a "popular" book than one for the thoughtful and enquiring mind'. However, it has a basic fault, not uncommon in books purporting to cover Britain, its history and local history; it neglects Scotland, Wales and Ulster: 'Scotland is rarely mentioned except when it erupts on the English stage'.

Indexes to reviews

The main sources are the indexes to the book-reviews in the journals themselves. The annual *Index to book reviews in historical periodicals*, compiled by John W. Brewster and Joseph A. McLeod (Metuchen, NJ, Scarecrow Press, 1972–76) has ceased, and the annual *An index to reviews in the humanities* (Williamston, Mich., Thomson, 1960-) has not covered historybook reviews since vol. 11 (1970). At period level we have *International guide to medieval studies: a quarterly index to periodical literature* (Darien, Conn., American Bibliographic Service, 1961–), and at countries level (USA and Canada), *America: history and life* (Santa Barbara, Calif., ABC-Clio, 1964–. 7 p.a.), part B: 'Index to book reviews'. *Arts and humanities citation index* (Philadelphia. Pa., Institute for Scientific Information, 1978–. 3 p.a. citing about 200 history journals ('+' = review) and *Historical abstracts* (ABC-Clio, 1955–. 4 p.a., pts a, b) are also of value. The more general indexing services help, to some extent: *Book review digest* (New York, H.W. Wilson, 1905–. 10 p.a., quarterly, annual cumulations); *Book review index* (Detroit, Mich., Gale, 1963–. 6 p.a., annual cumulation); *Social sciences index* and *Humanities index* (both H.W. Wilson, 1974–. 10 p.a., quarterly, annual cumulations); *Reference sources* (Ann Arbor, Mich., Pierian Press, 1977–. annual) and *Internationale Bibliographie der Rezensionen* (Osnabrück, Dietrich, 1971–. 2 p.a.).

Reviewing journals

The American historical review (Washington, DC, American Historical Association, 1895–. 5 p.a. Circulation: 23,000) devotes over 50 per cent of its text to historical reviews. Vol. 89 (3), June 1984 (pp. 593–906), carries 202 listed reviews on pp. 733–893 in 10 sections: General (7), Ancient (1), Medieval (11), Modern Europe (81), Near East (1), Africa (7), Asia and the East (18), United States (65), Canada (2), Latin America (9). Items reviewed include works in French, German and a few other European languages. The *AHR* has a book-review editor, and reviews are signed, with affiliations. Review length ranges from 600 to 1,200 words, comment being analytical and evaluative, indicating readership but only occasionally comparative. A book on authoritarianism in Greece is described as an oversimplification; another, as regrettably outdated in its findings on peasant movements in India, 1920–50; but a third monograph, on Kenya, is commended for its heavy reliance on both oral and archival sources. Most of the reviewers are American. Bibliographical details omit ISBNs. Letters accommodate rebuttals to reviews, provoking lively replies by reviewers. The annual index, cumulated ten-yearly, covers authors, reviewers and subjects in one A–Z sequence.

The English historical review (Harlow, Essex, Longman, 1886–. 4 p.a. Circulation: 3,000) is the leading—and oldest—British historical periodical, respected for its impeccable traditional scholarship. Vol. 100 (394), January 1985 (246pp.) carries 14 lengthy book-reviews (1,000–2,000) words apiece) on pp. 120–50, plus 118 'Short notices' (150–700 words apiece) on pp. 151–246. The reviews are listed and signed, with affiliations, comments being closely analytical and critical. The scope is wide-ranging, including items in German, Dutch, French, Italian and Spanish. The reviewers, some eminent in their field, are virtually all British. *The Chartists*, by Dorothy Thompson (London, Temple Smith, 1984) is acclaimed as having succeeded admirably in its main aims: 'Mrs. Thompson has produced the definitive general study of the greatest working-class movement of the nineteenth century'. Bibliographical details omit pagination and ISBNs. The annual index, cumulated ten-yearly, includes a 'List of reviews of books' (under authors) and a 'List of writers' (names only, of authors and reviewers).

Deutsches Archiv für Erforschung des Mittelalters. Namens der Monumenta Germaniae Historica (Cologne, Böhlau, 1937–. 2 p.a. Circulation: 900) is a heavily documented, scholarly journal devoted to medieval Europe. Vol. 40 (2), 1984 (pp. 379–792), has about 300 book-reviews and notices, signed or initialled, on pp. 622–763. Length of reviews/notices varies from 50 to 1,200 words. The seven main sections, further subdivided, are: General; Auxiliary material and sources; Medieval political and ecclesiastical history; Legal and constitutional history; Social and economic history; Provincial history; Cultural and intellectual history. The longer reviews are analytical and critical, as well as comparative. *Henry VI*, by Bertram Wolffe (London, Methuen, 1981) is commended as the first modern scholarly biography of an English 'roi fainéant', although there does exist another study: *The reign of King Henry VI: the exercise of royal authority, 1442–1461*, by Ralph A. Griffiths (Berkeley, Calif., University of California Press, 1981). The biography confirms Henry VI's reputation as an incompetent and partisan king who generated factions. Bibliographical details lack ISBNs. The annual index, cumulated 10-yearly, has section entries for authors and subjects of books reviewed.

Historische Zeitschrift (Munich, Oldenbourg, 1859–. 6 p.a.) predates other scholarly history journals such as *Revue historique*, *The English historical review* and *The American historical review.* Vol. 240 (2), April 1985 (pp. 265–528), has 85 reviews, signed, with locations on pp. 363–495 in six sections: General; Ancient history; Middle Ages; Sixteenth to eighteenth centuries; Nineteenth century; Twentieth century. All reviews are in German, with an average length of about 900 words. Comments are analytical and critical, indicating readership. *Die Weimarer Republik*, by Eberhard Kolb (Munich, Oldenbourg, 1984) is praised for its wide-ranging and precisely written assessment of the first German Republic's achievements. The reviewer knows of no better introduction to the troubled history of the Weimar Republic, for teachers, students and lay persons alike.

History; the journal of the Historical Association (London, the Association, 1912–. 3 p.a. Circulation: 8,000) is addressed to academics and history teachers. Vol. 69 (227), October 1984 (pp. 375–544) has 141 reviews and notices (not listed), pp. 443–544, in four sections: Ancient and medieval (34); The Americas (54); Early modern (21); Late modern (32). All reviewers are British, with two review editors. The reviews, between 350 and 1,000 words in length, are signed, with affiliations. The analytical and critical comments are written in an easy style and less in-depth than those in the *English historical review*. Several books are judged inadequate, for providing only 'straight' history. Thus a work on the age of Elizabeth draws no new conclusions, although it tells a story accurately, copiously and well. A trio of books on Prince Albert are usefully compared. Some issues of *History* carry review-articles (e.g. vol. 69 [226], June 1984). Bibliographical details omit ISBNs. The annual index includes an author-list of 'Books received or noticed' and a list of contributors (both authors and reviewers of books reviewed).

The journal of Asian studies (Ann Arbor, Mich., Association for Asian Studies, Inc., 1941–. 4 p.a. Circulation: 9,000) was formerly *Far Eastern quarterly*. Vol. 44 (2), February 1985 (pp. 267–479) has 83 listed book-reviews on pp. 359–476, signed, with affiliations. The six sections cover Asia, General (1); China and Inner Asia (21); Japan (11); Korea (2); South Asia (28); South-East Asia (20). Reviews, between 600 and 1,500 words apiece, analytical and critical, are mostly by US academics. *India within the Ganges*, by Susan Gill (New Delhi, Jayaprints, 1983) is found to be a remarkably thorough catalogue of maps of India, 1477–1800: 'an essentially sound piece of historical scholarship'. Comparison is made with two other works on early Indian maps by the same author. *Education and social change in the People's Republic of China*, by John N. Hawkins (New York, Praeger, 1978), is a composite work, criticized for unevenness of style and quality of contribution. Much of the material is available elsewhere, although one chapter is singled out for praise. Bibliographical details omit ISBNs. The annual index has a 'Book reviews' section and a list of contributors (including reviewers).

The Classical review (Oxford University Press, for the Classical Association, 1887–. New series, 1951–. 2 p.a. Circulation: 2,000) is the major English-language reviewing journal in its field and companion to *The Classical quarterly*. New series vol. 36 (1), 1985

(237pp.), has 79 reviews (1,000 to over 3,000 words each) on pp. 1–176, and 71 'Notices' in smaller type. Comments are closely analytical and critical. S. Hornblower's *The Greek world, 479–323 BC* (London, Methuen, 1983) is given detailed scrutiny, noting misprints and other technical faults. 'If my review has suggested that this is a Jekyll-and-Hyde of a book, that is the impression it creates...It will stimulate thought. But on occasion a wish to make us think approaches intellectual perversity' (examples follow). In the correspondence section, Professor O. Mandel defends his book, *Philoctetes and the fall of Troy* (Lincoln, University of Nebraska Press, 1981) against misconceptions by a reviewer. Bibliographical details omit ISBNs. The annual index comprises a general index (names in bold indicate reviewers) and an index locorum. A cumulative index to vols. 1–64 covers 1887–1950.

Journal of American history (Bloomington, Indiana University Press, 1914–. 4 p.a. Circulation: 12,500) was formerly *The Mississippi Valley historical review.* Vol. 71 (1), June 1984 (262pp.) has 83 listed book-reviews on pp. 101–77, with a review-essay preceding. The reviews, about 600 words in length apiece, are signed, with affiliations, comments being analytical and critical. The reviewers, predominantly US, include four British and one Canadian. One reviewer observes, 'I have always thought it unfair and unprofessional to take an author to task for not having written the book that he [the reviewer] might have written, and I have not followed such a practice in my own reviews'. Bibliographical details are full, apart from lack of ISBNs. 'Communications' includes letters challenging the verdict of reviews; some have the reviewers' replies appended. The annual index includes entries under reviewers as well as under both authors and titles of books reviewed.

The historian: a journal of history (Allentown, Pa., Phi Alpha Theta International Honor Society in History, 1938–. 4 p.a. Circulation: 10,500) is a scholarly periodical, with articles focused on American history, but books reviewed are wide-ranging. Vol. 47 (1), November 1984 (174 pp.), has 50 reviews (500–600 words in length), signed, with affiliations, on pp. 93–139. There is a book-review editor, and most of the reviewers are American. The reviews, analytical and critical, are in seven sections: Greece; Rome; Europe; Far East; Africa; USA; Central and South Asia. *Late Roman fortifications*, by Stephen Johnson (London, Batsford, 1983) is applauded for being 'abundantly illustrated with distribution maps, plans of cities and other fortified sites, and plans of important features like gates'. *European imperialism in nineteenth and twentieth centuries*, by

Woodruff D. Smith (Chicago, Ill., Nelson-Hall, 1982) is faulted for relying mainly on English secondary works. The older surveys, by Betts, Hyam, Fieldhaus 'have not been superseded'. Bibliographical details omit ISBNs. Reviews are listed per issue, but not indexed annually.

The Middle East journal (Washington, DC, The Middle East Institute, 1947–. 4 p.a. Circulation: 4,400) is a well-documented and organized scholarly periodical. Vol. 39 (1), Winter 1985 (226 pp.), has 56 book-reviews (500–800 words each) on pp. 123–86, preceded by a review-article. Sections are: Arabian Peninsula; Egypt; Israel; The Gulf; Maghreb; Pakistan; Palestine and Palestinians; Syria and Lebanon; Turkey; Modern history and politics; Arab-Israeli conflict; Pre-twentieth-century history; Economic conditions; Religion; Anthropology; Art; Science and law; Literature. *Pakistan's nuclear dilemma: energy and security dimensions*, by Akhbar Ali (Karachi, Economist Research Unit, 1984) has a clear-eyed look at Pakistan's nuclear options, but the author 'does not adequately detail or analyze the modalities of his recommended intiative'. In addition, the book is badly proof-read. Bibliographical details lack ISBNs. Appended to the book-reviews are 'Shorter notices' (pp. 186–97), averaging 300 to 400 words apiece.

Greece and Rome (Oxford, Clarendon Press, for the Classical Association, 1931–. 2nd series, 1954–. 2 p.a. Circulation: 1,800) is an interdisciplinary journal. Vol. 31 (2), October 1984 (pp. 119–242) has 3 major reviews (500–800 words), on pp. 203–6, with appended notes. 'Brief articles' (pp. 207–31) has running commentary, with notes, on about 100 titles in eight sections: Greek literature; Roman literature; Greek history; Roman history; Archaeology and art; General; School books; Reprints. Entries for books specially recommended for school libraries are asterisked; double-asterisked, to indicate suitability for advanced students only: and marked 'B' if a bibliography is included. Bibliographical details omit place of publication and ISBNs. There is no annual index; reviews are listed on the two contents-pages.

Archivio stórico italiano (Florence, Olschki, 1842–. 4 p.a.) covers medieval and modern Italian history. No. 522, 1984 (4), pp. 511–682, has 11 longer, signed reviews, averaging 1,250 words, on pp. 623–51; 42 shorter reviews follow, in three sections (General history; Medieval history; Modern and contemporary history). All reviews, descriptive rather than critical, are signed. *Il nazionalismo in Italia e in Germania fino alla prima guerra mondiale*, edited by R. Lill and F. Valsecchi (Bologna, Il Molino, 1983) invites a 2,500-word close analysis. It gives equal consideration to Italian and German nationalism and their foreign policies. Of the various contributions, several are selected for discussion. Bibliographical details lack prices, full pagination and ISBNs. Reviews, listed per issue, are not indexed annually but in the cumulative indexes for 1842–1941 and 1942–67.

History today (London, History Today, Ltd, 1951–. 12 p.a. Circulation: 22,000) is a popular, fully illustrated magazine, with wide-ranging articles. Vol. 34, October 1984 (64 p.) has headed and signed reviews of 16 books, with an appended list of affiliations of reviewers (university research fellows and lecturers, tutors and authors of history books). Five of the items, on the history of English family life and women, are grouped. Reviews, between 400 and 1,000 words in length, are vividly written and analytical, with critical comment. Bibliographical details omit full pagination and ISBNs. A further feature, 'Paperback history', comprises six short reviews. The annual index has a book-reviews section.

Speculum: a journal of medieval studies (Cambridge, Mass., The Medieval Academy of America, 1926–. 4 p.a. Circulation: 5,650) devotes more than half of its scholarly contents to reviews, signed, with affiliations. Vol. 60 (2), April 1985 (pp. 251–503), has 43 main book-reviews on pp. 373–468, followed by 'Brief notices', pp. 469–97. The main reviews, averaging about 1,800 words apiece, are analytical and critical. Comments on *Stained glass in thirteenth-century Burgundy*, by Virginia Chieffo Raguin (Princeton, NJ, Princeton University Press, 1982) begin, 'This is a detailed study of fundamental importance, concentrating chiefly on the stained glass windows of the Cathedral of St Étienne of Auxerre. The author had explored the stylistic connections of this glass not only with that of other Burgundian monuments, but also that of Chartres, Bourges and Paris and with Parisian manuscript illumination' – such comparison is one of the great merits of this study. Bibliographical details omit ISBNs. The annual index has a 'Review' section, with entries under authors of books reviewed.

The journal of modern history (Chicago, Ill., University of Chicago Press, 1929–. 4 p.a. Circulation: 4,300) deals with post-Renaissance European history. Vol. 57 (1), March 1985 (184p.) contains 43 book-reviews, signed, with affiliations, on pp. 97–184, and 500–2,500 words apiece in length. The review of *The Jews of East Central Europe between the World Wars*, by Ezra Mendelsohn (Bloomington, Indiana University Press, 1983) begins., 'This book is a major achievement in synthesizing existing but fragmentary scholarship about an important, complicated, fascinating, and ultimately tragic period in Jewish and East European history'. For each country Mendelsohn outlines the political history of both the Jewish and general communities. Jewish participation in the general culture varied considerably from one country to another. The chapters on Poland and Hungary are noteworthy for their treatment of demographic, economic and political issues. One shortcoming is the cursory treatment of Jewish culture. Bibliographical details omit ISBNs. Reviews are listed on the quarterly contents pages.

Victorian studies (Bloomington, Indiana University, Program for Victorian Studies, 1957–. 4 p.a. Circulation: 2,400) is a journal of history, literature and art in Victorian England. Vol. 27 (2), Winter 1984 (pp. 155–286) has 42 reviews, signed, with affiliations, on pp. 237–81. The reviews are analytical and critical, with occasional comparisons. Criticism is directed against subjectivity, failure to live up to the the book title, and uneven analysis, while praising use of primary sources (e.g. on Victorian India). Bibliographical details lack full pagination and ISBNs. The annual index has author and title entries for books reviewed, with cross-references from reviewers' names.

Canadian journal of history/Annales canadiennes d'histoire (Saskatoon, University of Saskatchewan, 1966–. 3 p.a. Circulation: 600) is international in scope but excludes Canadian history, being complementary to *The Canadian historical review* (see below). Vol. 19 (2), August 1984 (pp. 167–347), has three review-essays and 59 listed reviews, signed, with affiliations, on pp. 264–347. The reviews concern Europe and European countries, range from 600 to 1,200 words in length and are analytical and critical, some with comparisons. *The chancelleries of Europe*, by Alan Palmer (London, Allen and Unwin, 1983) is given a cool reception as being 'a competent, succinct retelling of things long since held to be true, with no new perspectives, no altered vision'. Bibliographical details lack ISBNs. There is no annual index, but book-reviews are listed in *Humanities index, Arts and humanities citation index* and *Internationale Bibliographie der Rezensionen*.

Cahiers de civilisation mediévale: x^e–xiie siècles (Poitiers, Centre d'Études Supérieures de Civilisation Mediévale, 1958–. 4 p.a.) is a scholarly journal on a vital formative period in the Middle Ages. Vol. 28 (1), January/March 1985 (100pp.), has 18 signed book-reviews, pp. 63–89, plus 24 short notices that include contents-listing of proceedings, and so on. The reviews average 1.500 words, are analytical, critical and, at times, comparative. *Griechisch-lateinisches Mittelalter von Hieronymus zu Nikolaus von Kues*, by Walter Berschin (Berne, Francke, 1980) will long be 'the obligatory reference on Hellenism in the West during the Middle Ages'. It differs from P. Courrelle's approach, which focuses on the prolongation of Greek philology in Western Europe. Bibliographical details omit ISBNs. The annual index has a reviews section (authors and reviewers).

Zeitschrift der Deutschen Morgenländischen Gesellschaft (Wiesbaden, Steiner, 1847–. 2 p.a.) is the long-lived journal of the German Oriental Society. Vol. 135 (1), 1985 (212, 28pp.), includes 41 reviews (about 1,000 words apiece) on pp. 104–78, signed, with locations. About 80 short notices (about 200 words each) follow. Most of the reviews, often analytical and critical, are in German. Mehdi Keyvani's *Artisans and guild life in the later Safavid period: contributions to the socio-economic history of Persia* (Berlin, Schwarz, 1982) discusses the sources, classification and number of guilds, structure, methods of government control, social action, special guilds, cultural and religious functions, and relations between merchants and guilds. The monograph is criticized for lack of definition of 'guild' and of the necessary socio-economic background. The text is that of the author's doctoral thesis and lacks further and analytical treatment: 'However, the book is useful because of the orderly arrangement of his material, which no doubt will facilitate further research in this field'. Bibliographical details are usually full. The annual index has sections for reviews and short notices, and a list of contributors includes reviewers.

Journal of American studies (Cambridge University Press, for the British Association of American Studies, 1967–. 3 p.a. Circulation: 1,400) covers US history, politics, foreign policy, economy, industrial relations, constitution, literature, and so on. Vol. 18 (3), December 1984 (pp. 343–497), has 52 reviews (500-900 words apiece) on pp. 453–97, preceded by four review-essays. Reviews are signed, with affiliations, and are closely analytical, sometimes with quotations and footnotes. *The growth of federal power*, edited by R. Jeffreys-Jones and Bruce Collins (De Kalb, North Illinois University Press, 1983) contains essays by 12 British academics. 'While it is certainly possible to quarrel with the judgments of some of the authors, they all have something to say', some introducing British comparisons. Bibliograhical details are in full. The annual index has author, title and reviewer entries for books reviewed.

Revue historique (Paris, Presses Universitaires de France, 1876–. 4 p.a.) is the leading French general-history journal. Vol. 272 (951), July/September 1984, has 11 signed book-reviews on pp. 191–214 and 26 shorter notices. The main reviews, 700 to 3,500 words long, are closely analytical and evaluative, some with comparisons. *Prix et* salaires à Florence au XIVe siècle, by Charles de la Roncière (École Française de Rome, 1982) is acclaimed as a remarkable achievement. While it is narrower in scope than the author's thesis on fourteenth-century Florence, it gives an in-depth insight into Florentine social life then, with data on poverty, food shortages, high interest-rates and the like. Bibliographical details omit prices and ISBNs. The annual index has sections for both reviews and notices.

Russian review: an American quarterly devoted to Russia past and present (Cambridge, Mass., 1941–. 4 p.a. Circulation: 1,000) is sponsored by Syracuse University, New York). Vol. 43 (4), October 1983 (pp. 369–469), has 33 listed reviews, signed, with affiliations, on pp. 417–69. Books reviewed, nearly all in English, cover aspects of Russian history and culture, as well as East–West relations. Reviews (350–1,000 words) are analytical, with quotations, and critical, some with quotations and noting readership. A monograph on Polish–American relations is praised for 'being based on extensive research in primary materials'; another, on Gogol, is commended for its style and flair; a third, on the influence of Christian philosophy on a Soviet writer, requires greater detail, cohesion and clarity of outline. Bibliographical details omit ISBNs. The annual index has a 'Book-review' section, with author entries.

Reviews in American history: a quarterly journal of criticism (Baltimore, Md., Johns Hopkins University Press, 1973–. 4 p.a. Circulation: 2,000) is almost wholly devoted to reviews. Vol. 13 (1), March 1985 (156pp.) has 32 book-reviews (1,500–3,000 words) on pp. 1–141, plus a review-article. The reviews are signed, with appended data on reviewers. Comments are closely analytical, with quotations, critical, and fluently written. *Women's activism and social change in Rochester, New York, 1822–1872*, by Nancy A. Hewitt (New Haven, Conn., Yale University Press, 1984) is praised as a valuable model for historians of women and antebellum reform. But there are 'inaccuracies and inattention to the historical meanings of terms like "radicalism" and "equality"', and the author confesses to being pressured into hasty production'. 'Correspondence' contains an aggrieved author's letter regarding a review. Bibliographical details omit ISBNs. The annual review lists reviews under authors and reviewers.

Journal of the Royal Asiatic Society of Great Britain and Ireland (London, the Society, 1834–. 2 p.a. Circulation: 1,600) includes northern Africa. 1985 (1), with 140pp., has 64 signed book-reviews on pp. 67–138, plus 'Books received for review'. The reviews (500–1,200 words) are written in an easy style, analytical and critical. *The development of Islam in West Africa,* by Mervyn Hiskett (London, Longman, 1984) is intended primarily for students, but is also for the general reader. Much reviewing space is devoted to discussing Vincenzo Matteo's search for Prester John. 'Obviously much of this book is beyond the competence of this reviewer or the scope of this journal.' Bibliographical details lack ISBNs. The annual index includes sections for reviewers and authors of books reviewed.

Bibliothèque d'Humanisme et Renaissance. Travaux et documents (Geneva, Droz, for Association d'Humanisme et Renaissance, 1941–. 3 p.a. Circulation: 600) is a leading scholarly journal for the period 1350–1550. Vol. 47 (1), 1985 (303pp.), has 42 book-reviews, signed, with locations, and average 1,200 words. Reviews, mostly in French, are analytical and critical. Comments on R. Starn's *Contrary Commonwealth: the theme of exile in medieval and Renaissance Italy* (Berkeley, University of California Press, 1982) compliment Professor Starn on having written 'an extraordinarily well conceived, well researched and well written book...Although more could have been written on some aspects [e.g. law, literatue], in all that has been written on the subject of exile, Starn has shown the way'. Bibliographical details omit prices and ISBNs. Each issue has contents pages listing reviews.

HAHR/The Hispanic American historical review (Durham, NC, Duke University Press, 1921–. 4 p.a. Circulation: 2,400) is a scholarly periodical published in co-operation with the Conference on Latin American History of the American Historical Association. Vol. 64 (3), August 1984 (pp. 421–631), has 29 listed book-reviews on pp. 555–92, each with 500–750 words, signed and with affiliations. Sections are: General (2); Background (2); Colonial (10); National (15). Fourteen book notices follow. There is a book-review editor and most reviewers are American. *Life in provincial Mexico,* by Carlos B. Gil (Los Angeles, University of California Press, 1983) is commended for being 'primarily based on archival sources and documents generated locally and regionally; it draws on interviews over a six-year period'. Bibliographical details omit prices and ISBNs. The annual index carries entries under both books reviewed and their reviewers.

The journal of interdisciplinary history (Cambridge, Mass., Massachusetts Institute of Technology, 1970–. 4 p.a. Circulation: 1,500) aims 'to review books of importance to the growth of history and historical research, whether published originally as history or as psychology, political science, sociology, anthropology, numismatics, and so on'. Vol. 15 (1), Summer 1984 (184pp.), has 26 listed reviews, signed, with affiliations, and averaging 800 words apiece, some with footnotes. Comments are analytical and critical. *The Black Death: natural and human disaster in medieval Europe*, by Robert S. Gottfried (New York, Free Press, 1983) is commended as 'a successful book, as an interdisciplinary study', but is 'marred by inconvenient placing of the notes at the end of the book, lacking any running heads to connect them to pages in the text'. Bibliographical details omit full pagination and ISBNs. The annual index has 'Reviews'.

The mariner's mirror: the international journal of the Society for Nautical Research (London, c/o National Maritime Museum, 1911–. 4 p.a. Circulation: 2,200) deals with nautical antiquities and customs, as well as with seafaring and shipbuilding worldwide and in all ages. Vol. 70 (4), November 1984 (pp. 347–460), carries 26 signed reviews on pp. 396, 414, 448–60. Reviews (100–750 words) are analytical, in one instance noting that 'the maps are almost illegible', and in another that a title is most misleading and that 'quite a lot of knowledge seems to be assumed'. Bibliographical details lack full pagination and ISBNs. Three unsigned short notices follow the reviews proper. The annual index, cumulated 10-yearly, has a 'Reviews' heading.

Asian affairs: journal of the Royal Society for Asian Affairs (London, the Society, 1903–. 3 p.a. Circulation: 3,500) was originally the *Royal Central Asian Society journal*. Vol. 16 (Old series, vol. 72), pt 1, February 1985 (119pp.), has 32 signed book-reviews on pp. 76–113, in six sections: General; Central Asia; South Asia; South-East Asia; Middle East; Far East—concerning their history, economies and cultures. Reviews (700–1,400 words) are analytical, with quotations, and critical. *The Japanese colonial empire, 1893–1945*, edited by Ramon H. Myers and Mark R. Peattie (Princeton, NJ, Princeton University Press, 1984), has a lengthy introduction and 11 essays by various hands, containing much information on an area often neglected by historians: 'However, as in many similar compilations, the general reader would I am sure have welcomed a short narrative summary of events and some expansion of the notice taken of major occurrences'. The maps are good, illustrations poor, and the price (£43.90) extortionate. Four short notices follow the main reviews. Bibliographical details lack full pagination and ISBNs. The annual index includes entries for reviewers and for titles (italicized) of books reviewed.

The Canadian historical review (University of Toronto Press, 1920–. 4 p.a. Circulation: 3,000) concentrates on the history of Canada. Vol. 66–(1), March 1985 (124pp.), has 19 book-reviews, signed, with affiliations, on pp. 103–24. The reviews, written in an easy style and averaging 600 words, are analytical and critical. The 1,000-word review of *An introduction to Canadian–American relations*, by Edel E. Mahant and Graeme S. Mount (Toronto, Methuen, 1984), begins, 'This book has three purposes: to bring the story of Canada's relationship with the United States up to the 1980s; to tell the story comprehensively; and to cast it within a framework that makes the character of the relationship intelligible'. However, cultural aspects are only briefly dealt with, and Canada's response to US dynamism is insufficiently appreciated — 'a book that is a good deal less than it might have been'. Bibliographical details lack ISBNs. The annual index has a 'Reviews' section and also lists reviewers.

Journal of African history (Cambridge University Press, 1960–. 4 p.a. Circulation: 2,370) is a leading scholarly journal in its field. Vol. 25 (3), 1984 (pp. 241–368) has 15 listed reviews (700–2,000 words) on pp. 343–64, plus four short notices. A review-article precedes. The team of reviewers (names, with affiliations) is international, and reviews, under headings, are closely analytical, with quotations. French and German titles are included. Some reviews praise extensive use of archives or indicate readership. One monograph is blamed for lack of maps, while another is recommended as 'an essential starting point'. Bibliographical data omit ISBNs. The annual index has entries for authors, titles and reviewers.

The local historian (Matlock, Derbyshire, British Association for Local History, 1952–. 4 p.a. Circulation: 2,500) was formerly *The amateur historian*. Vol. 16 (5), February 1985 (pp. 257–320), has 16 signed reviews on pp. 303–16. Coverage is not confined to the British Isles. Most of the reviews (200–1,000 words) are grouped — for example, Medieval overview (2); By word of mouth (3); Local history up to date (5); Gallic comparisons (2); Small town histories (4)— being analytical, critical and comparative. The longest review, of *The art and architecture of London*, by Ann Saunders (Oxford, Phaidon, 1984), is complimented for its well-chosen and excellently reproduced photographs, and its clearly-drawn maps, but it is faulted for its non-portability as a guide: 'Perhaps this book is destined to be more a work of reference on the shelves of branch libraries or on the coffee tables of relatives'. Bibliographical details omit date of publication and ISBNs. Volumes are two-yearly, and the author and subject-index entries italicize titles of books reviewed.

International journal of Middle East studies (Cambridge University Press, 1970–. 4 p.a. Circulation: 2,200) is published under the auspices of the Middle East Studies Association of North America. Vol. 16 (4), November 1984 (pp. 447–587), carries 16 book-reviews, signed, with affiliations, on pp. 565–87, each 800–1,400 words in length. Comments are closely analytical, with quotations, and critical, indicating readership. *Eastern Armenia in the last decades of Persian rule, 1807–1828*, by George A. Bournoutian (Malibu, Calif., Undena Publications, 1983) is highly commended for its detailed yet broad approach, 'made possible largely by the author's ability to deal with sources in Persian, Armenian, Russian, French, English and German languages'. Joseph Heller's *British policy towards the Ottoman Empire, 1908–1914* (London, Cass, 1983) is queried for its final chapters, 'absolving Great Britain of any responsibility for the fateful decisions of the Ottoman rulers in 1914'. Bibliographical details omit prices. The annual index includes a reviews section.

Archaeology

Archaeological research — a form of information retrieval — embodies prehistory, anthropology, post-medieval and industrial archaeology, as well as the more recent 'rescue' archaeology (the salvaging of evidence, artefacts, etc., during excavation, preparatory to building construction on the site). For archaeological-book reviewing, a first-hand acquaintance with 'digs' and a sense of period are essential.

New scientist[16] provides a helpful comparative review of two fairly recent dictionaries of archaeology: *The Penguin dictionary of archaeology*, edited by W. Bray and others (Harmondsworth, Middlesex, Penguin Books, 1982), and *The Macmillan dictionary of archaeology* (London, Macmillan Press, 1983). The latter provides more detailed coverage, but it omits entries found in the *Penguin dictionary*. The *Macmillan dictionary* also lacks line-drawings, and its higher price (£25, against £3.50 for the Penguin paperback) will put it beyond the reach of libraries, whereas the Penguin's low cost 'makes it available to the mass market'.

The *Aslib book list*[17] review of Kenneth Hudson's *World industrial archaeology* (2nd edn. Cambridge University Press, 1979), labelled 'A', 'for general reading', runs to 62 words:

> The author has widened the field of industrial archaeology to include, besides the technical appeal of old machines, their place in the social and economic conditions of their times. This does not lessen the attraction of the book to those whose idea of industrial archaeology is more specific and makes its appeal to a wider public to whom it can be recommended.

The following mini-review is more informative, in 62 words:

The writer, author of *A guide to the industrial archaeology of Europe* (1971), etc., here outlines the discovery, recording and study of the physical remains of yesterday's industries and communications, by types of activity (extractive industries; food and drink; construction; metal processing; transport; textiles, clothing, footwear; power; chemicals) in various countries. Excellent illustrations, a select bibliography and an index support the text.

Industrial archaeology review[18] adds the caution: 'Readers desire more attention to detail—perhaps they will get it in the third edition'.

Indexes to reviews

As in the case of history journals, the main sources are the indexes to the journals themselves: *Combined retrospective index to book reviews in humanities journals, 1802–1974* (Woodbridge, Conn., RP/Research Publications, Inc., 1982–84, 9 vols.); *Arts and humanities citation index* (1978–. 3 p.a.) and *Science citation index* (1961–. 6 p.a.) (both published Philadelphia, Pa., Institute for Scientific Information and cumulated annually); *Art index* (New York, H.W. Wilson, 1929–. 4 p.a., cumulated annually), and more general review-indexing services (see under the section History, above) are also of value. *Katalog der Bibliothek des Deutschen Archäologisches Instituts. Zeitschriften Authorenkatalog* (Rome, 1969, 3 vols.) includes review-article citations.

Reviewing journals

The Antiquaries journal, being the journal of the Society of Antiquaries of London (Oxford University Press, for the Society, 1921–. 2 p.a. Circulation: 700) is an authoritative review of British and European archaeological and antiquarian subjects. Vol. 64 (2) (pp. 251–623) carries about 90 listed and signed reviews, on pp. 425–523. The reviews, 250 to 1,200 words in length, are analytical and critical. *Excavations in Chios, 1938–1955: prehistoric Emporio and Ayio Gala*, by Sinclair Hood, with others (London, Thames and Hudson, for the British School of Archaeology at Athens, 1981–82. 2 vols.) is described as a monumental excavation report, cataloguing over 3,000 pottery items. Its most remarkable feature 'must be the catholicity and details of the comparanda cited for nearly every find'. The report richly deserves to be on every Aegean archaeologist's bookshelf, but for the price (£130). Correspondents are invited to

184 A.J. Walford

contact reviewers direct. Bibliographical details are full. The annual index, an A–Z sequence, has entries for both authors and reviewers.

The journal of Hellenic studies (London, Society for the Promotion of Hellenic Studies, 1880–. Annual. Circulation: 3,000) covers ancient, medieval and modern Greek language, literature, history, biography, art and archaeology. Vol. 103, 1983 (248pp.), carries some 100 reviews, signed with affiliations, on pp. 161–236. Reviews range from 300 to 6,000 words apiece, and are analytical and critical. Books reviewed are faulted for insufficient thematic illustrations or for the inaccuracy of the publisher's blurb. A book on dating Greek manuscripts elicits the remark: 'Much remains to be done'. Items reviewed include editions of texts. Bibliographical details are full, apart from omitting ISBNs. The index of books reviewed has author-entries, with references from reviewers' names.

Antiquity: a periodical review of archaeology (Cambridge, Heffer, for Antiquity Publications, Ltd, 1927–. 4 p.a. Circulation: 4,000) is wide in scope, not only invaluable to specialists, 'but also accessible to the rest of us'*.[19] Vol. 59 (228), March 1985 (79pp), has 28 listed and signed reviews on pp. 57–79. Reviews average around 1,300 words and are analytical and critical, sometimes with comparisons. *National Trust guide to prehistoric and Roman Britain*, by Richard Muir and Humphrey Welfare (London, G. Philip, 1983) has a chronological narrative, 'peopling it with the societies which built and utilized the area'. One surprising omission: illustrations of Celtic metalwork and discussions of its place of manufacture, which, 'coupled with the hillforts is the best evidence for a local iron age aristocracy'. Bibliographical details lack full pagination and ISBNs. The annual index italicizes titles reviewed and includes reviewers' names.

Bulletin of the Institute of Archaeology (London, the Institute, University of London), 1958–. Annual) is mainly British and European in scope. No. 20, 1983 (246pp.), includes 57 book-reviews on pp. 195–243, signed, with affiliations and (sometimes) references. Reviews are closely analytical and critical, indicating readership. Length ranges from 250 to 2,000 words. Some items are criticized for high price or 'relegation to the coffee-table'. One monograph is reproved for 'promising more than it can deliver'; another is praised for its illuminating illustrations and admirable bibliography. Bibliographical details are full, apart from lack of ISBNs. The reviews are neither listed nor indexed, but they are covered in *Internationale Bibliographie der Rezensionen*.

The archaeological journal (London, The Royal Archaeological Institute, 1845–. Annual. Circulation: 2,500) covers British archaeology only. Vol. 139, for 1982 (498.p.) has 56 reviews and short notices on pp. 441–86, signed and 600 to 1,600 words in length. One monograph is criticized for its high price; another, for a lack of any explicit statement on selection policy; and a book on Philip of Macedon overstresses the pictorial angle: 'the enquiring mind is kept on short rations'. But an atlas of the Greek and Roman world in antiquity is recommended for its clarity, authority and comprehensiveness. The bibliographical details are full, apart from ISBNs. The annual index, cumulated 25-yearly, italicizes titles of books reviewed and has entries for reviewers' names.

American journal of archaeology (Archaeological Society of America, c/o Thomas Library, Bryn Mawr College, Bryn Mawr, Pa., 1885–. 4 p.a. Circulation: 5,000) is concerned only with Old World (mostly Classical) archaeology. Vol. 89 (2), April 1985 (pp. 191–372), has 13 reviews, signed, with reviewers' full official addresses, on pp. 357–70. Reviews are analytical and critical, averaging around 1,000 words in length. The 2,000-word review of *Architecture et société de l'archaïsme grec à la République Romaine. Actes de colloque de Rome, 2–4 décembre 1980* (Paris, CNRS; and Rome, École Française de Rome, 1983) is a detailed examination of various papers read. 'In the final analysis it is gratifying to see in this publication such a close adherence to the central theme by the contributors.' The volume is 'superbly edited and organized, with illustrations well chosen and reproduced'. A few minor deficiencies and inconsistencies are pointed out. Bibliographical details omit prices and ISBNs, and lack full pagination. The annual index has a 'Book-reviews' section, with author entries.

The journal of Roman studies (London, The Society for the Promotion of Roman Studies, 1911–. Annual. Circulation: 2,800) covers Roman history, art, archaeology and literature to about AD 700. Vol. 74, 1984 (270pp.), has a review-article and 44 reviews of books, including titles in French, German, Italian, Latin and Greek, on pp. 209–56. Reviews are listed and signed, with affiliations, and occasionally appear in batches. (Thus four books on Julius Caesar are compared.) The reviews are closely analytical and critical, ranging from 400 to 4,000 words in length. Frequency of misprints and gaps in coverage are prime targets for criticism. All but two of the reviewers are British. Bibliographical details omit prices and ISBNs. The reviews are listed; there is no index, as such.

Medieval archaeology; journal of the Society for Medieval Archaeology (London, the Society, University College, 1959–. Annual. Circulation: 1,700) 'exists to further the study of British his-

tory since the Roman period'. Vol. 28, 1984 (302 + 6pp.), has 21
signed reviews, averaging 1,200 words, plus 11 short signed notices,
pp. 295–301. Longer reviews are analytical, critical and, at times,
comparative. Thus *Viking Age Denmark,* by Else Roesdahl (London,
Colonade Books, for British Museum Publications, 1982), is
acclaimed for providing for the first time in English a comprehensive
and reliable summary of the archaeology of Viking Age Denmark,
and 'fundamentally different from Klavs Randsborg's *The Viking
Age in Denmark*, — also written in 1980'. Roesdahl's work is that of
a specialist in full command of material. While the translation is a
credit to the original and illustrations are of good quality, there is the
inevitable danger of overcompression (e.g. in the chapter 'Art and
ornament'). Little basic knowledge is assumed, and the book is ideal
as an undergraduate text-book. Bibliographical details omit only
ISBNs. In lieu of an index, the contents page lists both longer and
shorter reviews.

Revue archéologique (Paris, Presses Universitaires de France,
1844–. 2 p.a.) is a leading, long-standing French archaeological journal. 1984 (2), pp. 357–77, has 14 signed reviews on pp. 357–77. The
reviews are closely analytical and critical, 700–2,500 words in
length. Norman Hammond's *Ancient Maya civilisation* (Cambridge
University Press, 1982) is praised for its lucid survey of the achievements of archaeological research over the last 10 years on Maya civili-
zation, and also for the concluding bibliographical essay. The author
is congratulated for keeping his personal hypotheses under restraint.
Prominence is given to the work of British archaeologists. Some
small omissions (e.g. on the role of the Maya merchant class) are
noted, but the work certainly deserves a French translation. Bibliographical details omit prices and ISBNs. Reviews are listed on the two
contents-pages.

Industrial archaeology review (Oxford University Press, with the
Association for Industrial Archaeology, 1976–. 3 p.a. Circulation:
1,000) concerns 'history and technology in the period of the Industrial Revolution, emphasis being on the surviving material evidence'.
Vol. 6 (3), October 1982 (pp. 161-238) has eight book-reviews, listed
and signed, with affiliations, on pp. 245–50. Length varies from 400
to 800 words. Comments are analytical and critical. *Technical
Americana: a checklist of technical publications printed before 1831,*
by Evald Rink (Millwood, NY, Kraus International, 1981) is warmly
recommended: 'I have enjoyed reading through this work and realis-
ing how helpful it would be to have a similar work for the UK'. *The
first industrial nation: an economic history of Britain, 1700–1914,* by

Peter Matthews (London, Methuen, 1983) is criticized for being a 'less than thorough revision of the first edition' [1969]. Seven examples of shortcomings are given. The reviewers are all British. 'Also received' (26 items, each with 50–100 words of annotation) covers books and latest issues of other journals. The bibliographical details are full. The annual index has a 'Book-reviews' section, with entries under both authors and reviewers.

Post-medieval archaeology: the journal of the Society for Post-Medieval Archaeology (London, the Society, 1967–. Annual. Circulation: 850) covers British and continental archaeology of the sixteenth century onwards (including industrial archaeology). Vol. 17. 1983 (226pp.), carries 17 signed reviews, analytical and critical, pp. 211–24. Length ranges from 500 to 1,600 words. Comments, in one case, note lapses in grammar and style; a favourable review of a book on Oxfordshire mills 'points the way for those many other counties where nothing at all has yet been published'; regarding a third book, the reviewer suggests that the author could perhaps be persuaded to write an 'industrial landscape study for earthworks, building styles and remains'. Bibliographical details lack full pagination, place of publication and ISBNs.

The South African archaeological bulletin (Cape Town, The South African Archaeological Society, 1945–. 2 p.a. Circulation: 1,700) carries articles restricted to Southern Africa, unlike the books reviewed. Vol. 39 (139), June 1984 (80pp.), has 14 listed reviews, signed, with affiliations/locations, on pp. 73–9. Review length extends from 250 to 700 words, and books reviewed range from Roman Britain and Stonehenge to Egypt, Greece, Western Europe and South Africa. The reviews are briefly analytical and critical, indicating readership. Spelling standardization of Egyptian names is called for by one reviewer; another praises a monograph for filling an important gap: 'it sets a high standard for future analysis'. Bibliographical details lack pagination and ISBNs. The annual index has a 'Book-reviews' section.

Geography

The last two decades of the nineteenth century were momentous for the development of geographical studies. Lectureships were created at Oxford in 1887 and at Cambridge in 1888. Between the First and Second World Wars geography was establishing itself as an Honours School in many universities, and the Royal Geographical Society presidential addresses were often wide-sweeping reviews of the discipline and its functions.[20] The literature of geography, and its reviews, have kept pace.

If the prime concern of archaeology is with man in time, then that of geography is with man in terrestrial space.[21] Hence the positive nature of the discipline. Area studies, political and human geography, landscape, geomorphology, oceanography and cartography are its major components. Expeditions, exploration, travel and local topography serve as its fieldwork.

Geographical literature reviewers, like the authors themselves, will comprise professionals (academics; school teachers; cartographers) as well as travellers and free-lance journalists. Illustrative matter, especially maps and photographs, diagrams and tables, form the necessary visual approach. The reviewer is normally allowed some latitude in his critical treatment, although editors do not assume responsibility for reviewers' assessments of the work they evaluate.[22]

The 1,500-word review of *Collins' atlas of the world,* edited by Andrew M. Currie (London, Collins, 1983) in *The cartographic journal,*[23] sets definite limits to the work's usefulness as one of several recent family atlases for the non-specialist:

> This atlas is not...particularly suitable for reference purposes, neither for the location of names of places (using the index), nor for the naming of places located (using the maps), mainly because the choice of names does not fully support the publisher's contention that 'full recognition has been given to the many different purposes that currently call for map reference during home study, school and college work, business enquiries, travel planning, current affairs background information and quiz solving and so on.

The use of preferred place-names is urged by the reviewer: 'It does not help the lay user if his atlas is made the means of insinuating new words into the language that might never finally take root'.

The London region: an annotated geographical bibliography, by Philippa Dolphin and others (London, Mansell, 1981), is given a 27-word mini-review in *The geographical magazine:*[24] Nine sections of this book deal with sources from general bibliographies to statistical sources of the metropolis and beyond. The subjects covered environmental problems, conservation and control'. Such a brief résumé allows the reviewer no room for evaluation. The *Library review's* 600-word critical review[25] recommends this annotated list of 1,909 items, arranged under broad subjects; for example housing, transport, recreation. It also approves the 'very informative' section-introductions, the accurate subject and name indexes, and the handsomeness of the volume. But would not a series of subject pamphlets, as necessary, have been more useful to the enquirer — and much cheaper? Topical themes such as flood control and ethnic minorities are 'very poorly represented'. The bibliography is historically weighted, the contemporary scene being less well served.

Indexes to reviews

Apart from the indexes in the journals themselves, there is, according to Chauncy D. Harris,[26] one specific source, and that largely American and for a short span of years: John Van Balen's *Geography and earth science publications, 1968–1972: an author, title and subject guide to books reviewed, and an index to the reviews* (Ann Arbor, Pierian Press, 1978) and its successor, *Geography and earth science publications, 1973–1975* (1978). Of the more general indexes, the following offer some guidance: *Reference sources* (Ann Arbor, Mich., Pierian Press, 1977–. Annual), *Arts and humanities citation index* (Philadelphia, Pa., Institute for Scientific Information, 1978–. 3 p.a.), *Book review index* (Detroit, Mich., Gale, 1965) 6 p.a., cumulated annually and for 1969–79); *Current book review citations* (New York, H.W. Wilson, 1976–82) and *Internationale Bibliographie der Rezensionen* (Osnabrück, Dietrich, 1971–.).

Reviewing journals

The geographical journal (London, Royal Geographical Society, 1893–. 3 p.a. Circulation: 10,000) is one of the world's leading scholarly geographical periodicals. Vol. 151 (1), March 1985 (153 pp.) has 28 longer reviews (600–1,500 words apiece) on pp. 101-22, plus seven shorter notices, six 'Cartographic survey' reviews and two Expedition Advisory Centre items. Coverage is international, main sections comprising Europe (6), Africa (2), Indian Ocean (1), Asia (1), The Americas (1), Physical and biological geography (3), Social and economic geography (3), Historical geography (1), Travel and biography (1), General (5). Major reviews are signed, without affiliations, but authoritativeness is attested by the inclusion of eminent contributors. Reviews are analytical, critical and, at times, comparative. *Rural geography,* by Michael Pacione (New York, Harper and Row, 1984) succeeds in offering a contemporary and comprehensive text, updating Hugh Clout's *Rural geography: an introductory survey* (Oxford, Pergamon, 1972), but the 20 chapters read like the lecture course on which it is based. Pacione has provided width rather than depth of treatment: 'Like a springboard with no spring, this book provides a solid foundation, but little progressive energy'. Bibliographical details are full. The annual index, cumulated 10-yearly, includes book-reviews under both authors and subjects, reviewed titles being italicized.

The professional geographer (Washington, DC, Association of American Geographers, 1949–. 4 p.a. Circulation: 8,000) is aimed primarily at the US lecturer. Vol. 136 (1), February 1984 (142pp.), has 44 listed book-reviews, signed, with affiliations, pp. 106–41. Nearly all reviewers are North American, and there is a book-review editor. Books chosen for review are in English. Comments, averaging 800 words each, are analytical, evaluative and comparative, indicating readership. *The natural environment of Newfoundland past and present,* edited by A.G. Macpherson and J.B. Macpherson (St John's, Department of Geography, Memorial University of Newfoundland, 1981), is criticized for a major omission: the marine flora and fauna. Many of the deficiencies stem from producing a text from only one department of the University. *Cities of the world: world regional urban development,* edited by Stanley D. Brunn and Jack I. Williams (New York, Harper and Row, 1983), attempts to cover too many cities. Selection of at most two cities per region would have avoided travelogue-type treatment. Bibliographical details are full, and the appended key-word/descriptors throughout are helpful. There is an annual index of reviews.

Annales de géographie (Paris, Colin, 1891–. 6 p.a.), a key international geographical journal, is published with the support of the Centre National de la Recherche Scientifique. Vol. 39, November/December 1984 (pp. 649–783), has 32 headed and signed reviews on pp. 719–78. The reviews, 500-2,500 words long, are analytical and critical. D. Sugden's *Arctic and Antarctic: a modern geographical synthesis* (Oxford, Blackwell, 1982) gives a detailed analysis of Polar geomorphology, oceanography and population, as well as of political and economic factors. The theme is well handled and the illustrations often outstanding. One drawback is the almost exclusive use of English-language material, omitting Gierloff-Emden, Lorius and Malaurie as sources. Bibliographical details omit prices and ISBNs. The annual index has subject-grouping, entries being earmarked 'A' ('articles') or 'N' ('notes et comptes rendus').

Geography: journal of the Geographical Association (Sheffield, the Association, 1901–. 4 p.a. Circulation: 9,000) 'exists to foster the knowledge of geography and the teaching of geography in all categories of educational institutions, from school to university, in the United Kingdom and abroad'. Vol. 70 (1), no. 306, January 1985 (96 pp.) carries 31 non-listed book-reviews, each 300–500 words, on pp. 81–96. Reviews, signed (without affiliations) are analytical and critical, indicating readership. *The outer city,* by John Herington (New York, Harper and Row, 1984) is praised as well-researched and a clear guide to a complex subject, 'probably more useful to the undergraduate and the teacher than the A-level student'. Michael Pacione's *Rural geography* (also reviewed in *Geographical journal,* above) is faulted for devoting 'very little space to analysis, interpretation and discussion of the issues raised'. Bibliographical details include ISBNs but not illustrative matter. The annual index, cumulated for Vols. 1-54, covers authors and subjects of books reviewed.

Journal of historical geography (London and New York, Academic Press, 1975–. 4 p.a.) is a scholarly interdisciplinary periodical, with both British and US editors and book-review editors. Vol. 11 (2), April 1985 (pp. 115–240), has 21 listed and signed book-reviews on pp. 210–36, plus five shorter notices. The three main sections comprise: The British Isles and the European mainland (12); The Americas (6); Other studies (3). The reviews average about 700 words in length and are analytical and critical. Comments on *Place-names in the landscape,* by Margaret Gelling (London, Dent, 1982) begin, 'Dr. Gelling's book makes a major contribution towards the more efficient use of place-names in landscape study. It is much more than a dictionary; topographical terms are grouped under such headings as 'rivers, springs, pools and lakes' or 'ploughland and pasture'. The review finds deficiencies: 'the need for more maps, to clarify many of the arguments put forward', and the 'tendency to necessarily equate an estate name with an early settlement site'. Specific terms are queried. Nevertheless, here is 'a serious book for the investigation of landscape development'. Bibliographical details omit ISBNs. Reviews (listed quarterly) are indexed in *Book review index* and *Internationale Bibliographie der Rezensionen.*

Progress in human geography (London, Edward Arnold, 1977–. 4 p.a.) is 'an international review of geographical work in the social sciences and humanities'. Vol. 8 (3), September 1984 (pp. 313–471), has 22 listed book-reviews (600–1,500 words apiece) on pp. 429-71, signed, with affiliations. The team of reviewers, mostly British, include five Americans, one Irish, one African and one Australian. Treatment is analytical (with quotations), markedly critical and also comparative. A book of readings on *The internal structure of the city,* by L.S. Bourne (New York, Oxford University Press, 1982), is faulted for inattention to planning and policy. On the other hand, *Industrial organization and location,* by P. McDermott and M. Taylor (Cambridge University Press, 1982) could well turn out to be the most important book on geography in this decade, 'at least from the perspective of conceptionable and theoretical reviews'. Bibliographical details omit illustrative data. The annual index has two sections, one recording titles reviewed, the other, authors and reviewers.

The geographical review (New York, American Geographical Society, 1916–. 4 p.a. Circulation: 3,500) is a key international journal, at one time (1956–65) also of value for its annual review of new geographical journals.[27] Vol. 74 (4), October 1984 (pp. 388–503), has 14 'Geographical reviews', signed and averaging about 700 words apiece. The five sections comprise: Regional; Cultural; Physical; Geographical education; Geographers. Reviews are analytical and evaluative, with some comparisons. *The geography of warfare,* by Patrick O'Sullian and Jesse W. Miller Jr (New York, St Martin's Press, 1983) is wide-ranging: 'the geographical dimensions of guerilla operations and urban conflict, missile strategy, the domino theory and defensive–offensive tatics', as well as the geographical aspects of various battles. The reviewer objects to the high price ($20 for 172pp), a solitary, poorly designed and reproduced map, some typographical errors and factual mistakes. 'Even so, the book is a most welcome addition to the literature on military geography' (similar efforts being few). The 900-item index 'makes it an even more valuable reference'. Bibliographical details omit ISBNs. The annual index, cumulated 10-yearly, includes author, title and reviewer entries for books reviewed.

Erdkunde. Archiv für wissenschaftliche Geographie (Bonn, Dümmler, 1947–. 4 p.a.) is a leading continental geographical journal. Vol. 39 (1), March 1985 (72pp.), has 16 signed book-reviews on pp. 63–7 (150–450 words each), briefly analytical and evaluative, with some indication of readership. The short review of *Géographie des régions arides,* by Jean Dresch and Christiane Motsch (Paris, Presses Universitaires de France, 1982) deals with three aspects of arid zones: climatological, geomorphological and biogeographical. The text concludes with a chapter on desertification and selected further reading. The work is welcomed as a stimulating handbook, a valuable source of information for both students and lay persons. Following the book-reviews proper are 18 short notices, (pp. 67–9). Bibliographical details omit only ISBNs. Reviews are indexed in *Internationale Bibliographie der Rezensionen.*

Regional studies: journal of the Regional Studies Association (Cambridge University Press, 1967–. 6 p.a.) is the organ of the

Association, an independent, interdisciplinary body exclusively concerned with urban and regional planning and development. Vol. 19 (1), February 1985 (84pp.), carries 10 book-reviews, signed, with affiliations, analytical and critical, with some footnotes. *Internal colonialism: essays around a theme,* edited by D. Drakakis-Smith and S.W. Williams (Department of Geography, University of Edinburgh, 1983) claims to seek 'meaning and utility' in the concept of internal colonialism: 'But it fails to consider spatial dimensions, racial, ethnic and cultural differentiation as well as an analysis of the centralisation of means of production'. Bibliographical details omit illustrative matter. Reviews are indexed in *Internationale Bibliographie der Rezensionen.*

Bulletin Geography and Map Division, Special Libraries Association (New York, the Association, 1947–. 4 p.a. Circulation: 950) is aimed mainly at geography and map librarians. No. 135, March 1984 (80pp.), contains 13 signed book-reviews (pp. 66–73), 200 to 800 words in length. Editorial staff includes a book-review editor, and reviewers' affiliations are shown. Entries are analytical and critical, indicating readership. *Map user's source book,* by Lance Feild (New York, Oceana, 1982) brings together many map sources but cites no new material, 'nor are there any new insights into the problem of map acquisition'. *Dictionary of human geography,* edited by R.J. Johnston (New York, Free Press, 1981) is, on the other hand, praised as an excellent reference book, not confined to definitions; illustrations are helpful, but few; 'this dictionary is also quite readable'. Appended is an annotated list of 'Recent publications of interest' (pp. 62–5). Bibliographical details are given in full. The annual index, cumulated, lists books reviewed under both authors and titles, as well as under reviewers' names.

The cartographic journal (London, British Cartographic Society, 1964–. 2 p.a. Circulation: 1,800) is highly regarded for both scholarship and production. Vol. 21 (1), June 1984 (90 pp.), has 11 signed reviews (500–1,500 words each) on pp. 76–8, with an appended list of reviewers, all British, and their affiliations. The 11 shorter notices (200–400 words apiece) are unsigned. There is a book-review editor; and the major reviews are analytical and critical, indicating readership. *Cartographic relief presentation* , by Eduard Imhof; edited by H.J. Steward (Berlin, de Gruyter, 1982) is a translation of *Kartographische Geländsdarstellung* (1965). The 1,000-word review acclaims it as 'what must be the most thorough and authoritative text-book available in the English language', the illustrations and diagrams bringing the subject to life. Bibliographical details are in full. The annual index includes sections 'Recent maps and atlases' and 'Reviews'.

Annals of the Association of American Geographers (Washington, DC, the Association, 1911–. 4 p.a. Circulation: 8,500) is 'the leading substantial, scholarly geographical periodical in the United States'. Vol. 74 (2), June 1984 (pp. 193–352), has 10 signed reviews (800–1,000 words apiece) on pp. 331–52, with fuller affiliations than is usual. Book-reviews are analytical and critical. Thus *Anglo-American landscapes*, by Christopher Mulvey (Cambridge University Press, 1981) is accused of being badly titled; it is a study of the reactions of some Americans to some 'English' landscapes and of some English men and women's reactions to some 'American' landscapes, based on 70 or more travel surveys of a subjective and 'literary' kind, to the neglect of the social theme. A volume on *Sport and place: a geography of sport in England, Scotland and Wales*, by John Bale (London, C. Hurst, 1983), although considered one of the most provocative books on the topic so far, is criticized for its illustrations — 'the poorest I have ever seen in a published book'. Bibliographical details are in full. Annual reviews, cumulated 10-yearly, cover articles, reviews, map supplement and commentary.

Journal of geography in higher education (Oxford Polytechnic, Faculty of Modern Studies, 1977–. 2 p.a. Circulation: 750) is devoted to the teaching of geography in polytechnics and universities. Vol. 8 (1), 90pp., has a section 'Resources', pp. 49–78, comprising review-essays by three reviewers. 'Textbooks in environmental geomorphology: a review' (pp. 49–53) evaluates and compares 14 textbooks for coverage of various geographical topics and encapsulates results in a table. Other sections review a video-disc on physical geography, and 28 films on the nuclear energy dispute. Bibliographical details on the text-books omits ISBNs. A subject index to reviews of text-books so far covered in the *Journal* is on p. 61.

References

1. *TLS*, no. 4211, 16 December 1983, p. 1399.
2. Kenney, Louis A. 'Reviewing of history books', *Illinois libraries*, vol. 41, May 1959, p. 355.
3. Hay, Denis. 'The historical periodical: some problems', *History*, vol. 34, June 1969, p. 173.
4. *American historical review*, vol. 60, 1954/55, p. 258.
5. Paves, Richard (editor, *English historical review*). Letter, 9 November 1954, quoted in Kenney, *op. cit.*, p. 359.
6. *Harvard guide to American history*. Cambridge, Mass., 1954, p. 50.
7. Paves, Richard, *op. cit.*, p. 359.

8. *History,* vol. 34, June 1969, pp. 170–1.
9. Clark, Sir George Norman. 'Historical reviewing', in *Essays in history presented to Reginald Lane Poole,* ed. H.W.C. Davis, Oxford, Clarendon Press, 1927, p. 124.
10. *The local historian,* vol. 16 (3) August 1984, pp. 131–2.
11. *The Times,* 3 June 1982, p. 26.
12. *Choice,* vol. 21 (9), May 1984, p. 1368.
13. *Choice,* vol. 22 (4), December 1984, p. 528.
14. Cole, Fred C., in *The journal of Southern history,* vol. 20 (3), August 1954, pp. 434–5.
15. *Books in Scotland,* vol. 17, Winter/Spring 1985, p. 21.
16. *New scientist,* 12 April 1982, p. 47.
17. *Aslib book list,* vol. 45 (1), January 1980, item 23.
18. *Industrial archaeology review,* vol. 6 (3), October 1982, p. 245.
19. *TLS,* no. 4211, 16 December 1983, p. 1400.
20. Beaver, W., in *Geographical journal,* vol. 148 (2), July 1982, pp. 179–81.
21. *Geographical journal,* vol. 149 (3), November 1983, pp. 316–33.
22. *Annals of the Association of American Geographers,* vol. 74 (2), June 1984, p. 331.
23. *The cartographic journal,* vol. 24 (1), June 1984, pp. 75–6.
24. *The geographical magazine,* vol. 54 (8), August 1982, p. 477.
25. *Library review,* vol. 31, Summer 1982, p. 157.
26. Harris, Chauncy D. *Annotated world list of selected current geographical serials,* 4th edn. Chicago, Ill., University of Chicago, Department of Geography, 1980, p. 133.
27. Harris, Chauncy D. *Bibliography of geography,* pt 1. Chicago, Ill., University of Chicago, Department of Geography, 1976, p. 138.

13.   Children's books

Grace Hallworth

The reviewing of children's books has grown in stature and also in the considerable number of intermediaries available since Dorothy K. Robertson's seminal survey, *The reviewing of children's books in Britain*.[1] The proliferation of reviewing journals gives the impression that children's books and children's book reviewing belong once again in the market place with reviews 'speaking' on behalf of divers issues.

Among the burgeoning growth of publications is the in-house journal *Recent children's fiction*, bi-annual product of an Avon and Gloucestershire reviewing team drawn from education, who provide pertinent and succinct reviews ranging from those for preschool picture books to those for novels for young adults. Many education authorities offer some degree of guidance through regular publications, such as the practical tips on craft and activity books in *Contact*, vol. 13 (21) 7 December 1984, and the sensitively written reviews on children's published poetry in *Language matters*, numbers 1/2 (one issue) 1984, or the in-depth reviews on world fiction in the *English magazine*, all published by Inner London Education Authority. Other helpful guides for teachers at nursery to primary-age schools include *Child education* and *Junior education*, both monthly journals published by Scholastic Publications.

A new generation of 'cultural crusaders' has broadened the debate of the 1960s on the provision of relevant literature for working-class children, to embrace black and Asian minority groups now living in Britain. Gillian Klein's *Multicultural teaching*, one of the journals of this genre, is committed to 'combat racism in school and community'. Articles covering all aspects of teaching and learning in a multicultural society predominate, but it does contain a few reviews of children's books and other resources and vol. 11 (2), Spring 1984, has an interesting survey of recent children's books entitled 'Fictional people, political facts'. There is less evidence of journals which evaluate the work of Scottish, Irish and Welsh children's authors as cultural groups, but the quarterly journal *Books in Scotland* has occasional reviews and articles on children's literature by Scottish writers.

The Essex review of children's literature, one of the early home-spun initiatives, provides reviews of fiction for primary and secondary teachers. *Learning resources*, the published assessments from Leicestershire Libraries and Information Service, includes fiction and non-fiction for primary and secondary teachers, and also films, video- tapes and computer resources.

Some periodicals do not review books in the strict sense of the word but present valuable overviews which 'move into the broader form of literary discussion'[2] with ample room to explore and develop ideas. *Children's literature in education*, a joint British and American publication, *Signal: approaches to children's book* and *Bookmark* are outstanding examples of this ilk. Similarly, the specialist journal *Schools poetry review* surveys and evaluates the work of poets, past and present. A unique journal is *Bookbird*, an Ibby production which is primarily an international news magazine on the children's book-world but includes reviews of books suitable for translations.

In an article on reviewing, Stuart Hannabuss deftly sums up the activity thus: 'the very best reviewing, short or long, implies sound critical standards. These often impose the obligation on the reviewer of putting the work in context, indicating its significance, examining its tone and stance and the ways in which it engages the imagination of the reader'.[3]

Divergence of approach and viewpoint is most marked in the reviewing of imaginative literature, as is demonstrated in the following reviews of Mairi Hedderwick's *Katie Morag delivers the mail* (London, Bodley Head, 1984). In *Books for your children*, vol. 19 (1), 1984, it is introduced with a comparison to Arthur Ransome's stories in its clearly defined community, and the review continues, 'This picture book's for a younger age group but Kate's adventure on the small Scottish Isle of Struay when she falls in the river on her way to deliver the mail to the other side of the island will start children's imagination wondering about the island in much the same way' In *Material matters*, vol. 8 (9), April 1984, the full review reads, 'When Katie Morag has to deliver the mail, a catastrophe follows — she drops the parcels, the labels smudge and the wrong things get delivered to people. Grannie comes to the rescue and all ends well. The storyline is weak and the illustrations rather wishy-washy, but the idea of living on an island may appeal to children'. In *The Horn book magazine*, vo. 60 (5), September/October 1984, the reviewer sets the scene with a description of life on an island, followed by a literary synopsis of the story and concludes with the evaluation:

> A slight, winsome story is greatly enriched by lively, descriptive watercolours, many of them double-page spreads, giving a delightful sense of the island, its residents, and their domestic arrangements. End papers add their own significance, showing a panorama of the setting by day and night. The author-artist will be remembered for her illustrations for Jane Duncan's *Brave Janet Reachfar*...and for Rumer Godden's *The old woman in a vinegar bottle*.

Whereas books on computers and other modern communication gadgets tend to receive serious and full treatment in reviewing journals, books about other lands and peoples receive scant attention. Whether titles of such books are grouped by series for collective reviewing, or individually assessed, the approach can be slight and subjective. In *Junior bookshelf*, vol. 48 (1), February 1984, G. Burns' *Let's go to New Zealand* (London, Watts, 1984) is reviewed as follows: 'This addition to the "Let's go to" series is plentifully illustrated and the information in the text is appropriate and accurate. As a visitor to New Zealand over a period of years I can vouch for both the detail and general impression given by this little volume. It is first class'. *In British book news: children's books Autumn '84*, four books in the same series on Antarctica, Indonesia, Malaysia and Singapore are grouped for composite reviewing. A critical listing of specific shortcomings comprises most of the review of 170 words, which reads in part,

> Each book has a map of the country itself and one locating it within the world. However, the maps are consistently placed on page 9, which is difficult to find...Each book also refers to at least one place not on the map! Indonesia, Malaysia and Singapore sketchily cover population, produce, geography, religion, customs and education, but home-life (mentioned on the back cover of the series) is not touched on. In Indonesia and Singapore the photos on each page illustrate the text, which is less bitty than in Malaysia.

In *Children's book bulletin* reviewers have more space to explore and develop a theme than in most journals, though it is the reviewer's percipience which makes for the balanced and informative review of Carol Barker's *Arjun and his village in India* (Oxford University Press, 1979) in no. 3, Spring 1980. Our attention is drawn to the 'decorative drawings of doe eyed children...which have the...effect of mitigating any sense of hardship of people's lives in this arid region' and to 'several confusing inconsistencies of detail — reference to male and female drummers in the text when only male drummers are shown' (in the illustrations).

Indexes to reviews

Children's book review index, ed. Gary C. Tarbert (Detroit, Mich., Gale, 1975–.) is based on Gale's *Book review index* and includes all citations for children's books listed in *BRI*. A few periodicals included in *Children's book review index* are not listed in *BRI*. Three issues are published annually, with a compilation at the end of each year. Another publication in this field is *Children's literature review: excerpts from reviews, criticism, and commentary on books for children*. Vol. 8, which was published in 1985 (Detroit, Mich., Gale),covers 14 authors and author-illustrators. Each work is represented by an average of two to six reviews, and complete bibliographical citations facilitate the location of each original review. There are cumulative indexes to authors, titles and nationalities, and an appendix identifies the sources from which material has been excerpted in the volume. *Library literature* (New York, H.W. Wilson, 1921–) is an index to library information science published six times per year with an annual cumulation. In addition to periodicals listed, it also indexes non-library science periodicals covered by other Wilson indexes. All entries are arranged in one A–Z sequence and citations to individual book-reviews are listed in a separate alphabet following the main body of the index. Book-reviews which appear as part of a review-article are also indexed under subject headings. In-depth assessment of American reviewing journals was obtained from Mary Meacham's *Information sources in children's literature* (Westport, Conn., Greenwood Press, 1978).

Reviewing journals

This selection of reviewing journals of children's books in English attempts to be representative of the broad spectrum of book material currently evaluated. I have therefore included educational journals which review a substantial number of essentially 'library' books in addition to their staple diet of text and professional books, journals which reflect the ideologies of groups within the society, and a selection of notable journals from Australia, New Zealand and North America, in view of the increased movement of books which takes place between those countries and Britain.

In order to obtain a wider view of the use and usefulness of children's journals circulating in Britain, a questionnaire was sent to librarians in nine library and education authorities, which included large city authorities and counties. Response from over one hundred librarians indicate that reviewing journals serve such disparate functions as 'reminders of basic stock and popular materials', 'a supplement to the local assessment scheme', 'a means of shaking you out of your complacency', and simply 'to keep in touch with the professional scene at home and abroad'. Such multi-faceted use militates against a system of arrangement which satisfies all practical requirements. However, responses do imply that discrimination of use is influenced by the schoolage levels of books reviewed, and the journals (under titles A–Z) are grouped as follows:

> *Reviewing journals: pre-school to mid-secondary* which review books for babies to approximately 13 to 14 years, and may contain reviews for non-book and professional resources.
>
> *Reviewing journals: all ages* which review books for very young children through young adults, and may contain reviews for non-book and professional resources.
>
> *Annual book guides and reviewing journals* which are particularly selective in their choice of books for children and young people, and may contain reviews for non-book and professional resources.

Reviewing journals: pre-school to mid-secondary

Bookquest (Brighton, East Sussex County Library, 1976–. 3 p.a. Circulation: 2,000), also produced for Brighton Polytechnic, receives contributions from librarians, teachers and members of children's book groups. Reviewers' names, with affiliations, are affixed to reviews. Mainly fiction is covered, but poetry and drama may be included. Each issue contains about 40 reviews, some clustered, which average 200 words. The style of reviewing is a combination of children's responses and teachers' perceptions of book and story requirements expressed in the confident voice of the practitioner. In vol. 7 (1), 1984, Geoff Abbott's *Pond life* (London, Macmillan, 1983) was used by a class of '7–9 year olds [who] tended to use the photographs as their main talking point rather than the general text', but the reviewer is confident that 'older juniors would find the more detailed explanations useful to them, especially as part of a project'. Bibliographical details omit pagination, but age range and ratings are provided. The practice of reviewing in-use increases the usefulness of this journal but also determines the extent to which current books are reviewed. A commissioned article treats an aspect of literature in an educational context, and notices of courses, exhibitions and opening hours of centres are carried. Vol. 7 (3) has cumulative indexes to vol. 6, 1983, and to vol. 7, 1984. Advertisements.

Books for your children: a magazine for parents about books for children (Birmingham, 1965–. 3 p.a. Circulation 25,000), organ of the Federation of Children's Book Groups, contains a plethora of reviews and annotated lists. Reviewers' names but not affiliations are given and reviews are initialled. The main review-section is divided into six age categories, ranging from preschool to 12 years and upwards, but there are often additional reviews of non-fiction books. Vol. 19 (3), 1984, has 86 fiction titles in the review section, plus a section of 22 information books suitable for presents, and an evaluation of poetry books for primary children. Reviews average 50 to 120 words and the style is mainly descriptive. The editorial of vol. 19 (2), Summer 1984, informs that a need for 'hard literary criticism' has been expressed but that the philosophy of the magazine is to 'advise and recommend rather than review in a more strictly critical sense'. Bibliographical details omit year of publication, pagination and ISBNs. Other features include announcements of courses, children's book awards, exhibitions, and correspondence is invited. Black-and-white and some colour illustrations help to make this an attractive browsing magazine of particular use to parents. No index. Advertisements.

British book news: children's books (London, British Council, 1983–. 4 p.a.) was formerly *Children's book review.* Names of reviewers but not their affiliations are given and reviews are signed. Coverage of books includes picture books through fiction and non-fiction suitable for middle secondary children, plus professional reading. Spring 1984 issue reviews 232 titles, with as many as six titles grouped by genre, format, theme or series for composite reviewing. Reviews average 100 to 120 words and the approach is a blend of descriptive and critical, with a keen eye for the authenticity of facts and qualification of authors. A reviewer of Terry Jennings's *The wild life in your home* (London, Young Library, 1984) points out that 'there are a few inaccuracies and misleading statements here and there', whilst another regrets 'that the publishers include no information as to the qualifications of these authors' in assessing four social history books. Bibliographical details are full, mentioning the inclusion of maps, index, bibliography. A regular feature is 'Booklist', a two-part list of books to be published within the year. Black-and-white illustrations, superimposed on coloured paper which differentiates review sections, enhance the text. Sound reviewing and interesting articles find equal favour with librarians and teachers. Each issue has a title and author-index. Advertisements.

Junior Bookshelf (Huddersfield, 1936–. 6 p.a. Circulation: 3,000) was until 1949 the only children's reviewing journal in the United Kingdom. There are ten regular reviewers but neither names nor affiliations are given, though reviews are intialled. An average of 95 books per issue are reviewed covering a range from picture books through ages fourteen to fifteen, plus a section on new books for librarians. Length and style of reviews vary depending on reviewer as well as on the type of book. For picture books and under tens, the average length is 80 to 100 words, while professional reading and books for older children receive, on the whole, much longer and more balanced reviews. Many titles are grouped for reviewing, although not necessarily with the aim of linking similar books or reviewing comparatively. Each issue carries one or two articles and brief news items. Bibliographical details omit year of publication, series title and ISBNs. The final number of each year is issued with an author and title-index, and there is a separate index for contributors of articles. Advertisements.

Primary education review (London, National Union of Teachers, 1975–. 3 p.a.) includes reviews of children's literature, and reviewers' names with affiliations are listed. Issue no. 20, Summer 1984, has reviews on pp. 20–31 covering about 30 fiction and folktales, and 68 non-fiction resources, including professional reading. Reviews are grouped under headings which reflect the interdisciplinary nature of education and comments emphasize concerns of teacher and classroom. Michael Rosen and Graham Round's *How to get out of the bath* (A Hippo Book, London, Scholastic Book Services, 1984) is assessed as encouraging 'reading, thinking and creative writing'; and two books in 'The Living world' series, *Grasslands* and *Mountains* by Clive Catchpole (London, Walker, 1984) are 'better suited to older juniors' because 'at times, the vocabulary would be a little above the reading ability of younger children'. Suggested lists of books for further reading often append reviews. Bibliographical details omit pagination. Photographs, diagrams, cartoons connected with the many informed articles on educational matters, enliven the appearances. No index. Advertisements.

Tried and tested: books to be read aloud (London, Centre for Language in Primary Education, 1978–. 3 p.a. Circulation: 1,500–2,000) has a small selection of reports on books which have been read to children in the classroom by nursery and primary teachers in Inner London schools. Each issue covers about 12 to 15 stories and the reviews, signed, with affiliations, average 200 words. Comments provide practical information, citing responses gleaned from the classroom and describing activities developed from sharing books. The nature of reviewing precludes an overly concern with current publications. Bibliographical details omit year of publication and pagination, but the various editions of a work are frequently given. Black-and-white illustrations complement the text of this helpful guide to shared reading. Index cumulates periodically, and CLPE publications are advertised.

Reviewing journals: all ages

Booklist (Chicago, Ill., American Library Association, twice a month September to July, and once in August. Circulation: 36,980) is the official review organ of the ALA. The editor and two full-time reviewers evaluate 50 to 70 books per issue, ranging from pre-school through adult books suitable for older children, and fiction and non-fiction are integrated. A section of specially assessed easy-to-read books with reading and interest levels provided, appears in every other issue. Reviews average 150 words and adopt a stance between 'critic and librarian'[4] reflecting the Association's principle of 'intellectual freedom'.[5] The journal's policy is to review only those books which can be recommended for purchase, and an asterisk denotes a highly recommended book. Bibliographical details are full for books as well as audiovisual resources reviewed; classification number and subject headings are suggested, and grade levels given, except for pre-school books which have age ranges. Special reading lists of foreign-language children's books, paperback reprints of children's books, and professional reading are included. Each issue has an index, and a cumulative index appears in the August issue of each year.

Books for keeps: the magazine of the School Bookshop Association (London, 1980–. 6 p.a. Circulation: 4,000) places emphasis on the reviewing of paperback fiction. Six regular reviewers, named with affiliations, are also identified by photographs, and reviews are initialled. In the main review-section reviews are grouped under teaching range, beginning with 'Nursery/infant' through older readers. Reviews average 100 words and are mainly pragmatic but also seek to extend the literary experience of the child. In issue no. 24, January 1984, the reviewer of Naomi Lewis and Tony Ross' *Hare and Badger go to town* (London, Methuen, 1984) observes that 'the artist's humour and the writer's style combine to *show* rather than *tell* that the theme is an important and timely one. I'll read this to juniors along with extracts from *Wind in the willows* and *Dream days* — to show them the things a children's book can say'. Bibliographical details omit year of publication and pagination. Many articles are included, some of which cite fiction and non-fiction books in both editions. A regular feature is 'Authorgraph' which highlights an established author or author-illustrator. A lively journal with many illustrations in black-and-white and colour, which is accessible to older children and a veritable mine of information for teachers and librarians. No index. Advertisements.

Bulletin of the Center for Children's Books (University of Chicago Press, 1945–. 11 p.a. Circulation: 9,500) is a source of current book reviews. The editor, assisted by an advisory committee, reviews about 60 to 75 fiction and non-fiction books for children and young adults each month, and the arrangement is an integrated author sequence of fiction and non-fiction. Reviews, which average 120 to 130 words, are highly discriminating on the basis of literary value and express a concern with the child as reader. In vol. 37 (5), January 1984, Joan Phillips's *Peek-a-boo! I see you!* (New York, Grosset, 1983) is described as 'A tall book with heavy board pages, this has a rhyming text that is related to a series of pictures in which baby animals or children are concealed and then visible. "Kitten's putting on her clothes/Getting dressed from head to toes..." The illustrations are...laden with anthropomorphism...and the small merit in the book lies in the ramification of the concept that creatures aren't gone just because they can't be seen'. Bibliographical details are full, providing all editions of a work with relevant prices. Symbols are used to indicate various aspects of books; an asterisk denotes a book of special distinction. Reading range is for grade level rather than age of child, except for preschool books. The list of sources about children's literature which appears regularly on the inside back cover, is much appreciated by librarians and teachers. An index is published once a year as part of the July–August issue. Advertisements.

Canadian materials for schools and libraries: an annotated critical bibliography (Toronto, Canadian Library Association, 1971–. 6 p.a. Circulation: 2,000). A policy statement in November 1984 issue claims that 'All obtainable materials, including text-books in all media formats published and/or produced in Canada since January

1, 1973, will be evaluated and included'. However, initial exceptions to this policy include French-language materials. Names of reviewers, with affiliations, are given and reviews are signed. Each issue contains 100 to 120 reviews of book and non-book resources, ranging from elementary to secondary school age, plus a few post-secondary and professional resources. Detailed guide-lines for reviewing all resources are provided. Reviews, which average 200 words, are fully documented and the style is a blend of critical, descriptive and analytical, achieving a balanced viewpoint on the whole. A 'not recommended' rating is given at the end of a review of 286 words. Bibliographical details are full and place of publication is stated; reading levels refer to school grades. The journal also carries a few professional news items, and correspondence is invited. Each issue has an index and there is an additional cumulative index in the final issue of each volume. Only professional publications are advertised.

Children's book bulletin for news of progressive moves in children's literature (London, 6 issues from 1979 to 1981, publication to be recommenced soon) is described as the 'review journal for news and reviews of non-sexist children's books, children's books for the multi-ethnic society and children's books which reflect the history and present day contribution of working people as well as other areas not covered by mainstream children's journals'. Names of reviewers, with affiliations, are given and reviews are signed. Resources covered range from preschool through young adults, plus professional materials and include non-book resources. Issues no. 6, Summer 1981, reviews 73 items, of which six are published and/or distributed by non-established sources. Grouping books for comparative assessment is employed and particularly appropriate for conveying the subtlety and similarity of social issues dealt with in this journal. Jan Needle's *A fine boy for killing* (London, Deutsch, 1979) is compared and contrasted with Peter Carter's *The sentinels* (Oxford University Press, 1980) to demonstrate the plight of the English working class and the African at the turn of the nineteenth century, in a review of 646 words. Reviews are stringent and uncompromising, and positive in tone. The articles are often themselves exemplars of extended analytical and literary reviewing. Bibliographical details omit year of publication and pagination. Some issues carry correspondence, and news and comments inform of related developments and activities. Black-and-white illustrations relieve long dense columns of text. Each issue contains an index of authors, titles and illustrators.

Dragon's tale (Aberystwyth, Dyfed, Welsh National Centre for

Children's Literature, 1984–. Annual), Vol. 1 appeared in January 1984 and the editorial expresses a hope that the magazine will inform teachers, parents and librarians of available books in Wales written both in English and Welsh. Names but not affiliations of reviewers are given and an average of 19 books are reviewed per issue, covering mainly fiction and folklore for children of primary and secondary age levels. The style of reviewing is not noticeably critical, tending to dwell on the more literary and cultural aspects of works. Bibliographical details are full, and age suitability is suggested within the review. A literary article on traditional Welsh materials in modern fantasy cites Alan Garner, Susan Cooper and other notable children's authors. A regular feature is a list of Tir na n -og prizes awarded annually to the author of the best original book in the Welsh language and to the author of the best English book with an authentic Welsh background. Black-and-white illustrations complement the text. No index.

Dragon's teeth (London, National Committee on Racism in Children's Books, 1979–. 4 p.a.) sets out to 'faithfully represent the experience of black people...and to tap the rich oral tradition of Africa, Asia and the Caribbean'. Names but not affiliations of reviewers are given, and it is a tenet of the editorial board that books about a particular community be reviewed by a member of that community. The journal devotes most of its space to articles which are often controversial and 'essential reading', but each issue carries about a dozen book-reviews of children and adult resources. Signed reviews are lengthy expositions, averaging 300 words, which set the scene and provide background information for the multi-layered approach to reviewing typical of this journal. The tone, essentially supportive to Third World writers, offers constructive criticism. A young poet's work is said to have 'the attraction of being rough and ready, there is no polish, no smoothness, no sophistication, just directness. This avoidance of poetic craft and subtlety can be a genuine strength', but the reviewer rejects the blurb's claim that 'the poems reflect a maturity of sustained poetic expression'; rather, the publication of the work is seen as a genuine inspiration to 'others who feel that they have similar things to say'. Bibliographical details omit pagination. Black-and-white illustrations, cartoons, photographs enliven the journal. No index.

Growing point: Margery Fisher's regular review of books for the growing families of the English reading world and for parents, teachers, librarians, and other guardians (Northampton, 1962–. 6 p.a.). All books are reviewed by the editor except where otherwise stated, and resources covered range from preschool through young adult fiction and non-fiction. Literary discourse links clusters of fiction to develop a hypothesis. In vol. 23 (3), September 1984, ten stories and concept books for the very young are grouped under the heading 'To begin with' and introduced with the question 'What is a concept?' In the 1984 issues an average of 40 additional fiction and non-fiction titles are individually reviewed under graphic headings, and the arrangement in these sections is A–Z by author. Full-length reviews averaging 500 words feature an oustanding book, professional publications which merit attention, and an old favourite, but other reviews average 120 to 130 words. The composite nature of reviewing some fiction titles does not inhibit the scrupulous attention to detail and clear-sighted observation for which this editor is noted and whose aim is 'to give anyone concerned with children's books some guidance about literary types and approximate readership'.[6] There is a cumulative index to each volume.

Horn book magazine: about books for children and young adults (Boston, Mass., 1924–. 6 p.a. Circulation: 20,000) maintains its reputation of being 'one of the most scholarly and literate publications in children's literature'. An editorial staff of six members whose names but not affiliations are given, review 50 to 70 publications including non-book items in each issue. Reviews are initialled and average 180 to 200 words, and arrangement is an A–Z sequence of fiction in four sequences. Resources range from preschool through young adult, with parallel arrangement for recommended paperbacks and for new editions and reissues; a limited number of non-fiction for 12 year-olds and upwards is also reviewed. There are special reviews on science books and adult books of interest to young adults, and an out-of-print list reminds librarians of significant books which may still be in stock. Reviews focus on literary and aesthetic aspects of works, and criticism, where it occurs, is oblique and balanced. In vol. 60 (4), August 1984, the reviewer of Brian Wildsmith's *Daisy* (New York, Pantheon, 1984) writes, 'The author-artist continues to be more inspired by colour than by words. Still, despite the perfunctory writing, his use of the expansive technique of half-page pictures alternately bound with full pages create some of his most varied and animated illustrations'. However, a more forthright tone is adopted for another author-illustrator, who is advised to 'turn her impressive talents to something fresh and new'— thus reflecting the personal tone which frequently sounds through the formal literary style. Bibliographical details are full, and all editions of a work are given. Many librarians value this journal especially for 'its excellent articles', including the Newberry and Caldecott medals acceptance speeches. Sample illustrations in black-and-white pervade. Each number has an index of authors and books, and there is a yearly index in December issue of each year. Advertisements are also indexed.

Material matters (Hertfordshire Library Service, 1976–. 9 p.a. Circulation: 1,947) is a journal in which 'current publications are evaluated' by members of the library service, teachers, educational advisors, parents and children'. Book and non-book resources are grouped according to broad age ranges for fiction, and by Dewey Decimal Classification for non-fiction, and cover preschool to young adult materials. Popular foreign-language books in French, German, Italian and Spanish are included and there is an increasing number of publications from community groups and small publishers. There are 247 items in vol. 9 (6), of which 210 are evaluated, and reviews, which are not signed, average 50 words. Despite the excellent guidelines, resources are briefly assessed. In vol. 9 (6) a reviewer fails to clarify the content of a book on a relatively unfamiliar theme, and Janis Hannaford's *Ramadan and Id-ul-fitr* (Oxford, Pergamon, 1982) is assessed, 'Although slightly patronising and simplistic in approach, many of the chapters are interesting and informative at a basic level. They can be used in a study of Islam but would require further material for an in-depth study'. A supplement of 'Not recommended' books is circulated with each issue. There is a separate cumulative index for each volume as well as one for the 'Not recommended' supplements. This is a journal particularly appreciated for its broad coverage of materials and learning resources.

Reading time (Curtin, ACT 2605, The Children's Book Council of Australia, 1957–. 4 p.a. Circulation: 4,000) reviews children's books published in Australia. Reviewers' names but not affiliations are given and reviews are initialled. No. 93, October 1984, contains 49 reviews in sections representing picture books through older readers, collections and non-fiction. Reviews average 150 to 200 words and are mainly descriptive. In issue no. 90, January 1984, the review of Dr Zsolt Harsanyi and Richard Hutton's *Genetic prophecy: beyond the double helix* (London, Granada, 1982), although 275 words long, is confined to a detailed description of the work, with no evaluation or indication as to level of specialism required for comprehending the work. Articles on approaches to children's literature feature regularly. A cumulative index of authors and their publications, contributors of articles, titles and series is issued with the final number of each volume in October. This is a valuable bibliographical tool which covers American, Australian, British and New Zealand publications. Advertisements.

School Librarian: official journal of the School Library Association (Oxford, 1937–. 4 p.a. Circulation: 5,000) is a forum for matters on librarianship and education, aspects of literature, and a reviewing journal of books and resources for children and young people. Names but not affiliations of reviewers are given and reviews are signed. Resources covered range from picture books to novels for 11- to 15-year-olds, and non-fiction suitable for 16- to 19-year-olds. Lists of reprints and new editions parallel fiction and non-fiction sections. Vol. 32 (4), December 1984, carries 117 signed reviews and clustering is employed to discuss books which share a common feature. Two books about dinosaurs are grouped to illustrate 'the problem of presenting information at basic reading levels' and to compare approaches. The educational slant is reflected by the inclusion of students' texts, reading schemes and reference works at all levels. Reviews average 150 to 200 words; a Newberry winner receives a review of 370 words. Concerned, personal voices describe, analyse and criticize as is appropriate, *vide* vol. 32 (3), on Elvig Hansen's *In the barn* (Hove, Wayland, 1983): 'From time to time the author steps outside the narrative to present us with somewhat indigestible information about straw and the history of corn...The personal voice and involvement of the author seems to be missing (lost presumably in the translation from Danish into English)'. Bibliographical details are full, providing the various editions of a work. Miscellany, the vehicle of committee proceedings and other professional news, is distributed to members, and the lists of recent articles in periodicals about children's books and reading, are invaluable. Each number has an author-index and the final number of each year has a cumulative index under contributors and titles. Advertisements.

School library journal (New York, Bowker, 1954–. 9 p.a. Circulation: 44,000). Four full-time reviewing editors assisted by librarians and subject specialists, named with affiliations, review over 2,500 titles annually. Fiction and non-fiction reviews are grouped in two sections: Pre-school and primary grades; and Grades 3 to 6 (plus a few professional books). Reviews average 100 words, are compact and critical, and may even be unfavourable, but retain a personal tone. An outstanding book is denoted by an asterisk, and grade levels are provided. The journal also reviews paperback titles and non-book resources. Regular features include interesting articles, correspondence, children's book awards and special bibliographies. Bibliographical details are full, giving month as well as year of publication. Once a year all the reviews from *School library journal* are published in one volume, and there is an index in each issue as well as an annual cumulative one.

School library review (Wellington, New Zealand, 1980–. 4 p.a.) is a reviewing journal of the School Library Service. The number of reviewers, whose names are listed in each number, varies but they are mainly members of the School Library Service. Resources reviewed range from picture books through books for young adults, and there are sections for multicultural and professional books. Arrangement is an A–Z sequence within graded levels for fiction, and subject order for non-fiction, with classification numbers provided. Reviews average 80 to 120 words, but multicultural resources and professional literature are reviewed in greater detail. Vol. 4 (3) has a selection of 81 fiction, 83 non-fiction, 9 items with a multicultural focus, and 5 books on professional literature. Reviews are clear and concise, fusing critical and descriptive styles effectively, particularly when applied to non-fiction. Bibliographical details omit ISBNs, and level of user is suggested. An 'Also recommended' list of titles is appended to some reviews. Other features include announcements of awards, correspondence and matters of professional interest. This is an attractively produced journal which appeals to teachers and librarians. No index.

Times educational supplement (London, Times Newspapers, Ltd, 1910–. Weekly. Circulation: 132,000). The *Children's literature extra* appears three times a year and there is a special *TES* 'Information awards' section. Reviews contained are mainly fiction, folklore and poetry, and reviewers, whose names but not affiliations are given, include writers, teachers, specialists. Issue no. 3545, June 1984, carries three interviews — with Geoffrey Trease, Dick Bruna and Judy Blume — and composite reviews on space fiction, teenage fiction, school stories, new series, life and death, poetry anthologies and picture books. Reviews average 180 to 200 words in length, with two individually evaluated reviews averaging 260 words, and about 70 books cited and/or reviewed per issue. Authoritative evaluation of literature is the dominant style and the practice of reviewing current publications alongside earlier works in the same genre provides the long view which is demonstrated in the review of John Christopher's *Tripods trilogy* (London, Kestrel, 1984) under 'Space challenge'. The works are seen 'to have worn surprisingly well...[and to be] a more impressive achievement than I had remembered, though not as challenging'. Also, in juxtaposing Ron Morton's *The squeeze* (London, Hamish Hamilton, 1984) with Gene Kemp's *Charlie Lewis plays for time* (London, Faber and Faber, 1984), another reviewer both compares and contrasts approaches to the 'school story' genre. Other features include announcements of children's book awards, celebrations and advertisements. Black-and-white illustrations do not necessarily represent books reviewed. List of contents compensates to some extent for lack of index.

TLS: children's books supplement (London, Times Newspapers, Ltd, 1949–. 2 p.a. Circulation: 38,000). The original criteria for selection of reviewers still apply; that is, that 'they have a wide knowledge of, and interest in, children's literature and, which is also important, can write well'.[7] They include writers, teachers, librarians, specialists, and names but not affiliations are given. Every fortnight the *TLS* carries a page of four to six reviews of children's fiction, but the supplement, which appears in March and November, contains an average of 50 fiction and non-fiction titles. Issue 4,261, November 1984, reviews approximately 55 books, including a section of 12 picture books and some professional reading. Reviews average 500 to 600 words for older books and 200 to 250 words for picture books, and some titles are clustered for composite reviewing under such imaginative headings as, 'Final horrors', for a clutch of supernatural tales in the March issue. Most of the books reviewed are fiction and books discussed in composite reviews are frequently listed with full bibliographical details. Academic reviews are mini-analyses and discourses combining an awareness of child psychology, artistic and aesthetic dimensions, literary influence and educational concerns. Bibliographical details are full, and suggested ages tend to be incorporated within the review. Information about new editions and reprints is also provided, and other features include announcements of children's book awards, of conferences and exhibitions, and impressive scholarly articles make this a 'must' for all those interested in literature, even if 'not particularly relevant in a more practical sense'. Black-and-white illustrations pervade as well as advertisements, and each issue has an author-index of books reviewed.

Annual book guides and reviewing journals

Children's books of the year (London, National Book League, 1970–1983; rev. edn. 1985–. Annual) is the first issue of the series and reviews 269 books selected from 1984 publications covering picture books through older novels and non-fiction. An interesting introduction which surveys new trends in children's literature, also provides the selector's criteria for the inclusion of works. The new format is attractive and easy to consult, and entries are arranged by author in an A–Z sequence within various categories. Reviews, which average 100 words, convey, with economy, the essence and mood, and by sensitive choice of quotations encourage an interest in the books selected. There is a key to symbols employed and indexes of authors and illustrators, and of titles of books contained. Bibliographical details omit series title but provide all editions of a work. Advertisements.

Good book guide (London, Braithwaite and Taylor, Ltd, 1983–. Annual) is an independent, colourful catalogue, edited by Bing Taylor and Peter Braithwaite, advised by Elaine Moss, which is designed for parents and children. It contains approximately 600 titles, some of which are selected from the year's publications. The magazine provides advice for parents on selecting books in relation to stages of child development, and includes a list of books 'that provide concerned parents with information about reading techniques and an understanding of the problems that children encounter at home and in the school'. Books covered range from board books for the very young through fiction and non-fiction for 13- to 14-year-olds, and paperbacks are included. Entry is by title, and annotations are concise and descriptive, with matching colour photographs of book-covers on each double page. Bibliographical details omit year of publication, series title and ISBNs. The 1985 edition has a survey of 28 encyclopaedias for children and young adults, and there are two articles on children's reading. the index is an A–Z sequence of author, title and series entries.

Signal selection of children's books (Gloucester, Thimble Press, 1985–. Annual). The 1984 edition is a streamlined production of the former *Signal review of children's books*. This guide to significant books published within the year contains about 140 review entries, as well as listings of paperback editions which are not reviewed. Names of reviewers with affiliations are given and the foreword states that the basis of selection is an awareness of 'needs and perspectives'. Book-notes introduce and intersperse reviews which fall into five main sections, and reviews are initialled. Lay-out of text and type-face are used as assessment indicators, and the focus is on fiction and literature, with information books in the minority. The strong representation of teachers on the panel gives a practical balance to a house style which is markedly literary and philosophical, and which speaks primarily to the cognescenti of children's literature. Bibliographical details are full (year of publication omitted) and give age range. The journal also contains a list of children's book awards for 1984. Black-and-white illustrations complement the text, and there is an index of author, title and series entries. Dual 'teacher cum librarian viewpoints broaden its usefulness as a practical and exhibition tool'.

References

1. Robertson, Dorothy K. *The reviewing of children's books in Britain.* London, Library Association, Youth Libraries Group, 1969 (Pamphlet no. 4).
2. Hannabuss, Stuart, 'Reviewing reviews', *Signal*, no. 35, May 1981, p.104.
3. *Ibid.*, p. 106.
4. Moulton, Priscilla. 'Children's book reviews and reviewing', in *Encyclopedia of library and information science*, vol. 25, pp. 373–80.
5. Meacham, Mary. *Information sources in children's literature.* Westport, Conn., Greenwood Press, 1978.
6. Fisher, Margery. Letter, 15 June 1985.
7. Robertson, Dorothy K., *op. cit.*, p. 22.

14. Audiovisual materials

Helen P. Harrison

Audiovisual materials (AVM) have many applications. They can be used for leisure or learning and instruction. The dividing lines between the applications are not drawn rigidly and an entertainment film or video can sometimes be used for purposes of discussion and discovery in an educational situation. Also a training or instructional film often has entertainment value — for example the Video Arts productions on management featuring John Cleese. It is reasonable to say that this leads to a variety of choices for the reviewer of AVM, but in making this distinction between entertainment and education the reviews should be designed to match both the original purpose of the material as well as its peripheral uses and the purpose of the journal in which the review is to appear.

Reviewing AVM is becoming a matter of the reviewer contacting the journal concerned. A glance at Ulrich's *International periodicals directory* for 1984 will find no entry under audiovisual materials, nor even a reference. Motion pictures, yes, Communications — radio and television, music — but no 'audiovisual' journals, as such.

A previous article on the reviewing of AVM published in 1978 in the *Encyclopedia of library and information science*, entitled 'Reviews and reviewing of multimedia materials', by Estelle Jussim, was based on the US experience and concentrated on film materials: 'The discussion is centered on film as the single most important media form in the nonprint area'.[1] This statement does not reflect the situation in the UK. Regrettably, film is one of the lesser influences in the current canon of AVM. Even in the entertainment area, film has declined as an influence and television has achieved an importance. For various other reasons video-recordings have become the major carrier of moving images in the educational sector.

Another reference which includes examples of review techniques is Evelyn Oppenheimer's *Oral book reviewing to stimulate reading: a practical guide in techniques for lecture and broadcast.*[2] This contains descriptive outlines of the author's oral reviews of popular novels, plays, biographies and histories.

The AV field has advanced considerably since 1950. Previously it was almost wholly film and sound recording, which is to say expensive 35mm, 16mm or 8mm film and 33, 45 or 78 rpm discs and open-reel audiotape. Audiocassettes were not in sufficient evidence in the early 1970s to be of more than a passing concern.

Today, only 15 years later, the situation has changed almost out of bounds. We now have moving images as opposed to film. Moving images encompass film, television, videotape, cassette and disc. Sound recordings have to take account of gramophone records, radio programmes, audiotape, audiocassette and compact disc. The digital technologies enforce another dimension on us.

With the advancing technology has come an outburst of activity in the AV field. But this does not mean that there has been a parallel activity in publishing articles about the effect or educational performance of the materials and the media in which they are transmitted, and many of these journals carry reviews of books about the materials, their use and effectiveness. Few journals have concentrated upon or even included reviews of the materials themselves. Journals for reviewing AVM have been found wanting in certain areas, but not all. We have some very detailed reviews for current productions in film and sound recording — usually reviewed from the aesthetic point of view. But over and above these materials there is a large volume of audiovisual material threatening to overwhelm us — of AVM presented in video, tape–slide and kit format.

AVM include:

Moving images	Films
	Videotapes
	Videodiscs
Sound recordings	Gramophone or phone recordings
	Audiotapes
	Audiocassettes
	Compact discs
Still visuals	Photographs
	Slides
Mixtures	Tape–slides
	Kits/packs
	Videodiscs (some)

Of the AVM, those most likely to receive reviews are the moving visuals, sound recordings, tape–slide presentations, packs and kits. There is not a great deal which can be said about the still visuals over and above their quality. Reviews of slide packs, sets of slides or books including slide materials are usually confined to a comment on the quality of slides, an indication of the extent of the material and its availability. Regular users quickly come to be aware of the standard of many slide production companies, and the most a reviewer can do is to indicate the range and technical quality of production companies or the availability of material in certain subject areas. Journals like the *ARLIS news-sheet*, published by ARLIS in the UK, or the ARLIS/North American publications for slide librarians, will carry review- or appraisal-articles which usually compare and contrast a range of material available.

The next problem is where to find critical reviews of all this variety of material. Should we divide between entertainment and education, the transmission media, or such factors as the age levels of suitability? False demarcations are always a danger in this respect. Decisions taken to omit reviews of entertainment materials in educational journals might result in the loss of valuable study material. This is especially true of film studies materials, where feature film is as important as many documentary films.

The type of AVM for which reviews are required include:

— Entertainment films or television programmes
— Film and television documentaries
— Current affairs programmes
—Gramophone records, audiocassettes or compact discs
— Educational videos
— Videodiscs
— Tape–slide programmes
— Kits or packs of materials which incorporate AV and instructional notes
— Language tuition packages

Not all AVM do all jobs adequately. The medium of transmission of information or entertainment has to fit the message. A film or television programme, shown continuously with little or no opportunity for the viewer to stop the action and recap sections which are unclear is, or should be, quite different to a videocassette which has been designed for instructional purposes. Although the material may be the same, the purpose of it is different, and the programme will be designed and produced differently. The reviewer should therefore be aware of the purpose of the production and try to match it with the review.

These changes in the purpose and the increased use of AV for instruction and learning, plus the rapid advances in the technology, have meant changes in the pattern and type of reviewing necessary.

Some AVM are better served by review journals than others. As already stated the film and gramophone record are fairly well served. The educational video is also becoming a more prominent part of review journals, and sometimes the tape–slide, but there is often a lack of adequate reviews for other materials. It is more likely to be an indicative statement of content than a considered review, concentrating more on the design of the package than its ultimate effectiveness as a learning package.

It is worth raising the question whether or not reviews of AVM are necessary. Reviews are certainly valuable for several reasons, not least the expense of many AVM to purchase or even hire. Reviews can help to prevent expensive mistakes being made in the selection of AVM in libraries and other areas. Librarians and users select material for inclusion in many situations. They need as much information as possible about the materials if they cannot handle them or preview them before purchase. It was once possible to obtain material on approval, or at least to be given the opportunity to preview, but with the increased costs of the material and transport, not to mention the possibilities of copying video programmes, however illegally, previewing and approval copies are becoming a rarity. The expense of the material and sometimes the restricted market for the material militate against supply before demand. Reviews may have to replace preview facilities, and the reviewer's capability will be called upon. Reviewing journals and appraisal indexes are an essential part of the selection process.

It is at this point that we should begin to make a distinction between objective and subjective reviews. Both may have validity, but in widely different circumstances. 'Educational' material almost certainly requires an objective review, stating clearly the intended purpose of the material, its format, its subject content and the level of this content — that is, primary, secondary, tertiary or further education — with an indication of its academic merit in as objective a manner as possible. This is no area for idiosyncratic flights of fancy. Of course, it can be said that no review should indulge itself to this extent, but with entertainment or cultural film material some critical licence is allowed the reviewer. This is especially the case for feature films with the detailed reviews in the Sunday papers and in the journals such as *Sight and sound, Films and filming* or the *Monthly film bulletin* of the British Film Institute. Reviewers in these outlets may even elevate their craft to an art form, and the reader of the reviews will quickly become aware of the particular approach of the reviewer. Such reviews are not normally used in the same way as reviews for educational material. The user reads the review to see if he wants to see the film in a cinema, borrow the video or view the programme on television; sometimes even to see if the reviewer agrees with his own reaction.

Reviews vary widely from the brief indicative preview which is found in daily newspapers, indicating the content of the programmes to be seen on television, to a rather more expansive review of the material after showing, once again in the newspapers. The reader will be aware of the bias of the production companies for their own products, which may invalidate some of the broadcast journals writing reviews of their own products (e.g. *Radio times*, and *TV times*). *The listener* covers a wider area, including reviews of programmes on all television channels, radio, cinema (presumably because many of the films will appear on the television screen in time) and records as well. The reviews are less biased than the broadcasting companies own reports. Other reviewing styles include the very detailed critical review of feature film productions or recordings in film journals or record reviewing journals such as *Records and recording* or the *Gramophone*. In the educational sector the reviewing style may range from a detailed analysis of the material in the film studies area, to a shorter review which indicates the subject content, educational level and educational quality of the material concerned. This latter is the most prevalent type of review in the educational area. Often the material is not reviewed, as such, but appraised for use in certain situations; for example, in *HELPIS*, the catalogue and database produced by the British Universities Film and Video Council, the material is normally included after appraisal as to its usefulness in higher education.

The elements which are required in a review of AVM will include the format of the material, the duration, the subject content, the educational level or the general applications of the material and, in the headings, the availability of the material (i.e. hire or purchase arrangements and the distributor).

Competence of reviewers in the educational sector is required in two areas: they need both a knowledge of the subject and also of the medium used for transmission of the information. As noted already, not all AVM do all jobs adequately. The message or subject content of the programme can be obscured by the technicalities of the medium. Some television tuition programmes are better seen in cassette format, where there is an opportunity to view, review and check the content and the users' understanding at intervals. This is the case with the interactive materials, programmed learning, computer-assisted learning and interactive videodisc. The reviewer should have sufficient knowledge of the medium used to be able to indicate how successful the choice of medium has been, or whether a different medium would have produced a better programme.

AVM usually require playback equipment, therefore reviews of AVM, especially the newer ones, require a definition of the system employed to alert the user to the playback machine he will need. This definition may cover only one system or the material could be available for purchase on several systems. In the latter case, all the systems should be delineated and, if the costs vary, this is another essential item to include; for example, U'matic cassettes recorded on high band *will* play back on low-band machines, but the results could be interesting (i.e. colour may turn to black and white), and the cost of purchase will certainly be different. It is necessary for the user to acquire material which he can play back adequately on his existing machinery, and a review should carry sufficient information for him to order the correct material.

This leads on to one of the many problems in dealing with audiovisual materials: the transferability of AVM, especially video material, from one country to another. It is by now axiomatic that if one video system *can* be different to another, it will! It is of course possible to transfer different line and cycle systems from one to another, but at a considerable cost, which it may not be possible to meet for the limited market the material may have in other countries. Transfer of colour systems is also possible, and many library machines have a switch facility to go from the American NTSC to the British PAL or European SECAM systems. But the resulting pictures will be in black and white, and this may seriously affect the usefulness of the programme content. The reviewer should alert the user to this fact and indicate where programmes are not transferred to other systems and distributed in their transferred form.

Another problem in this area of crossing national boundaries with AVM is also a resource question. The cost of transport, customs duties, import taxes and the expense of time involved in obtaining many of the materials may make it uneconomic of time and resources to acquire certain materials. The situation is improving but can still present difficulties for remote countries with good AV facilities to acquire up-to-date, useful teaching material. A reviewer embarking on film and video materials will be well advised to delineate the extent of the market envisaged and be aware of the possible difficulties of availability to alert the user. This is one of the chief difficulties of a reviewer in an international journal, but it is also one of the major responsibilities to the 'remote' user, who has little information on the programmes involved other than by review. Preview is seldom if ever possible for the 'remote' user. No one wants to ship off expensive material on approval with scant chance of its either arriving or the risk of it not replaying properly at the far end. Distribution agents do exist, but not always in the areas which are interested, or with the necessary resources to deal with 'one-off' orders. Thus reviews in international journals have to pay close attention to detailed synopses or contents lists, format availability and even on occasion cross-cultural information.

The British Council, for example, employ trained appraisal staff to look at UK material and vet it for overseas consumption. The British Council journal is *Media in education and development* (1967–. 4 p.a.).

Length of reviews varies according to type and nature. If the review is in fact an appraisal, short, succinct statements of between 150 and 200 words are necessary. It should also be remembered that some of the appraisal types of review will appear in online databases, where economies in style will be appreciated by the user being charged connect time. Critical reviews may run into 1,000 words, although 500 would be a more appropriate length. Not all reviews are of single works, and some reviews delineate particular subject areas: a guide to the best audiovisual tools in physics, or the spread and relative merits of different audiovisual materials in medicine, or the usefulness of the tape–slide or the training film in the teaching of particular subjects. These may extend to articles rather than reviews, but they nevertheless can be defined as reviews of the available materials.

Indexes to reviews

Before embarking on the review journals themselves, some mention should be made of the literature and journals which index reviews of AVM in several subject areas.

The international index to film periodicals: an annotated guide (1972–. Annual), which is a FIAF (International Federation of Film Archives) publication, provides information on articles and reviews appearing in film periodicals. A major section of the index is devoted to individual film reviews. The companion publication is *The inter-*

national index to television periodicals (1979–. Annual), which deals with television materials, including review-articles on films and programmes appearing on television.

Reviews of specific journals are included in several indexes; for example, *Sight and sound*, the film periodical, is indexed in the *Arts and humanities citation index*, *Book review index* and *Humanities index*; *Educational media international* reviews are indexed in *Education index*; *Film library quarterly* reviews, in *Library literature*: and *Films in review*, in *Book review index*. More specialized subjects are indexed elsewhere; for example, the *Journal of audiovisual media in medicine* reviews appear in the *Internationale Bibliographie der Rezensionen* (Osnabrück, Dietrich, 1971–. 2 p.a.). *Health media review index: a guide to reviews and descriptions of commercially available nonprint material for the medical, mental, allied health, human science, and selected counselling professions* provides excerpts from reviews of over 4,000 audiovisual items in journals during the period 1980–83.[3]

Reviewing journals

Because of the differing nature and purpose of reviews of many AVM, the review journals will be divided into those dealing with particular AV forms and also into the target audience of the reviews. This may at times be an arbitrary distinction as there is considerable overlap in reviewing film and documentary video.

Feature-film reviews appear in several journals, including the *Monthly film bulletin* of the British Film Institute (1934–. 12 p.a.). This covers feature films, both British and foreign, which were released during the particular month in the UK. It carries signed reviews by competent film critics. The description of each film is given in three sections: first, a detailed and lengthy credits list gives information about the country of production, date of release, production details, director, technical and artist credits (the artist credit indicates the role played by the actor); the second section is a detailed synopsis of the storyline and action; and finally a critical review is appended. The *MFB* is indexed annually. Reviews are lengthy (up to 1,000 words) and authoritative.

Sight and sound, also issued by the British Film Institute (1932–. 4 p.a.), is a critical journal with lengthy film-reviews (not always of feature films) and articles which review the work of particular directors or genres.

Film library quarterly, now merged with *Sightlines* (1985), published by the Educational Film Library Association in America, gives reviews of material of sociological and educational significance. *FLQ* is now incorporated as a supplement to *Sightlines* and the reviews give a detailed 200-word résumé of the films involved plus articles covering film materials and critical comment upon the contemporary film scene, especially from the library point of view in America, where film is still used widely for educational and recreational purposes.

Other film-review journals includes: *Films and filming* (1954–. 12 p.a.); *Film* (1952–. 12 p.a.), the journal of the British Federation of Film Societies; *Screen international* (1912–. Weekly. Ed. Peter Noble); and *Films in review* (1950–. 12 p.a.), a United States publication from the National Board of Review of Motion Pictures.

On the audio scene there are the very well-known publications of the *Gramophone* — principally an index to current releases and including details of production and versions released. Beyond this there are the critical reviews contained in *Records and recording* and *Music and musicians*. Once again, these are reviews written from the aesthetic point of view with a bias towards the artistic content of the recording and of value to the connoisseur of music. The *Gramophone* publication, *Recommended recordings (best buys of the popular classics on record and cassette)*, which includes a guide to a basic classical record collections, is as close as most people in libraries will come to a definitive list of the best recordings of the year, but these represent an appraised list of current recordings and are not reviews in any sense of the word.

Coming to the review journals which cover AVM in general, the scene becomes more sparsely populated, although it is improving. There are review journals which cover AVM in particular subject areas or for particular sectors of the community, but in most cases the journals will be devoted to education where the major emphasis of AVM as a tool worth reviewing is centred.

The reviews in this area are very often of the appraisal type — this film/video/tape–slide or whatever will suit certain purposes for the educator, learner or enthusiast — but this is not to denigrate the review. It cannot be said too often that good audiovisual material which achieves its main objective is worth a thousand words of a lecturer's time. But that lecturer or teacher needs to be made aware of the potential of the material and also of its existence. Reviews which alert a teacher to the materials available, and which also give him an idea of the content, level of competence needed to gain benefit from them and the technical level of presentation achieved by the material, are of greater value than all the finely phrased critical prose often used by people who do not understand the purpose of a programme.

Since the unfortunate demise of *Visual education* in 1980, the reviewing of *AVM* in general has been found wanting. Gradually, and fortunately, the professions involved (for there are more than one) have been trying to bridge this gap. But there is still a long way to go. The journals can be divided into those which give objective and very straightforward synopses of contents of programmes with details of format, age levels, duration and subject content, and those which attempt further critical coverage.

The British national film and video catalogue (1963–. 4 p.a.) is a catalogue rather than a reviewing journal, but it indicates the elements of format, duration and availability and gives a brief synopsis of the content, plus the level of British and foreign films and videocassettes made available for non-theatrical screening in the UK. An example will indicate the type of entry to be found:

WHAT THE JOB NEEDS
dist.; Local Government Training Board. Sale, 1984, pc: Local Government Training Board in association with Southampton City Council for Local Government Training Board.
25 mins. sd. col. viodeocassette.
Designed to help Youth Training Scheme trainees to identify skills and attitudes which will be helpful when looking for permanent employment. Focuses on employer requirements in a number of different situations, both local authority and commercially based. Uses interviews by a group of YTS trainees with supervisors, personnel staff and managers.

NICEM (National Information Center for Educational Media, USA) publishes a series of indexes which give even briefer details of the contents of a wide range of materials. Although the NICEM indexes are useful to indicate that material exists, the user has always to question the availability of the material within countries other than the US. NICEM indexes cover educational videotapes, audiotapes, films and slides.

The British Universities Film and Video Council *BUFVC catalogue* with approximately 5,500 entries covers the field of higher education. By implication, researchers and subject specialists understand that the materials contained within the catalogue are suitable for higher education and at certain levels within higher education. The catalogue entries are not signed, but in most cases the material has been appraised by an academic working within the particular subject field before inclusion in the catalogue. Appraisals may be consulted by members of BUFVC and viewing copies are sometimes available in the Audiovisual Resources Centre (AVRC) of BUFVC. But, of course, this service, excellent though it may be, cannot cover the whole UK, as it is based in London, nor can it satisfy all demands which might be placed upon it. The following is an example of an entry in the BUFVC catalogue:

WATERWHEELS IN WALES AND THE WEST COUNTRY
dist.: Mr J. Rogers, Hire or Sale; 1978: pc: J. Rogers (Technical Films) with support from the Welsh Industrial & Maritime Museum. Credits: p.d., sc., ph., ed. J. Rogers. comm.s, Dr E.S. Owen Jones.
Film. 16mm. sd. col. 20 min.
Shows sixteen waterwheels seen working in 1976 and others no longer in use. Outlines the development of waterwheels in Britain and shows some applications in cornmilling (watermills operating commercially), the woollen industry (3 mills driven by waterwheels), pumping, ore crushing and driving tilt hammers and grindstones. A tidemill is also shown as is corn grinding by hand-quern, wool carding and spinning by hand.
Uses: Introductory courses in Industrial Archaeology.
Attractively filmed and well edited survey of the principal types of water-wheel and waterpowered engine. Should be useful for explanations. Only the very early history (eg. treatment of horizontal waterwheel — not represented among those filmed) is rather out of date. As a survey of the main types in a particular region, using the evidence of survivors, it is excellent.
Signed.

Associated with the catalogue there is an online database, *HELPIS*, with approximately 5,700 entries, which represents the only AV database of currently available material in the UK at present. Although full details of appraisals are not available on the database, the user can assume certain standards and the level of competence required for use in higher or tertiary education. The following is an example of an entry:

MOTION: NEWTON'S LAWS
dist. Guild Sound & Vision, Off air recording licence or sale; 1980; p.c. British Broadcasting Corporation Open University Productions.
Videocassette. Standard formats. col. 25 min. (Science Foundation course)
Presents practical demonstrations of Newton's laws of motion and of the principle of conservation of momentum. Item number: S101/03F.
Uses: First year mechanics courses for demonstration; schools and colleges of education.*
* indicates item available in the AVRC.

The synopses used by BUFVC to compile their entries are not just the distributors' own synopses but reviewers' comments are also included. Detailed reviews, signed, and covering a wide range of materials are published in the BUFVC *Newsletter*.

The *Journal of educational television* (1975–. 3 p.a.), published by the Educational Television Association in the UK, carries reviews of selected programmes or AVM, especially video, which are suitable for use in educational situations.

The *Audiovisual librarian* (1973–. 4 p.a.) has recently begun to review material in AV format in general. Previously the policy was to review only AVM which related directly to audiovisual librarianship, but recently the *AVL* editorial board realized that so few journals were reviewing AVM, especially those for educational and library uses, that it was decided to widen the field to material which could be of use to libraries. This is of course a much wider field. The reviews are signed, and written from the point of view of how useful they can be to a library, but this includes entertainment (leisure) and education, and it is hoped that the non-book reviews column will expand as more producers realize its value.

This last point is one with which most producers will agree. The difficulties of making products, useful in themselves, known to the user is one which besets the AV producer. It is useful for some of the AV journals to receive unsolicited reviews of materials in the present hiatus. Not only are some producers reluctant to send out expensive review copies (in some instances they may send out only a sample, or a section of a pack with explanatory notes for the remainder) but also the journals themselves may not be known targets. In this way the casual reviewer can assist both producer and journal.

Educational media international (1971–. 4 p.a.), the journal of the International Council for Educational Media, carries reviews of AV.

In addition to the journals which review general AV publications, there are those which specialize in particular subject areas. Of these areas in the AV field, none has been so prominent as the medical publications. Medicine has led the way in its many uses of AVM: medical illustration, videos of surgical operations and treatments which could not be shown in other ways because of the particular conditions of a surgical theatre or the microphotography needed to explain certain techniques, or the before and after instances of medical conditions.

A journal such as the *Journal of audiovisual media in medicine* (1951–. 4 p.a.), formerly the *Journal of medical and biological illustration*, carries reviews, while another journal such as *BLAT Informa-*

tion (British Life Assurance Trust) published by the BMA (British Medical Association) carries brief notes of appraisal. Both journals indicate material suitable for various levels of the medical profession, from nursing to teaching hospitals to advanced studies in medicine. A recent publication of the Medical, Health and Welfare Libraries Group of the Library Association, *Health libraries review* (1984–. 4 p.a.), published by Blackwell Scientific Publications, although it does not as yet review AVM, has no editorial policy against such reviews. Only the reviewers are missing!

Other subject areas which have journals carrying reviews of AVM include: *Education in chemistry* (1964–. 6 p.a.), published by the Royal Society of Chemistry, which carries detailed, signed reviews; *Physics education review*; *The school science review*, journal of the Association for Science Education; and the Royal Anthropological Society *News*.

References

1. Jussim, Estelle. 'Reviews and reviewing of multimedia materials', in *Encyclopedia of library and information science*, vol. 25, pp. 330–50.
2. Oppenheimer, Evelyn. *Oral book reviewing to stimulate reading: a practical guide in techniques for lecture and broadcast.* Metuchen, NJ, Scarecrow Press, 1980.
3. Proven, Jill E., and Hunter, Joy W., (eds.) *Health media review index.* Metuchen, NJ, Scarecrow Press, 1985.

Appendix A

Select list of indexes to reviews

1. *Indexes wholly devoted to reviews*

Book review digest. New York, H.W. Wilson, 1905–. 10 p.a., cumulated quarterly and annually.

Book review index. Detroit, Mich., Gale, 1965–. 6 p.a., cumulated annually; master cumulation, 1969–79, 1980–81, 7 vols.

Children's book review index. Detroit, Mich., Gale, 1975–. Annual; master cumulation, 1960–81, 1982.

Children's literature review: excerpts from reviews, criticism and commentary on books for children. Detroit, Mich., Gale, 1976–. Annual

Guía a las reseñas de libros de y sobre Hispanoamerica, 1972–. Detroit, Mich., Blaine Ethridge, 1976–. Annual

Index to Australian book reviews, 1965–. Adelaide, Libraries of South Australia, 1965–. 4 p.a.

Index to book reviews in the humanities. Wilmington, Mich., Thomson, 1960–. Annual.

Index to book reviews in the sciences. Philadelphia, Pa., Institute for Scientific Information, 1978–. 4 p.a.

Index to reviews of bibliographical publications: an international annual. Boston, Mass, G.K. Hall, 1976–. vol. 1–. (vol. 6: 1981. 1984).

Index to scientific reviews. Philadelphia, Pa., Institute for Scientific Information, 1974–. 2 p.a., cumulated annually.

Indian book review index. Gurgaon, New Delhi, Indian Book Service, 1975/76–. [1978?] Annual.

Internationale Bibliographie der Rezensionen, wissenschaftliche Literatur. Osnabrück, Dietrich, 1971, 2 p.a. (preceded by *Bibliographie der Rezensionen und Referate*, 1900–43. Leipzig, Dietrich, 1901–44).

Media review digest. Ann Arbor, Mich., Pierian Press, 1971–. Annual, cumulated 2-yearly.

Reference sources. Ann Arbor, Mich., Pierian Press, 1977–. Annual. (preceded by *Reference book review index*, 1970–75).

Technical book review index. Pittsburgh, Pa., JAAD, 1917–29, 1935–. 10 p.a.

2. Indexes that include a book-review section, entries or references

America: history and life. Santa Barbara, Calif., ABC-Clio, 1964–. 7 p.a., cumulated 5-yearly.

American reference books annual. Littleton, Colo., Libraries Unlimited, 1970–.

Applied science and technology index. New York, H.W. Wilson, 1958–. 11 p.a. quarterly and annual cumulations.

Art Index. New York, H.W. Wilson, 1929–. 4 p.a. cumulated annually.

Arts and humanities citation index. Philadelphia, Pa., Institute for Scientific Information, 1978–. 3 p.a.

Bibliographie linguistique de l'année, 1939/47–. Utrecht, Spectrum, 1947–. Annual.

Biological and agricultural index. New York, H.W. Wilson, 1964–. 11 p.a. cumulated annually.

Business periodicals index. New York, H.W. Wilson, 1958–. 11 p.a. cumulated annually.

The Catholic periodical and literature index. Haverford, Pa., Catholic Library Association, 1930–. 6 p.a., cumulated 2-yearly.

Education index. New York, H.W. Wilson, 1929–. 12 p.a., cumulated quarterly and annually.

Film literature index. Albany, NY, Filmdex, 1973–. 4 p.a., cumulated annually.

General science index, 1978–. New York, H.W. Wilson, 1978–. 10 p.a., cumulated quarterly and annually.

Hispanic American periodicals index, 1975–. Los Angeles, University of California, 1977–. Annual.

Historical abstracts. Santa Barbara, Calif., ABC-Clio, 1955–. pts A, B. each 4 p.a., cumulated annually.

Humanities index. New York, H.W. Wilson, 1974–. 4 p.a., cumulated annually.

The index to Jewish periodicals. Cleveland, Ohio, College of Jewish Studies Press, 1963–. 2 p.a.

Index to legal periodicals. New York, H.W. Wilson, with American Association of Law Libraries, 1908–. 11 p.a. cumulated quarterly, annually, 3-yearly.

International guide to medieval studies. Darien, Conn., American Bibliographic Service, 1961–. 4 p.a.

International index to film periodicals. London FIAF/International Federation of Film Archives, 1972–. Annual.

International index to television periodicals. London, FIAF/International Federation of Film Archives, 1979–. Annual.

LLBA/Language and language behaviour abstracts. San Diego, Calif., Sociological Abstracts, Inc., 1967–. 4 p.a.

Language teaching. Cambridge University Press, 1968–. 4 p.a.

Music index. Detroit, Mich., Information Coordinators, Inc., 1949–. 12 p.a., cumulated annually.

The philosopher's index. Bowling Green, Ohio, Philosophy Documentation Center, Bowling Green State University, 1967–. 4 p.a. cumulated annually; also online.

RILA: répertoire international de la littérature de l'art. c/o Sterling and Francine Art Institute, Williamstown, Md., 1975–. 2 p.a.

RILM abstracts. New York, International RILM Center, 1967–. 4 p.a. (4th issue being annual cumulation; cumulated 5-yearly).

Religious index one: periodicals. Chicago, Ill., American Theological

Library Association, 1977–. 2 p.a., cumulated 2-yearly. (preceded by *Index to religious periodical literature*, 1949–76, 12 vols.).

Science citation index. Philadelphia, Pa., Institute for Scientific Information, 1961–. 6 p.a., including annual cumulation.

Serials review. Ann Arbor, Mich., Pierian Press, 1975–. 4 p.a.

Social science citation index. Philadelphia, Pa., Institute for Scientific Information, 1970–. 3 p.a. (3rd issue being annual cumulation).

Social sciences index. New York, H.W. Wilson, 1974–. 4 p.a., cumulated annually.

3. *Some retrospective indexes to reviews*

Bloomfield, Barry Cambray. *An author index to selected British 'little magazines', 1930–1939*. London, Mansell, 1976.

Book review index to social science periodicals [1964–74]. Ann Arbor, Mich., Pierian Press, 1978–80, 4 vols.

Combined retrospective index to book reviews in humanities journals, 1802–1974. Woodbridge, Conn., RP/Research Publications, 1982–84, 9 vols. (vols. 1–8, Authors; vol. 9, Titles).

Combined retrospective index to book reviews in scholarly journals, 1886–1974. Woodbridge, Conn, RP/Research Publications, 1979, 15 vols.

Easterbrook, David L. *African book reviews, 1885–1945: an index to books reviewed in selected English language publications*. Boston, Mass, G.K. Hall, [1979].

Henige, David. *Works in African history: an index to reviews, 1960–1974*. Waltham, Mass., African Studies Association, Brandeis University, 1974.

Henige, David. *Works in African history: an index to reviews, 1974–1978*. [Waltham, Mass], Crossroads Press, [1978].

Index Nordicus: a cumulative index to English-language periodicals in Scandinavian studies. Millwood, NY, Kraus Thomson, 1976, 8 vols.

Sader, Marion. *Comprehensive index to English-language little magazines, 1890–1970*. Series one. Millwood, NY, Kraus Thomson, 1976, 8 vols.

The Wellesley index to Victorian periodicals, 1824–1900. Toronto, University of Toronto Press, 1966–. (vols. 1–3. 1966–78).

Appendix B

Select and annotated bibliography

This bibliography includes a number of the basic items cited in the references and bibliographies at the end of individual chapters. Association of Learned and Professional Society Publishers.

Refereeing, commissioning and editing for journals and books. London, ALPSP, 1980. 41 pp.
Five papers (delivered at the ALPSP seminar, 17 April 1980) on: editing and refereeing for a learned journal; an author's view of learned journals; the refereeing of papers; the creative role of the commissioning editor; editing and editing standards.

Bateson, Frederick W. *The scholar critic: an introduction to literary research.* London, Routledge and Kegan Paul, 1972. xi, 202pp.
Maintains that literary criticism and literary scholarship are complementary and gives examples of unscholarly journalism and uncritical scholarship. Select bibliography, pp. 184–96.

Budd, John. 'Book reviewing practices of journals in the humanities', *Scholarly publishing*, vol. 13 (4), July 1982, pp. 363–71.
A survey of the editorial policy of 58 literary journals (nearly all US). All the editors were conscious of reviewing-space considerations. Examples are quoted from guidelines provided in three journals (not named). Six references.

Chen, Ching-chih. *Biomedical, scientific and technical book reviews.* Metuchen, NJ, Scarecrow Press, 1976. xv, 186pp.
Results of a comprehensive study of about 500 biomedical, scientific and technical reviewing journals, with particular reference to quantitative coverage, time-lag, adequacy and authoritativeness of reviews, etc. 19 tables, 4 diagrams.

Chen, Ching-chih. 'Current status of medical book reviewing', *Bulle-*

tin of the Medical Library Association, vol. 62 (2,3), April 1974, pp. 105–19; July 1974, pp. 296–308.
A survey in five parts of key medical reviewing journals with quantitative significance, their time-lag and duplication patterns, and a list of most frequently reviewed biomedical books in 1970.

Chen, Ching-chih. 'Reviews and reviewing of scientific and technical materials', in *Encyclopedia of library and information science*. New York, Dekker, vol. 25, 1978, pp. 350–72.
A comprehensive account that includes sections on 'Sources of scientific reviews' and 'The current status of scientific reviews and reviewing'. 72 references; bibliography of 44 items; tables.

Clark, Sir George Norman. 'Historical reviewing', in *Essays in history presented to Reginald Lane Poole*, ed. H.W.C. Davis. Oxford, Clarendon Press, 1927, pp. 115–26.
Sections: The rise of reviewing — Anonymous reviewing — The slashing review — Whether bad books should be reviewed — The impartial reviewer — The editor's responsibility for reviews — Methods of reviewing, by summarizing and by criticizing — The formula for historical reviewers — The function of the historical reviewer.

Colaianne, A.J. 'The aims and methods of annotated bibliography', *Scholarly publishing*, vol. 11 (4), July 1980, pp. 321–31.
'Annotated bibliographies are attractive to book compilers and publishers, but are apt to be uneven. Their most important attribute is usefulness — the ease with which accurate and complete information can be retrieved from their pages' (*abstract*). Concentrates on annotated literary bibliographies, giving guidelines. Two references.

Cole, Fred C. 'Book reviews: an editor's point of view', *The journal of Southern history*, vol. 13 (1), February 1947, pp. 264–74.
Points: What books should be reviewed? — Haphazard assignment of space — The choice of reviewers — Time taken in reviewing — Editing of reviews — 'Communications': rebuttal of reviews — General aims of reviews — Criteria.

Covey, Alma A. *Reviewing of reference books: an evaluation of the effectiveness of selected announcement, review and index media in their coverage of reference books*. Metuchen, NJ, Scarecrow Press, 1972. 142pp.
Explores the coverage, frequency, timing, review-length and indexing of 13 US reviewing sources dealing with reference books. But Covey is a realist: 'There is no single tool, nor a combination of tools

in existence today, that enables the conscientious reference librarian systematically and efficiently to select the best reference books for his or her reference library' (p.129).

Drewry, John. *Writing book reviews*. Boston, Mass., The Writer, Inc., 1966. xx, 230 pp.
Offers step-by-step guidance on how to evaluate books in fields such as fiction, biography, history, poetry and children's books, and on writing for newspapers, magazines and specialized periodicals.

Freeman, Susan Tax. 'On responsibility in reviewing', *American anthropologist*, vol. 79 (2), June 1977, pp. 441–2.
Urges that 'each reviewer show normal professional courtesy and responsibility in personally sending a copy of a review to the author reviewed, prior to submitting it to the editors, to make sure that errors and distortions do not occur'.

Gissen, M. 'Commercial criticism and punch-drunk reviewing', *Antioch review*, vol. 2, January 1942, pp. 232–41.
A devastating attack on standards of book reviewing at that time in the American press, as well as in national monthlies. 'The besetting sin of academic specialist reviewing is a fussy concern with the bits and pieces of research.'

Gray, R.A., comp. *A guide to book review citations: a bibliography of sources*. Columbus, Ohio State University Press, 1968. viii, 221pp.
512 numbered and annotated entries in eight classes, with subdivisions. Four indexes: subject, personal name, title and chronology. Annotations are in two parts: coverage; bibliographical details.

Haines, Helen E. *Living with books: the art of book selection*, 2nd edn. New York, Columbia University Press, 1950. xviii, 630pp.
First published 1935. A classic treatise that devotes Chapters 6–7 (pp. 99–136) to assessing the value of book reviewing and its place in book selection, plus Chapter 8, 'The art of annotation'. Analytical index, pp. 571–630.

Hannabuss, Stuart. 'Re-viewing reviews', *Signal: approach to children's books*, no. 35, May 1981, pp. 96–107.
Argues for a child-centred approach to the reviewing of children's books, criticizing intellectual overkill in reviews and examining the case for extended reviews. Cites numerous examples of reviewing.

Hargrave, Victoria E. 'A comparison of reviews of books in the social sciences and in scholarly periodicals', *The library quarterly*, vol. 18, July 1948, pp. 206–17.

Spells out the various stages of the reviewing process and concludes that there is 'relatively little difference between the interpretations given to the products of scholarship for popular as against technical consumption'. Four tables.

Hoge, James O., and West III, James L.W. 'Academic book reviewing: some problems and suggestions'. *Scholarly publishing*, vol. 11 (1), October 1979, pp. 35–41.
Maintains that scholarly-book reviewing deserves to be taken more seriously — by publishers, journal editors and the reviewers themselves.

Jussim, Estelle. 'Reviews and reviewing of multimedia materials', in *Encyclopedia of library and information science*. New York, Dekker, vol. 25, 1978, pp. 330–50.
Concerns non-print materials, especially films. Notes that the eight leading US and British journals in the field normally review only book about films, rather than films themselves. 21 references and notes.

Kamerman, Sylvia E. (ed.) *Book reviewing: a guide to writing book reviews for newspapers, magazines, radio and television, by leading abook editors, critics, and reviewers*. Boston, Mass., The Writer, Inc., 1978. xxvii, 215 pp. (reprinted London, Popular Press, 1985).
There are 21 chapters of varying quality, by 21 contributors. One chapter, 'Reviewing for specialized journals', gives specific guidelines. Four other chapters concern children's book reviewing. Appended 'Reference shelf' of 17 items.

Katz, William A. *Introduction to reference work*. Vol. 1: *Basic information services*, 4th edn. New York, McGraw-Hill, 1982.
Includes chapter sections (pp. 52–7) on reference-book reviews and major indexes.

Kenney, L.A. 'Reviewing of historical books', *Illinois libraries*, vol. 41, May 1959, pp. 355–61.
Summarizes a questionnaire completed by editors of 10 major historical journals. Topics at issue showed varying editorial practice as to length, analysis, praise/dispraise, essay form, provision of a 'communication' column, objectivity, payment, bias and editorial right to alter reviews.

Kinney, M.M., and others. 'The book review — a hybrid in literature and a stepchild in documentation'. *International Congress of Libraries and Documentation Centres*, Brussels, 11-18 September 1955.

The Hague, Nijhoff, 1955, vol. 2 (4), pp. 80–6.
Recommends that 'documentation be used as a lever to raise the ranking of the book-review in literature', by standardizing bibliographic presentation of book reviews in journals, by indexing reviews in subject areas and by resuming a comprehensive indexing service 'on and beyond the scale of the [then] defunct *Bibliographie des Rezensionen'*.

Kister, Ken. 'Wanted: more professionalism in reference book reviewing', *RQ*, vol. 19 (2), Winter 1979, pp. 144–8.
Reviewers of reference books are often librarians — volunteer reviewers content to have a review copy of a book and, perhaps, a byline. Basic requirements of the responsible professional book critic are enumerated.

Lee, Muna. 'Can't book reviewers be honest?' *Book abroad*, vol. 20 (4), Autumn 1946, pp. 370–4.
Asserts that while a book reviewer's responsibility is enormous, 'generally speaking, it is discharged lamentably'. The inadequate critic refuses to admit his own human limitations subject-wise, uses the publisher's blurbs, is dogmatic about the quality and accuracy of translations, is prejudiced and fails to place and evaluate a book 'in the stream of history'.

Macphail, Bruce D. 'Book reviews and the scholarly publisher', *Scholarly publishing*, vol. 12 (1), October 1980, pp. 53–63.
'Book reviews serve as an adjunct to the editorial process as well as an effective method of promotion. Publishers should systematically seek to get their books reviewed, authors, editors and reviewers should support their efforts' (*abstract*). Topics include pre-publication reviewing, and reviewing the reviewing media.

Manten, Arie A. 'Book reviews in primary journals', *Journal of technical writing and communication*, vol. 5 (3), 1975, pp. 227–36.
'Suggested general rules in editorial policy re publishing book-reviews in primary scientific and technological journals and the writing of such reviews' (*abstract*). The process, from obtaining books for review to review publication.

Martinelli, L.W. 'Book reviews in scholarly journals: report of a discussion group', *Journal of research communication studies*, vol. 3 (4), 1981/82, pp. 387–91.
Briefly considers such topics as length; reviewing from page-proofs; selecting reviewers; bibliographical details; editing of reviews; criticism of books, not their authors; evaluative rather than negative

reviewing; uncommissioned reviewing; and a journal correspondence column, to ventilate reactions.

Merritt, Leroy C., and others. *Reviews in library book selection.* Detroit,. Mich., Wayne State University Press, 1958. xv, 188 pp.
Contents: 'The pattern of modern book reviewing', by L.C. Merrill; 'The reviews and reviewers of bestsellers', by Martha Boaz; 'Staff reviewing in library book selection', by Kenneth S. Tisdel; 'Some historical sidelights in book reviewing', by Martha Boaz. US angle; rather dated.

Moulton, Priscilla. 'Children's book reviews and reviewing', in *Encyclopedia of library and information science.* New York, Dekker, vol. 25, 1978, pp. 373–80.
A short history of children's literature and its reviewing in the USA. The 'big four' US children's book-review journals are: *Booklist, Bulletin of the Center for Children's Books, Horn book magazine* and *School library journal.*

Oppenheimer, Evelyn. *Oral book reviewing to stimulate reading: a practical guide in technique for lecture and broadcast.* Metuchen, NJ, Scarecrow Press, 1980. xi, 156 pp.
Updates her *Book reviewing for an audience* (1963). The book-review, as written, is governed by spaced allowed; the suitability of a book to its audience is a vital factor in the case of oral reviewing. Topics: preparation and delivery techniques, and the art of interviewing.

Palmer, Joseph W, 'Review citations for best-selling books', *RQ*, vol. 19 (2), Winter 1979, pp. 154–8.
Book review digest, Book review index and *Current book review citation* [1976–82] complement each other, despite a very high duplication of coverage. 5 tables.

Pathania, M.S. 'The function of reviews in the dissemination of information', *Iaslic bulletin*, vol. 28 (3), 1983, pp. 123–30.
The review-article and its types fulfil two functions: 'that of forming an integral part of the development of science...and that of providing individual readers with information about the current development of science and its literature'. A framework for systematic and effective production of reviews concludes. Nine references. (This article owes more than a little to A.M. Woodward's 'The role of reviews in information transfer', *Journal of the American Society for Information Science*, vol. 28 (4), May 1977, pp. 175–80. 19 references.)

Rettig, James. 'Reviewing the reference reviews', *RSR/Reference services review,* vol. 9 (4), October/December 1981, pp. 85–102.
Surveys in turn Reference and Subscription Books Review Committee, *American reference books annual, Choice, RQ, Library journal* and *Wilson library bulletin.* Focuses on the people involved 'and the process by which these reviews came into being', rather than on time-lag, coverage and percentage favourable *v.* unfavourable judgement.

Riley, Lawrence E., and Spreitzer, Elmer A. 'Book reviewing in the social sciences', *The American sociologist,* vol. 5 (4), November 1970, pp. 358–63.
In the social sciences book reviews occupy a place subordinate to that of articles. They tend to be ranked alongside such 'prosaic forms' as abstracts, indexes and bibliographies, whereas they merit more attention as a form of professional recognition and evaluation. 43 references.

Robertson, Dorothy K. *The reviewing of children's book in Britain: a survey of current sources.* London, Library Association, Youth Libraries Group, 1968. 48 pp. (Pamphlet no. 4.)
Distinguishes five groups of reviewing sources: A. Special and general book-reviewing periodicals (7) — B. General monthly and weekly periodicals (7) — C. Periodicals intended primarily for educationalists and teachers (3) — D. National daily and Sunday newspapers (6) — E. Provincial newspapers (5). Tabular 'Analysis of numbers of books reviewed by periodicals and newspapers in 1967'.

S., F.H. 'What is a good review?' *Contemporary psychology,* vol. 8 (2), February 1963, pp. 43–4.
Outlines the essential, desirable and non-essential qualities of a review. Its main purpose is 'to improve communication of new ideas'.

Sadow, Arnold. 'Book reviewing media for technical libraries', *Special libraries,* vol. 61 (4), April 1970, pp. 194–8.
Identifies two kinds of book selection tools: detection aids (book lists) and evaluative aids. In science and technology recommended aids are: *Technical book review index, New technical books* and *Aslib book list.* (Maurice H. Smith, in *Special libraries,* vol. 61 (9), November 1970, pp. 515–6, adds other titles.)

Sarton, George. 'Notes on the reviewing of learned books', *Isis,* vol. 41, 1950, pp. 149–58 (reprinted in *Science,* vol. 131 [3408], 23 April 1980, pp. 1182–7.
A classic statement of the main points of a good review and the art of reviewing, including practices to avoid. He advises the scholar to

restrict his amount of reviewing; 'he should write a few and as well as possible'.

Serebnick, Judith. 'An analysis of publishers of books in six library journals', *Library and information science research*, vol. 6 (3), July/ September 1984, pp. 289–303.
Findings, based on two samples made in 1973–74 and 1978–80, showed that a core of 20–30 mainly large trade houses were responsible for the majority of books reviewed in six key US journals. About 70 per cent of the reviews were favourable.

Simon, M.R. (ed.) 'Analyses of bibliographies', *Library trends*, vol. 22, July 1973 (whole issue). 74 pp.
The six contributions include: 'Numerical methods of bibliographic analysis', by B.C. Brookes; 'The humanities: a state of the art report', by Lawrence S. Thompson; 'Information obtainable from analyses of scientific bibliographies', by R.T. Bottle; and 'Outlook: the analyses of bibliographies in the future', by M.R. Simon.

Simon, Rice James, and Mahan, Linda. 'A note on the role of book review editor as decision maker', *The library quarterly*, vol. 39, October 1969, pp. 353–6.
Aims to find out how decisions are made about *who* will review *which* book at *what* length at *which* location in the journal. Concludes that we need some kind of reviewing rating system (A, B and C grades).

Stueart, Robert D. 'Reviews and reviewing: introduction', in *Encyclopedia of library and information science*. New York, Dekker, vol. 25, 1978, pp. 314-24.
A compact informative survey of the field. Sections: Introduction — History — A current overview — General reviewing sources. 21 references.

Stueart, Robert D. 'Reviews and reviewing: library literature', *op.cit.*, pp. 324–30.
Sections: Favourable/unfavourable reviews — Review length — Time-lag — Signed/unsigned reviews — The reviewer — Sources for reviews. Seven references; two tables.

Subramanyam, K. 'Scientific literature', in *Encyclopedia of library and information science*. New York, Dekker, Vol. 26, 1979, pp. 376–548.

Section 'Review literature' (pp. 461-74) has headings: Introduction — Functions of reviews — Characteristics of reviews — Types and sources of reviews — Bibliographic control of reviews — Review authors and review preparation. Concentrates on review-articles and review monographs.

Swinnerton, Frank. *Authors and the book trade*, 2nd edn. London, Gerald Howe, Ltd, 1933. xiv, 144pp.
Chapter 8 (pp. 103–24), 'Reviewers' concerns 'star' reviewers, cliques and amateur reviewers. The chief charge against reviewers at that time was considered to be overenthusiasm, and a danger: advertising space encroaching on literary pages or reviews.

Walford, A.J. 'The necessity of scientific books', *TBR/Technical book review*, no. 40, February 1967, pp. 4–6.
Points to be noted in composing a review are analysed, with examples of good and bad reviews and notes on various types of science book. 17 references.

Walford, A.J. 'The reviewing of reference books', *The reference librarian*, no. 4, Summer 1982, pp. 165–9.
Examples are given of incompetent and competent reviewing, followed by a systematic analysis of J. Keegan's *World armies* (1979). Criteria for assessing reference books and qualities considered necessary for a good reference-book reviewer are then outlined. Six references.

Whittaker, Kenneth. *Systematic evaluation: methods and sources for evaluating books*. London, Bingley, 1980. 152pp.
Eight chapters, each with notes and references: 1. Critical approach to books — 2. Books: basic analysis — 3. The systematic method — 4. General criteria — 5. Specialized criteria: contents — 6. Published evaluations — 7. Evaluations in the book-weeding process — 8. Books compared with other materials [e.g. audiovisual]. Appended checklist of criteria and 'Guide to further reading' (20 items). Concise and informative, although necessarily focused on more general material and resources.

Wolper, R.S. 'A grass blade: on academic reviewing', *Scholarly publishing*, vol. 10 (4), July 1979, pp. 325–8.
An editor on reviewers: 'not only do they omit data and ignore house style; too often they are insensitive to language'. 500 words is a good average length for a review, the first sentence being important; clichés should be shunned; 'accuracy and succinctness are vital,

although brevity does increase pressure on the reviewer'.

Wolper, R.S. 'On academic reviewing: ten common errors', *Scholarly publishing*, vol. 16 (3), April 1985, pp. 265–75.
A valuable aide-mémoire, although Wolper confesses that his list is an arbitrary one.

Woodward, Anthony M. 'Review literature: characteristics, sources and output in 1972', *Aslib proceedings*, vol.. 26 (9), September 1974, pp. 367–76.
The 'core' of the review literature is stated to be of eight types: Annual review; Advances; Journal; Popular journals; Yearbook; Monograph series; Essay; 'Comments on...'. 17 references.

Woolf, Virgina. *Reviewing*; with a note by Leonard Woolf. London, Hogarth Press, 1939, 31pp.
Aimed at rousing discussion 'as to the value of the reviewer's office, and concentrating on the reviewing of poetry, drama and fiction. Leonard Woolf's note distinguishes between reviewing and literary criticism.

Young, Arthur P. 'Scholarly book reviewing in America', *Libri*, vol. 25 (3), 1975, pp. 174–82.
Three main themes: the characteristics of book-reviews and the dynamics of the reviewing process; the book-review journal (tabulating nine examples); bibliographical control of reviews. Introductory notes establish criteria for writing reviews, regional distribution of review authors, and review time-lag and duplication rates.

Index

Author and title entries for examples of books reviewed are omitted.